Louisa May Alcott
&
Charlotte Brontë

Transatlantic Translations

Christine Doyle

THE UNIVERSITY OF TENNESSEE PRESS / KNOXVILLE

Excerpts from *A Long Fatal Love Chase* by Louisa May Alcott, edited by Kent
Bicknell. Copyright © 1995 by Kent Bicknell. Reprinted by permission of Random House, Inc.

The paper used in this book meets the minimum requirements of ANSI/
NISO Z39.48-1992 (R 1997) (Permanence of Paper). The binding materials have
been chosen for strength and durability. Printed on recycled paper.

Library of Congress Cataloging-in-Publication Data

Doyle, Christine.
Louisa May Alcott and Charlotte Brontë : transatlantic translations /
    Christine Doyle.— 1st ed.
        p. cm.
    Includes bibliographical references and index.
    ISBN 1-57233-083-x (cl.: alk. paper)
    1. Alcott, Louisa May, 1832–1888—Knowledge—Literature. 2. Women
    and literature—United States—History—19th century. 3. Women and
    literature—England—History—19th century. 4. Brontë, Charlotte,
    1816–1855—Influence. 5. Feminist fiction—History and criticism. 6.Ameri-
    can fiction—English influences. 7. Feminism in literature. I. Title.
    PS1018 .D69 2000
    813'.4—dc21   99-050721

Louisa May Alcott
and
Charlotte Brontë

To my Mother,
whose life was also a long labor of love

CONTENTS

ACKNOWLEDGMENTS

Like Louisa May Alcott's *Work*, the work of preparing this book has been a narrative of community—or, more accurately, a narrative of several communities. I would like to extend my thanks to some of the people in those communities who have been especially instrumental in bringing this story to such a fulfilling end.

The project began during my graduate studies at the University of Connecticut, and I would first like to thank faculty there who encouraged, enlightened, and challenged me, especially Michael Meyer, Jean Marsden, Joan Joffe Hall, Feenie Ziner, Barbara Rosen, and Richard Peterson.

It would not have been possible to undertake this work if not for the modern editors who have made portions of Alcott's work accessible, sometimes for the first time in a century, sometimes for the first time ever—Madeleine Stern, Joel Myerson, Daniel Shealy, Kent Bicknell, and Sarah Elbert in particular—and the many scholars whose insightful studies of Alcott and Brontë and of nineteenth-century British and American culture laid so much of the groundwork upon which I could build. Reading through the Works Cited list gives some idea of the number of foremothers and forefathers a work such as this one must have. I would particularly like to thank Kent Bicknell, whose generosity with the manuscript of *A Long Fatal Love Chase* before it was published made it possible for me to complete the first version of this manuscript, and whose insights on Louisa and Bronson Alcott helped immensely as I wrote. Three other fine Alcott scholars, Beverly Lyon Clark, Daniel Shealy, and Elizabeth Keyser, read the entire manuscript at various stages and offered greatly appreciated support and suggestions.

It seems impossible that a writer deceased for more than a century could still have work under copyright, but due to the efforts of the modern editors mentioned above, that is indeed the case with Louisa May Alcott. I am grateful to the literary heirs of the Alcott family for permission to use quotations from Alcott letters and journals, and to Kent Bicknell and Random House for permission to quote from *A Long Fatal Love Chase*. Also, Garland Publishing kindly granted me permission to reprint material from my essay, "Transatlantic Translations: Communities of Education in Alcott and Brontë," which appeared in Little Women *and the Feminist Imagination*, edited by Janice M. Alberghene and Beverly Lyon Clark (New York, 1999).

I wish to thank staff members at the University of Tennessee Press for their enthusiasm and encouragement from the first query letter, and for their prompt and continuing responsiveness at every stage of the process thereafter. I am also grateful to Central Connecticut State University for a Faculty Research Grant that enabled me to complete revisions on this manuscript during the summer of 1999.

Finally, I must acknowledge the love and support of my community of friends and family, whose encouragement has been relentless. Thanks for always thinking I could. Jen, Kristin, and Mike, thanks for reminding me that scholars, like writers, are people, too.

CHRONOLOGY

Charlotte Brontë

1816   Born 21 April, Thornton

1820   Family moves to Haworth

1821   Maria Branwell Brontë (mother) dies

1824   Maria, Elizabeth, Emily and Charlotte to Cowan Bridge School

1825   Maria and Elizabeth die; Charlotte and Emily return home to Haworth

1839   Charlotte rejects two marriage proposals

1842   Charlotte and Emily go to Brussels to school

1844   Charlotte returns to Haworth for good after her second year at the Pensionnat Heger

Louisa May Alcott

1832   Born 29 Nov., Germantown, Pa.

1834   Family moves to Boston

1843   Utopian community at Fruitlands

Charlotte Brontë

1846 *Poems* published; sells two copies
1847 *Jane Eyre* published in Oct.
1848 Branwell and Emily Brontë die
1849 Anne Brontë dies; *Shirley* published
1853 *Villette* published
1854 Marriage to Arthur B. Nicholls, 29 June
1855 Dies, 31 March
1857 *The Professor* published; Gaskell's *Life of Charlotte Brontë* published

Louisa May Alcott

1851 First published poem, "Sunlight"
1852 First short story, "The Rival Painters," published
1854 First book, *Flower Fables*, published
1858 Elizabeth (Lizzie) Alcott dies; Anna and John Pratt engaged
1860 *Moods* written
1861 *Moods* revised; "Success" begun
1862 Louisa works at Union Hotel Hospital, Georgetown
1863 *Hospital Sketches* published
1864 *Moods* published
1868 *Little Women*, Part 1, published
1869 *Little Women*, Part 2, published
1871 *Little Men* published
1873 "Success" published as *Work*
1877 Mrs. Alcott dies
1879 May Alcott Nieriker dies, leaving baby Lulu to Louisa
1886 *Jo's Boys* published

Charlotte Brontë	Louisa May Alcott
	1888 A. Bronson Alcott dies 4 March; Louisa May Alcott dies 6 March
	1889 Ednah Dow Cheney's *Louisa May Alcott: Her Life, Letters, and Journals* published
	1975 First volume of thrillers, *Behind a Mask*, published

INTRODUCTION

Suppose you knew the novel open before you had been written by a woman in the middle of the nineteenth century. Suppose further that, in that novel, a woman seems to be urged in a chapter title to "Flee temptation"—that is, to flee the man she loves because he has lied to her and is already married. Suppose you noticed another scene in which an eighteen-year-old woman banters with an older man about societal rules, with one defiant character declaring, "Law and creation I know nothing of, public opinion I despise, & shame & fear I defy." You might be excused for beginning to wonder whether you misremembered *Jane Eyre*, for this novel might seem to be Brontë's famous work, and yet somehow not. The lines excerpted above appear in *A Long Fatal Love Chase*, a novel not written in 1847 by the British writer Charlotte Brontë but a generation later and an ocean away by an American admirer: Louisa May Alcott. They demonstrate some of the ways in which Alcott responded to her reading of one of her favorite writers during her own literary career. Alcott seems to adopt Brontë directly in the "Flee temptation" line, and indeed her heroine Rosamond Vivian does flee her lover, Philip Tempest; yet, within the chapter, Tempest himself uses the line to urge Rosamond not to flee him; Alcott's quotes around the phrase indicate that Tempest knows its source and is perverting it. As a matter of fact, the defiant speaker in the second quote, also from *Love Chase*, is not Rochester raging against marriage laws that bind him to a madwoman, or even Philip Tempest bemoaning divorce laws that will not allow him both his freedom and custody of his son, but Alcott's heroine Rosamond demanding freedom and independence and a place in the world for herself. She knew Brontë's work well enough to quote from it by heart, but was capable of using it to suit her own, sometimes very different, ends.

A Long Fatal Love Chase is one example of the wealth of Alcott's writing for adults now available for modern scholars to consider in conjunction with her consistently available children's novels. Having the wider breadth of Alcott's work accessible makes it possible to trace the influence of Charlotte Brontë in all phases of Louisa May Alcott's career and in all three of the major genres to which she contributed: children's fiction, adult sensation fiction, and adult novels. Pursuing such a project expands upon existing approaches to Alcott's writing, most of which focus on her either as a writer for children or as a feminist writer, in order to take a more comprehensive view of her as a nineteenth-century American author making her own way among the various influences of the transcendentalists among whom she was raised, the popular markets in which she participated, and literary models whom she admired.

An overview of previous critical and popular approaches to Alcott's work provides a clearer sense of both the value and the limits of existing scholarship, as well as how this study augments it. Essentially, critical assessments of Alcott have proceeded in three stages. For nearly one hundred years, Alcott's reputation was based on her children's fiction, particularly *Little Women*. Then, beginning in 1975, republication of her sensational thrillers, coinciding with important developments in the modern feminist movement, focused attention on Alcott's feminism—and sometimes the perceived lack of it—as expressed in her work. Only recently has scholarship turned to more encompassing approaches to Alcott's fiction.

It is ironic that only Alcott's children's novels have remained consistently in print for the perusal of popular and critical audiences, for she first established a literary reputation with adult stories. No less influential a reviewer than Henry James observed in reviewing her first novel, *Moods* (1864), that "With the exception of two or three celebrated names, we know not, indeed, to whom, in this country, unless to Miss Alcott, we are to look for a novel above the average" (281). However, the beginning of the March family trilogy with *Little Women* in 1868 established her through the rest of her lifetime and beyond as "the children's friend," as her first biographer, Ednah Cheney, called her. Indeed, it would be hard to overestimate the importance of *Little Women* to Alcott, personally and professionally. From her personal perspective, it was the children's novels, beginning with *Little Women*, that once and for all rescued her family from the financial distress that had been a part of their existence since the marriage of Abigail May to Amos Bronson Alcott. Louisa's income supported her parents, her widowed sister, Anna, and her two children, her sister May, a struggling artist in Paris, and eventually May's daughter, who came to live with her aunt after May's death when Lulu was only seven weeks old.

Little Women also broke new ground for children's literature in the United States. In a genre known for its relentless didacticism, Alcott found ways to demonstrate morality rather than merely to preach it. In a genre in which good children always triumphed and bad children never came to good ends, the March girls were "the first 'naughty' children allowed to survive and prosper in American children's literature" (MacDonald 19)— significantly before the arrival of either *Tom Sawyer* (1876) or *Huckleberry Finn* (1884). G. K. Chesterton attested to Alcott's continuing popularity with young women when he wrote in 1907:

> I have . . . hardly ever known a really admirable woman who did not confess to having read these books. Haughty ladies confessed . . . that they liked them still. Stately suffragettes rose rustling from the sofa and dropped *Little Women* on the floor. At learned ladies' colleges, it is, I firmly believe, handed about secretly, like a dangerous drug. (214)

While Chesterton's account may have been playful, there is no doubt that Alcott's popularity was immense; further, the children who read Alcott clearly did not forget her, for her children's books have had a lasting impact upon American popular culture—the most recent example being the third film version of *Little Women* that opened in December 1994 with stars of the stature of Susan Sarandon and Winona Ryder in leading roles.

Little Women continues to fascinate American critics as well as general readers. Well over a century after its first appearance, it has never been out of print; the fact that respected critic Elaine Showalter was called upon to write the introduction to the most recent Penguin edition of the book and that she devotes a chapter to it in her recent book on American women writers (*Sister's Choice*, 1991) suggests its significance in scholarly circles as well. Little Women *and the Feminist Imagination*, a collection of classic and new essays on Alcott's most famous work, was published in 1999. This is not to say that critics have neglected Alcott's adult writing entirely. Writers around the turn of the century such as Mary S. Logan, Frank Sanborn, and Lorenzo Dow Turner noted Alcott's contributions to the women's movement and her sympathy for abolition. But in the throes of the popular phenomenon generated by her children's writings, her adult novels and journalistic contributions faded in importance and, in fact, were lost or unavailable for many years.

The work of Leona Rostenberg and Madeleine Stern has helped to remind modern scholars of other dimensions of Alcott's work. In 1943, a Rostenberg article publicly acknowledged for the first time the possibility of retrieving Alcott's anonymous and pseudonymous contributions to the sensation literature of the 1860s. These writings are mentioned in Cheney's early biography, but only became traceable through Stern and Rostenberg's detective work on Alcott's complete journals, correspondences, and other papers, including the ledger in which she had recorded the names of the stories, to whom they were sold, and when. World War II interfered with Stern and Rostenberg's research, for many libraries put rare books and papers away for safekeeping during that time, and after the war Stern turned her efforts toward writing a modern biography of Alcott, which she published in 1950. In fact, a resurgence of interest in Alcott scholarship accompanying the *Little Women* centennial (1968) had come and gone before Stern began seriously to attempt the painstaking task of recovering and reprinting the lost stories. In 1975 Stern published the first collection of the "potboiler" tales, *Behind a Mask: The Unknown Thrillers of Louisa May Alcott*. More collections appeared over the next twenty years, culminating in *Louisa May Alcott Unmasked* (1995), a volume containing twenty-nine recovered tales. Also in 1995, Alcott's novel-length thriller, *A Long Fatal Love Chase*, was published for the first time, thanks to the perceptiveness of Kent Bicknell, a New Hampshire school principal who bought the unpublished manuscript and saw its delightful possibilities.

The appearances of these new materials rekindled interest in Alcott as a writer of adult fiction, which in turn spurred the reprinting of her novels *Work* and *Moods* in 1977 and 1991 respectively, making both available for the first time in this century. An unfinished novel, *Diana and Persis*, was edited by Sarah Elbert and published in 1978. The previously unpublished manuscript of the first novel Alcott attempted, *The Inheritance*, appeared in 1997.

The perceived dichotomy between the writer of children's books and the Louisa May Alcott revealed in the sensation stories evoked immediate response from feminist scholars such as Lynette Carpenter and Elaine Showalter (Introduction, *Alternative Alcott*), who largely tended to see the "thrillers" as a safe creative outlet for a culturally repressed woman writer who could not afford to have her reputation as a children's writer damaged by a connection with stories containing blood, sex, and violence. While no careful reader could deny that Alcott raises her voice against the Victorian repression of women in these stories, it is likely that in this case she was guarding her reputation as a serious writer as much as her reputation as a children's writer, for the overwhelming majority of the anonymous works recently recovered were written and published in the 1860s before *Little Women*. Although her first published book, *Flower Fables* (1854), was a collection of fairy tales, her literary reputation at that time was mostly based upon two adult works, *Hospital Sketches* (1863) and *Moods* (1865). Recasting the repression theory along more Freudian lines, critic Martha Saxton found that Alcott's thrillers were a means of venting her rage at the psychological damage inflicted upon her by the impractical ideas of her father; she could be "Duty's faithful child" (her father's term for her from a poem he wrote [Saxton 383]) as a writer of "acceptable" books and manifest the "real" Louisa in the anonymous tales.

The initial response to the whole of Alcott's work in light of the newly published materials was to label her a disappointment for having sold her artistic soul in order to placate Victorian patriarchal standards, a conclusion fed by the fact that one of Alcott's republished books was *A Modern Mephistopheles*, in which a struggling artist does sell his soul for fame. Martha Saxton, for example, comments on the fact that Alcott ceased to write sensation literature after the success of *Little Women*: "She gave up her pseudonymous gothics as unworthy. . . . Her writing rapidly lost its vitality and expansiveness as it became another extension of her entrapment" (331). Other critics, such as Angela Estes and Kathleen Lant ("Dismembering"), asserted that Alcott's radicalism was not lost but rather embedded as a subversive subtext in her children's writings, where anger and rebellion seethed beneath the "moral pap" (*Journals* 204) she provided for her young audience. While the great discrepancies, moral and otherwise, among the various genres in which Alcott participated provide much fuel for such interpretations and while the interpretations themselves do add a new dimension to our understanding of Alcott, many of these responses are limited by the critics' insistence on examining Alcott's work primarily on the basis of what her sensation stories demonstrate. Privileging the sensation stories in this way sets up a new dichotomy that demands that we look at her as a repressed Victorian *instead of* as a children's writer, merely leaving out a different aspect of the whole; this "new" look at Alcott is finally as incomplete as the image it seeks to replace.

Gradually, some critics have begun to address the issue of a cultural context for Alcott and the whole of her work. Charles Strickland's *Victorian Domesticity* (1985), for example, examines families throughout Alcott's work in the light of nineteenth-century ideals. Sarah Elbert's fine literary biography *A Hunger for Home* (1987) focuses on Alcott's interest in social reform and especially her feminism in a nineteenth-century context. Elizabeth Keyser's *Whispers in the Dark* (1993) takes its title from one of the sensation tales, but uses the whole body of Alcott's work to argue Alcott's consistent subversion of nineteenth-century conventionality regarding women's roles.

In examining Alcott as a feminist, as a Victorian woman, or as a divided personality, however, little of the recent Alcott scholarship has focused upon her as a reader of other writers (Jesse Crisler's 1994 essay on *Little Women* is a notable exception). This would seem to be an especially useful approach to a writer who frequently seemed to have literary models in mind when she wrote: *Pilgrim's Progress* for *Little Women*, *The Taming of the Shrew* for *Taming a Tartar*, and Goethe's *Faust* for *A Modern Mephistopheles*. Further, while biographers have consistently documented the extent to which Alcott shaped her life's events into her fiction, the extent to which she drew upon her life as a reader is an important part of Alcott as an artist which has been too little explored.

Significantly, the new primary sources now available to Alcott scholars show convincingly that Alcott as a reader of Charlotte Brontë's life and works saw both personal and literary ties between herself and the famous British author. In particular, Madeleine Stern, Joel Myerson, and Daniel Shealy recently edited and published Alcott's *Selected Letters* (1987) and *Journals* (1989), which had been available only partially, within Ednah Cheney's 1889 biography and Stern's more recent one. These materials offer concrete evidence that Charlotte Brontë's work as well as her life inspired Louisa May Alcott.

For example, at twenty years of age in 1852, Alcott followed her journal entry celebrating the sale of her first story, "The Rival Painters," with a "resolution to read fewer novels, and those only of the best." Among works by Carlyle, Goethe, and Milton, Alcott at that time listed *Jane Eyre* as one of the "books I like" (*Journals* 68; Brontë's novels *Jane Eyre*, *Shirley*, *Villette*, and *The Professor* all appeared between 1847 and 1857, formative years for Alcott, who was born in 1832). Two years before her death, she still counted Brontë among her favorite writers (*Letters* 296; 18 Dec. 1885); clearly, her interest in Brontë extended far beyond youthful fascination. Further evidence from her journals (*Journals* 85; June 1857) shows that she read, and was moved by, Elizabeth Gaskell's biography *The Life of Charlotte Brontë*.

While Alcott's comments in letters and journal entries suggest her long-standing interest in Charlotte Brontë, the recently republished sensation tales and adult novels, when looked at as a whole with her children's novels, make it clear that not only was Brontë one of Alcott's favorite writers, but that frequently and throughout her entire career, Alcott drew upon her reading of Charlotte Brontë in her own work. Alcott's allusions to Brontë have never gone totally unnoticed. For example, in the previously cited review of *Moods*, Henry James referred to the hero of Alcott's first novel as a Rochester-like character. But other than a few passing allusions, such as Elaine Showalter's contention that Tribulation Periwinkle's trip from Concord to Washington in *Hospital Sketches* "seems endlessly long, almost like Lucy Snowe's journey in *Villette*" (*AA* 27), or Madelon Bedell's vision of Jo's marriage to Frederick Bhaer as a "mentor-as-mate . . . female literary fantasy. . . . [like] Austen's Emma and Knightly [or] Brontë's Lucy and her professor" ("Introduction" xxiv), scholars have only begun to pursue the implications of the Brontëan connection. Notably, Sarah Elbert's introduction to the 1991 reprint of *Moods* clearly delineates connections between Rochester and Alcott's moody hero Adam Warwick, as well as some of the ways in which Alcott rewrites the situation between Jane and Rochester in her novel. Also, Elizabeth Keyser's *Whispers in the Dark* (1993) discusses Alcott's use of Brontë in several works. However, both of these recent works refer only to Alcott's interest in *Jane Eyre*, and Elbert applies it to only one Alcott work and Keyser to only one theme (the repressed subversiveness that, she contends, underlies Alcott's work). Examining the full extent of this influence, both in terms of how widely Alcott draws upon Brontë and the variety of ways in which she incorporates her reading of Brontë into her own writing, provides a new kind of lens through which to view the literary career of Louisa May Alcott.

Alcott's connections with—and disconnections from—Charlotte Brontë operate at two levels. Overt ties are discernible in biographical details and in Alcott's specific textual allusions to Brontë's plots and characters; more subtle parallels emerge in an analysis of each writer's recurring themes. At both levels and in all three areas, powerful connections and interesting disconnections appear. There were many similarities in the writers' backgrounds, but also some important biographical and cultural differences. In examining plots and characters in the whole range of Alcott's writing, a pattern emerges of Alcott's initial adoption, then as she became a more competent writer, adaptation, of her reading of Brontë's works. Alcott found herself attracted to the power of Brontë's characters, particularly her female characters, but eventually reacted with "troubled refusal" (Weisbuch 20) to the way those characters act out their destinies, and responded with an increasingly assured, increasingly American, literary voice. It is significant that at the height of Alcott's artistic powers, from the mid-1860s to the mid-1870s, she not only drew greatly upon Brontë for plots and characters but also adapted those influences—what I call "translating" Brontë—most dramatically. That is, Alcott's sleight-of-pen regarding her reading of Charlotte Brontë is interesting in itself, but more importantly it demonstrates her increasing artistic control.

The biographical and structural allusions are concrete matters which lead to the more subtle issue of the important themes that concerned both writers. As in her responses to Brontë's characters and plots, Alcott's themes also demonstrate a tension between fascination and contradiction; she frequently agrees with Brontë on which issues are worth writing about, but disagrees with her solutions to the problems raised—or even more precisely, on whether the problems have solutions— on grounds that often fall along the lines of British reserve versus American optimism. Individual attention is given here to each author's presentations of her characters' responses to specific issues that begin with the inmost soul and work outward; the relationship to the concept of God and spirituality leads to the presentation of their characters' lives in relation to other people and finally to their lives in relation to the working world. Alcott and Brontë wrestle with many of the same spiritual and social dilemmas that society, and especially women, on both sides of the Atlantic faced in their own time as well as in ours, but Alcott consistently takes a more optimistic stance toward the possibility of resolving these problems than does her British counterpart. Thus, her rewriting of Charlotte Brontë can be considered as a part of her attempt to rewrite life in general. Examining some specific ways in which Alcott deals with these ideas in comparison with Charlotte Brontë helps to clarify Alcott's position as an American writer by linking her attitudes more closely to American ideals, but it is no simple matter of opting for the tie of culture over the bond of gender. That the tension between acceptance and rejection of Brontë continues to be played out in Alcott's writing makes it impossible to dismiss the powerful transatlantic connections that gender forged between them. Thus, this study neither addresses Louisa May Alcott only as a woman writer nor only as an American writer, or only as children's writer or only as a writer of adult fiction. Rather, it gives fuller voice to the multiple dimensions—what Elaine Showalter calls the "hybridity" (*Sister's Choice* 20)—of her work as a nineteenth-century writer—a hybridity that argues convincingly for her importance as an American writer worthy of continued study.

Part One

Undisguised Affinities: Lives & Works

CHAPTER 1

Transatlantic Ties
The "Dear Girls" of Haworth and Concord

When twenty-four year old Louisa May Alcott read Elizabeth Gaskell's *The Life of Charlotte Brontë* in June 1857, she noted that the biography was

> [a] very interesting, but sad one. So full of talent, and after working long, just as success, love, and happiness come, she dies. Wonder if I shall ever be famous enough for people to care to read my story and struggles. I can't be a C.B., but I may do a little something yet. (*Journals* 85)

Louisa was not the only Alcott woman in whom Gaskell's book struck a chord of recognition. Louisa's mother, Abba May Alcott, later wrote in her own journal about the Brontës, "Their struggle reminds me of my own dear girls" (May 1869). Indeed, Louisa May Alcott's family circumstances resembled those of Charlotte Brontë in many respects. Examining the biographical parallels between Alcott, born in 1832, and Brontë, born just sixteen years earlier, reveals intriguing similarities in the life circumstances that shaped the writers they were to become. Further, as the earliest biographers of both Alcott and Brontë, Ednah Cheney and Elizabeth Gaskell, noted—and as the writers themselves acknowledged—Alcott and Brontë drew frequently from their own lives in creating their art. While life parallels need not necessarily imply literary parallels, a brief examination of the biographical similarities—as well as the disparities—between the two will serve as a means of bringing the personal and literary backgrounds of each into sharper focus and as a point of departure for exploring the literary parallels. Louisa May Alcott did have many reasons to acknowledge connections between herself and Charlotte Brontë in terms of family life, in terms of her personal life as a nineteenth-century woman, and in terms of her career as a woman writer. Some of the biographical connections are truly fascinating coincidences; others seem to be commonalities one might reasonably expect to find among many women whose formative years were spent in early- to mid-nineteenth century Victorian cultures.

In some respects, the differences between them, both personal and cultural, are as important as the similarities. In examining each, what becomes increasingly clear is that, at the same time she identified with Charlotte Brontë in a number of ways, Alcott as an American Victorian resisted and even refuted the influence of her British counterpart. The personal connections and divergences examined in this chapter, therefore, fuel the suggestion that even more meaningful comparisons and contrasts might emerge in a comparison of Brontë's work to the writing Alcott produced in this dual atmosphere of agreement and dissent.

Long before they were writers, both Louisa Alcott and Charlotte Brontë were daughters of committed moralists with eccentric ideas about child raising and little talent for, or even interest in, breadwinning. Patrick Brontë, a Cambridge-educated Anglican clergyman, stretched his modest income at Haworth to its limits in supporting a wife (briefly) and six children. Necessity and inclination seem to have gone hand in hand, however, for Gaskell reports that Brontë "thought that children should be brought up simply and hardily: so they had nothing but potatoes for their dinner" (38), and that he "wished to make his children . . . indifferent to the pleasures of eating and dress" (38). Other than as the voice of authority or the voice of religion (he led his family in prayer every evening), however, Patrick Brontë seems to have had limited contact with his children. Whether due to dietary problems, as Gaskell claimed, or to personal preference, he began to take his meals separately from the rest of the family even before the death of his wife, which occurred when Charlotte was only five years old. His one personal extravagance was a white silk cravat that "had begun as a modest affair," but each year, he kept adding to it until "eventually it enveloped half his head" like a monstrous cocoon, becoming his trademark throughout the countryside (Peters 40).

Gaskell also acknowledged, though, that however "eccentric and strange" Patrick Brontë may have been, "not one opinion that he held could be stirred or modified by any worldly motive; he acted up to his principles of action" (35). Gaskell's contention that he was active among and concerned for the people of his parish is affirmed by Rebecca Fraser's more recent portrait of the family. Fraser cites records of Brontë's lifelong social activism, from his efforts to force the Public Health Inspector to investigate the Haworth water supply to his seeking employment for his parishioners, even at age eighty-two. Further, he regularly contributed articles to local papers on political and religious issues that interested him (Fraser 22–24). It was Patrick Brontë, not his more politically conservative daughter Charlotte, who supported the English Reform Bill of 1832 (Peters 28).[1]

Louisa May Alcott may have found much in Elizabeth Gaskell's portrait of Charlotte Brontë's activist father that reminded her of her own father, Amos Bronson Alcott.[2] Though never a clergyman and, in fact, a great skeptic of organized religion from an early age, he was essentially a preacher, and certainly a philosopher, all his life. Mostly self-educated, in contrast to the Cambridge-educated Patrick Brontë, Alcott's remunerative employments included a brief career as a traveling salesman followed by a lifetime of work as an educator and a philosopher. The Romantic ideals of Swiss educator Johann Pestalozzi greatly influenced Alcott's educational theories, but, as Madelon Bedell notes, "Many of the innovations he introduced . . . were derived from his own fertile mind" (17). Alcott's educational innovations often involved connections between learning and real life that were a century and a half ahead of his time—children in his school, for instance, learned the concepts of geography by constructing a map of their own schoolyard—but in the mid-nineteenth century, his ideas led him into constant conflict with parents and school boards. After brief stints as an educator in Connecticut and in

Germantown, Pennsylvania (where Louisa May Alcott was born), he brought his family permanently to the Boston area. He continued to teach all his life, but with only marginal financial success, for his involvement with the transcendentalists and with reform movements, coupled with his often radical educational ideas, did not win him many friends among the populace. Like Patrick Brontë, he acted openly upon his ideals without seeming to consider the practical repercussions. His Temple School, for example, came under attack after Elizabeth Peabody transcribed and published children's conversations about God that had occurred in the school and shut down completely after Bronson enrolled a black child there. Abba Alcott's uncle Sam May and Ralph Waldo Emerson, who became Bronson's friend for life after the move to Concord, repeatedly rescued the family financially during Louisa's early years.

Bronson Alcott's educational philosophies emphasized the importance of early childhood education; unlike Patrick Brontë, who, Gaskell averred, turned much of his children's upbringing over to their Aunt Branwell after his wife's death, he put many of his educational ideas into practice through a high level of involvement with his own children during their infancy and early childhood. He supplemented his close attentions to his babies with copious journals documenting all aspects of their growth and development, journals which reached a length of twenty-five hundred pages in chronicling only about the first four years of his life as a parent. But whether because his main interest was in the formation of very young children, or because of the emotional breakdown he seems to have suffered when the utopian community in which he involved his family at Fruitlands collapsed in 1844 (Bedell 230–34), Alcott dedicated progressively more of his life to traveling and giving speeches on educational and transcendentalist philosophy, and less to personal involvement with his children. These speaking tours may have proved intellectually gratifying to Alcott, but they were seldom financially rewarding: Louisa recorded in her journal that her father once returned from a four-month speaking tour with one dollar in his pocket (*Journals* 71; 1854).

Notwithstanding his inability to profit materially from his

ideas, the recognizable depth of Bronson Alcott's spirituality is revealed in a comment from Ralph Waldo Emerson. When the founders of the Transcendentalist Club wanted to exclude Alcott from membership because they wished to restrict it to clerics or ex-clerics, Emerson successfully supported Alcott's right to participate, commenting, "He is a God-made priest" (Emerson, *Letters* II: 29; also see Bedell 115). The spiritual intensity of both Louisa Alcott's and Charlotte Brontë's fathers imbedded itself deeply in their daughters' writing lives; however, the differences between the British and American religious milieu in general, and between churchgoing Anglican and radical transcendentalist approaches to spiritual life in particular, also found expression there. As the discussion of spiritual issues in chapter 3 demonstrates, Alcott considered religion a matter of public action, while Brontë regarded public displays of religious fervor as suspect and considered religion an important but essentially private matter.

In addition to their influential fathers, Louisa Alcott and Charlotte Brontë had much in common within the families headed by those fathers. The lack of social opportunities due to poverty and, in the Brontës' case, to their isolation at Haworth (whether necessary or partially self-imposed), resulted in close sibling relationships, cemented by joint artistic endeavors, for both writers. Patrick Brontë reported in a letter to Elizabeth Gaskell that "When mere children, as soon as they could read and write, Charlotte and her brother and sisters used to invent and act little plays of their own" (Gaskell 36–37). The four younger children together created a journal modeled after *Blackwood's* magazine and filled it with the adventures of a place they called Glass Town. Later they wrote, in pairs, the chronicles of Angria (Charlotte and her brother Branwell) and Gondal (Emily and Anne). Eventually Anne, Emily, and Charlotte collaborated to produce their first publication, a volume of poetry that sold only two copies. When they turned to novels, Charlotte's *The Professor*, Emily's *Wuthering Heights*, and Anne's *Agnes Grey* were offered to publishers as one three-volume work "by Currer, Ellis, and Acton Bell." On their own side of the Atlantic, the Alcott daughters also produced a family newspaper together, and, as Louisa recorded in *Little Women*, they often wrote and acted in family theatricals. Her sister May (an aspiring artist, as was Charlotte's brother Branwell) even illustrated the first edition of *Little Women*.

Both writers were to endure the losses of many of these intense sibling relationships. Charlotte Brontë's two oldest sisters, Maria (later immortalized as *Jane Eyre*'s Helen Burns) and Elizabeth, died in 1825 when Charlotte was just nine years old. Her remaining three siblings all died within a period of nine months in 1848–49, leaving her and her father as the sole survivors. Although Louisa May Alcott's personal losses were nowhere as encompassing as Brontë's, her own sister Elizabeth (another sister immortalized, as *Little Women*'s Beth) died in 1858, an event followed shortly by her sister Anna's betrothal, an occurrence that at the time was almost as difficult for her to bear. She recorded the engagement in her May journal entry with the words, "I moan in private over my great loss" (*Journals* 89).

While Alcott's and Brontë's familial lives held many parallels regarding their fathers and siblings, their maternal backgrounds stood in marked contrast. Brontë, unlike Alcott, was motherless from the age of five. She only knew her mother from a packet of letters her mother had written to her father during their engagement; her father gave the letters to Charlotte twenty-nine years after his wife's death. She found in these letters evidence of "a mind of a truly fine, pure, and elevated order," and lamented, "I wish that she had lived, and that I had known her" (Wise and Symington III; 77–79). Patrick Brontë never remarried after his wife's death; instead, Mrs. Brontë's sister Elizabeth Branwell came to live with the family and care for the children until her own death. While both Gaskell (48–49) and Fraser (29–30) contend that Aunt Branwell inspired little affection from the Brontë girls — Fraser notes that "None of the Brontë children's letters except Branwell's includes an affectionate mention of her" (29) — Peters uses comments from Charlotte's friend Ellen Nussey to argue a somewhat less harsh assessment of her as "a Cornwall exotic, transplanted, but obliging enough to flourish in barren soil" (18). Even Peters acknowledges, however, that Aunt Branwell's "repressive brand of Calvinistic Methodism" (18) proved a dampening force on the spirits of the children at Haworth. According to Winifred Gérin, what nurturing was provided in the Brontë household came from their long-term servant Tabby (Tabitha Aykroyd), who "supplanted the dead mother in their hearts" (19).

Abba Alcott, on the other hand, lived to the age of seventy-seven. Her daughter's portrait of her as Marmee in the March trilogy, the dedication to her in *Work*—"To MY MOTHER, whose life has been a long labor of love"—as well as the many references to her in Louisa's letters and journals, attest to a close and affectionate relationship between them. Louisa Alcott also observed the loving bond between her two parents, despite their many difficulties both personal and financial. In response to the aforementioned incident in which Bronson Alcott returned from his lecture tour with only a dollar in his pocket, Louisa wrote in her journal:

> I shall never forget how beautifully Mother answered him . . . with a beaming face she kissed him, saying, "I call that doing very well. Since you are safely home, dear, we don't ask anything more."
>
> Anna and I choked down our tears, and took a little lesson in real love which we never forgot, nor the look that the tired man and the tender woman gave one another. It was half tragic and half comic, for Father was very dirty and sleepy, and Mother in a big nightcap and funny old jacket. (*Journals* 71; 1854)

Both the incident itself and Alcott's response to it indicate that, unlike Charlotte Brontë, she had firsthand access to both the comedy *and* the tragedy of the parental relationship, and to mother's love as well as duty as motivations for tending children.

Besides this important difference in Alcott and Brontë's private lives, their perspectives regarding relationships with people outside the family differed as well. While Patrick Brontë involved himself in his parish and in local politics, it was not an involvement his children shared. Relying greatly on one another's company, their relationships—at least the girls'—with others were few but intense. Charlotte Brontë did some traveling, including her important months at the Pensionnat Heger in Brussels, but she seems always to have had a great dread of strangers, and became as much exhausted as invigorated by the trips she made to London as her fame grew. Her close friend Mary Taylor told Gaskell that Brontë was never able to enjoy the fame her writing brought her because "Her solitary life had disqualified her for society. She had become unready, nervous, excitable, and either incapable of speech, or talked vapidly" (qtd. in Gaskell 286). But especially after the deaths of her siblings, Brontë found little solace at Haworth, either. Concern for her father and the discomfort of being among strangers drove her home, but home came to evoke "A reaction that sunk me to the earth; the deadly silence, solitude, desolation . . . the craving for companionship, the hopelessness of relief" (qtd. in Gaskell 313).

Louisa Alcott shared with Brontë a growing dread of the confines of home, but responded to it as befitted her more outgoing, gregarious nature. When her mother founded what was essentially an employment agency in Boston, Louisa herself took jobs at various times as a seamstress and a domestic servant, so she was exposed to a wide variety of people and situations. She traveled to Europe twice, and served briefly as a Civil War nurse. Like Brontë in her eventual restlessness at home, she grew more and more impatient with "stupid Concord" (Journals 228; October 1880), where family duties repeatedly summoned her. Nevertheless, with more options and more inclination toward sociability than Charlotte Brontë had at Haworth, Alcott was always part of the active life of Concord and of Boston, where she often lived for periods of weeks or months at a time, attending the theater and acting, attending meetings of the Radical Club, and participating in abolitionist and women's rights meetings. She lived most of her life in the Boston area, but hers was a life of great activity and variety, despite health problems that plagued her from the time she contracted typhus during her Civil War experience throughout the rest of her life. Alcott told both Ednah Cheney and Louise Chandler Moulton, "I was never ill before this time, and never well afterward" (Cheney 41–42; Moulton 137).

The convergences and divergences in Alcott's and Brontë's personal relationships within and without their immediate families manifest themselves in the way each characterizes human relationships in her work. Alcott seems to have been fascinated, as were many American readers, with the characters Charlotte

Brontë created—in Alcott's case, particularly the female characters. But as the detailed study of the characters themselves in the next chapter indicates, Alcott mixes assent with resistance when she responds to Brontë in creating her own characters. Alcott openly admires Brontë's strong female characters and seems particularly attracted to the way Brontë articulates, through them, the limits that Victorian society placed upon women. However, neither her natural inclinations, her own family life, nor the American cultural milieu caused her to despair of changing her society or her position in it, as did Brontë's, and neither do the characters she creates. Further, as chapter 4 explains, Brontë increasingly turns her attention to an exploration of the problems of solitude—an interest certainly dictated by the devastating losses in her own family—but Alcott moves in the opposite direction, increasingly examining the problems and the possibilities of relationships.

In attending to the role that personal and family backgrounds played in shaping these writers' artistic responses, it is important not to overlook the powerful impact of the larger cultural environment on their personal lives. Certainly, one personal problem for both women that was further complicated by cultural attitudes was that of inadequate financial support (although Patrick Brontë's income was at least steady), which eventually catapulted both women into the position of family breadwinners. However, the writing that was to bring them lasting fame was by no means their first source of income as adults. Louisa Alcott and Charlotte Brontë both worked as teachers and as governesses; neither relished either of these careers open to nineteenth-century women, but instead pursued them out of a sense of family duty and the desire for economic independence. Upon being offered a job as a kindergarten teacher, Alcott recorded in her journal, "Don't like to teach, but take what comes," and a month later pronounced it "distasteful work" (*Journals* 108; January, February 1862); nevertheless, she did what she could to shore up the "Alcott sinking fund," as she often referred to her family's income.

Brontë was not nearly so acquiescent as was Alcott in her response to her teaching duties. She wrote from a teaching job in 1836, "Am I forced to spend all the best part of my life in this wretched bondage, forcibly suppressing my rage at the idleness, the apathy, and the hyperbolical and most asinine stupidity of these fat-headed oafs?" (Wise and Symington II, 255–56). Unfortunately, Brontë had anticipated and answered her own question a year earlier when she first took employment as a teacher; in a letter to her friend Ellen Nussey, she wrote, "*Duty—Necessity—* these are stern mistresses who will not be disobeyed" (Wise and Symington I, 129; emphasis in the original).

Neither writer initially had reason to expect that a time would come when she could devote full energies to writing and so make a living in a less "distasteful" way. Publisher James T. Fields rejected one of Alcott's early stories about her experience as a domestic servant with the advice, "Stick to your teaching; you can't write" (*Journals* 109; May 1862). Charlotte Brontë received a more flattering assessment of her talents, but a no less discouraging assessment of their possible uses, when she sent some of her poetry to Robert Southey, then England's poet laureate. Southey acknowledged that his correspondent possessed "in no inconsiderable degree, what Wordsworth calls the 'faculty of verse,'" but cautioned her, "Literature cannot be the business of a woman's life, and it ought not to be. The more she is engaged in her proper duties, the less leisure will she have for it, even as an accomplishment and a recreation"; he especially warned against writing "with a view to celebrity" (Wise and Symington I, 154–56). Though each woman's career eventually vindicated her choice to pursue authorship despite such discouraging words, neither famous daughter was ever to escape from family cares, regardless of financial and critical success: Charlotte Brontë lived in her father's home all her life, even during the nine months between her marriage and her death; Louisa Alcott supported her mother, sisters, nephews, and niece, tended her father until the end of his life, and died herself only two days after him.

Having faced many obstacles themselves, Alcott and Brontë turned frequently in their art to considerations of the many obstacles facing women who wished to make their independent way in the world. The experiences they shared made similarities in the way they presented these themes almost natural; but again, while the bond of gender draws them together, culture sets them apart. Both writers protest the limitations their respective societies place upon women's work, but Brontë's novels indicate little hope of changing the situation; indeed, the rigidity of nineteenth-century class structure gave her little reason to hold any such hope. Her heroines must make their peace within such strictures or go mad in the attempt. Alcott, spurred on by her American perspective, identifies with Brontë's premises but resists her conclusions. Even her governesses control their own destinies; further, her experience of American life allowed her to propose many more options for women's work besides governess or teacher—sometimes even pushing the boundaries of American limitations—than those Brontë could imagine.

Some of the ways in which each writer articulated the problems of women in the working world are explored in detail in chapter 5. First, however, recall from the journal entry quoted at the beginning of this chapter that Alcott herself had followed musings on Brontë's biography with musings on their mutual impulse toward writing: "I can't be a C.B., but I may do a little something yet." Since the larger purpose here is to use the personal and cultural worlds these writers inhabited as a lens through which to examine the fiction each writer created, it is appropriate to consider the literary worlds in which they found themselves, as a bridge between the two. Actually, Alcott and Brontë described their own writing processes similarly. Brontë wrote to George Lewes in 1848:

> When authors write best . . . an influence seems to waken in them, which becomes their master—which will have its own way—putting out of view all behests but its own, dictating certain words, and insisting on their being used, whether vehement or measured in their nature; new-molding characters, giving unthought-of turns to incidents, rejecting carefully elaborated old ideas, and suddenly creating and adopting new ones. (Gaskell 236)

Brontë's masterful influence sounds much like what Alcott typically called her "vortex": "Fired up the engine, and plunged into a vortex . . . Can't work slowly, the thing possesses me, and I must obey till it's done" (*Journals* 183–4; November 1872).

A further similarity between their creative approaches was that, when publishing the results of these intense processes, both Alcott and Brontë used pseudonyms. All of Charlotte Brontë's novels, and even her contributions to the 1846 volume *Poems*, were attributed to "Currer Bell." Alcott published as Flora Fairchild, as A. M. Barnard, and anonymously, as well as under her own name. Beneath this surface similarity, however, lie major differences in how each woman conceived of herself as a writer, differences again shaped by background and culture. As Richard Brodhead argues in *Cultures of Letters*, "A writer can only become a writer by first constructing some working idea of what a writer is and does, an idea that is never merely self-generated but . . . formed in and against the understandings of this role that are operative in a particular space" (86). In Charlotte Brontë's "cultural space," mid-nineteenth-century England, she had already been admonished (by her country's poet laureate, no less), that there *was* no role for a woman who wished to be considered an artist. Perhaps, as Gilbert and Gubar suggest, Brontë's choice of the masculine-sounding pseudonym is her response to the "anxiety of authorship," that "radical fear that . . . the act of writing will isolate or destroy her" (49)—that is, it would destroy her *if* she presented herself as a woman author. In this vein, it is interesting to note that in her first attempted novel, *The Professor,* she even adopted (though not very successfully) the first-person narrative voice of a man, William Crimsworth. Her attempt to avoid censure and to be judged on the basis of art, not gender, is delineated in a remark to Elizabeth Gaskell regarding the Brontë sisters' choices of Acton, Ellis, and Currer Bell as the pseudonymous co-authors of *Poems:*

> [W]e did not like to declare ourselves women, because . . . we had a vague impression that authoresses are liable to be looked on with prejudice; we noticed how critics sometimes use for their chastisement the weapon of personality, and for their reward, a flattery, which is not true praise. (Gaskell 197)

The Brontës' concerns were well-founded, but the ruse drew more rather than less attention to their identities, and specifically to their gender. The *Critic* reviewer began, "No preface introduces these poems to the reader. Who are Currer, Ellis, and Acton Bell," then accurately conjectured, "Perhaps they desired that the poems should be tried and judged upon their own merits alone, apart from all extraneous circumstances" (rpt. in Allott 59). Not that this critic, or any others, could address the work of any of the "Bells" without speculating upon the gender of the authors: in the *North British Review,* James Lorimer speculated that

> if they [*Jane Eyre, Wuthering Heights,* and *The Tenant of Wildfell Hall*] are the production of a woman, she must be a woman nearly unsexed; and Jane Eyre strikes us as a personage much more likely to have sprung ready armed from the head of a man . . . than to have experienced, in any shape, the softening influence of female creation. (rpt. in Allott 116)

A *Sartain's* reviewer declared in June 1848 that "No woman could write *Wuthering Heights*" (qtd. in Baym, *Novels* 168), and a *Literary World* review of *The Tenant of Wildfell Hall* dubbed Acton Bell "a man of genius" in the first paragraph, then inexplicably downgraded the author to "some gifted and retired woman" when it decided "he" was a "she" later in the review (rpt. in Allott 258, 259).

Nor was this gender speculation confined to literary criticism; although Charlotte and Anne Brontë's impromptu visit to London in July 1848 cleared up the mystery for their publishers, Smith & Elder, and although other friends and acquaintances and reviewers gradually came to learn the truth as well, by 1850, according to Peters, "The game 'Who are the Bells?' became a favorite literary pastime" (205–6) in London society. Questions of whether they were one or three, male or female, were not settled conclusively until Gaskell's biography was published in 1857. Even then, literary criticism of Charlotte Brontë had a difficult time undertaking a dispassionate analysis of her writing, for Gaskell's book itself gave birth to the "'poor Charlotte' . . . school of hagiography," and critics who had previously castigated her for unwomanliness now excused every perceivable fault as attributable to her sufferings (Barker 797). The *North American Review,* with an incredibly short memory, it seems, criticized those who had dared to accuse Brontë of "coarseness and immorality" merely because she "dared to speak on certain topics with a plainness somewhat unusual among the fashionable lady-writers" (qtd. in Baym, *Novels* 269)—ironically, as Baym points out, "using one woman's work to denigrate the achievements of others" (*Novels* 269). As Charlotte Brontë had rightly predicted, critiques of her womanhood typically accompanied—even dominated—considerations of her art; unfortunately, her male pseudonym never had the effect of eliminating this problem, but instead caused problems of its own.

But if the *North American* reviewer's attitudes reveal a lack of understanding about women as writers, they also demonstrate a greater acceptance of at least the abstract notion of the woman as writer on Louisa May Alcott's side of the Atlantic than on Brontë's. As early as 1855, even *Godey's Lady's Book*, a Philadelphia periodical that generally "avoided politics and current events" (Baym, *Novels* 15), insisted that writing could indeed be "the business of a woman's life," asserting that "those gifted with a talent for literary pursuits should be encouraged and rewarded" ("Editor's Table" 368). Apparently *Godey's* practiced as it preached: Nye states that "[t]he swift growth of a huge market of educated, literate women promised great rewards for writers who could satisfy it" and that "*Godey's* itself at one time had eighteen regular female contributors" (98). The art of the time confirms that women writers were part of American life; both Catherine Sedgwick's "Cacoethes Scribendi" ("Scribbler's Itch," 1830) and Frances Harper's "The Two Offers" (1852), for example, feature female characters who are writers. Nina Baym's study of antebellum novels found that nearly 40 percent of the novels reviewed in periodicals were written by women (100)—which no doubt was one of the circumstances that prompted Nathaniel Hawthorne's infamous remark that "America is now wholly given over to a d——d mob of scribbling women." From a more positive perspective, recall Henry James's statement as he reviewed Alcott's *Moods*, "we know not, indeed, to whom, in this country, unless to Miss Alcott, we are to look for a novel above the average" (281); notwithstanding James's multiplicity of commas and his reluctance to be overly committal, his implicit assumption seems to be that an exceptional novel *could*, in fact, come from a woman's pen.

Even in an atmosphere so much more conducive to the idea of woman as writer, however, Louisa May Alcott, like Charlotte Brontë, used pseudonyms and even published anonymously at times. Nevertheless, as Elaine Showalter notes, Alcott largely ignored the model of the Brontës and of George Eliot, opting instead for the American convention of "hyperfeminine" pseudonyms (*Sister's Choice* 49); for example, her first publication, the poem "Sunlight," appeared under the name Flora Fairfield. Alcott's sensation stories were either published anonymously or with the masculine-sounding pseudonym A. M. Barnard; her children's stories and adult novels, however, appeared under her own name. Alcott even instigated her own "name game" when she contributed *A Modern Mephistopheles* to Roberts Brothers' No Name Series in 1877, when her own fame was well-established. The series was conceived as anonymous writings by well-known authors, and Alcott's contribution was much discussed by critics and the public; the *Atlantic* insisted it was the work of Julian Hawthorne. Although the *Woman's Journal*, to which Alcott frequently contributed, guessed the secret, it was not until Alcott later allowed it to be republished under her own name that her authorship was publicly affirmed (Stern, Introduction to *A Modern Mephistopheles*).

Using a variety of names suggests Alcott's practicality and her awareness of the many facets of herself as a writer—her "ultimate professionalism," as Madeleine Stern puts it ("Self-Criticism" 333). Stern's assessment of Alcott concurs with Nina Baym's assertion that American women writers before the 1870s "saw themselves not as 'artists' but as professional writers with work to do and a living to be made from satisfactory fulfillment of an obligation [that is, to entertain and to instruct] to their audience" (*Woman's Fiction* 16). Certainly Alcott's choices of names, like the breadth of her writing, reflected her ability to understand and to adapt to the conventions of genres. Indeed, Alcott's reading of her market, her attention to production details, even her adoption of her nephew John Pratt so that, as her direct heir, he could continue to apply for her copyright, attest to her practical professionalism.

However, the American "cultural space" in which Louisa May Alcott forged her career as a writer adds another layer of complexity to the issue of professionalism. The rise of the American periodical press, beginning in the 1840s, and the particulars of its early growth helped to shape the writing career Alcott was trying to shape for herself. The 125 or so American magazines that existed in 1825 burgeoned to 600 by 1850. Periodicals expanded their subscription bases at astounding rates; during the 1850s, several journals had over 100,000 subscribers (Baym, *Novels* 14). The *New York Ledger,* founded in 1855, had 180,000 subscribers by 1857, and its numbers doubled soon after (Brodhead 77–78). Further, while the various periodicals represented a wide range of reading tastes, from the lowbrow story-papers to the middle-class domestic fiction to the high art of magazines like the *Atlantic Monthly,* the fact that the periodicals came into existence at more or less the same time meant that, in the beginning, "writers were not in any necessary way aligned with one or another of these distinct cultures but faced an array of literary possibilities, and had several publics and several models of authorship equally available to them" (Brodhead 80). The lines dividing "high" literary art from "low" became more sharply drawn by about 1870, nearly the exact chronological midpoint of Alcott's career, but during the first half of her career, it was a fairly simple enterprise for a writer to participate at all the different levels; in fact, Brodhead uses Alcott as his prime example of a writer who did exactly that, publishing in the *Atlantic Monthly* at the same time she was producing sensation stories for *Frank Leslie's Illustrated Newspaper.* Her insightful understanding of the conventions of various genres and the ability to shape her talents to fit them carried her successfully through the mid-1860s. Brodhead suggests that the success of *Little Women* in 1868–69 was another stroke of fortuitous timing, coming at a time when the *Atlantic* was courting Henry James but not Louisa May Alcott. Cut off from high art, excelling at her own brand of domestic fiction—a genre whose conventions she "stretched" by her secularism, her humor, and her use of vernacular language, among other things—enabled her to be a recognized successful author and to stay afloat financially without having to continue to participate in the "sensation" genre, now becoming more clearly lower class (Brodhead 87–89).

Brodhead's cultural reasoning goes a long way toward explaining Alcott's choice of post-1870 genre, but he defines it almost completely in terms of the American marketplace, then adds the personal element that this also allowed Alcott to fulfill her need for self-sacrifice, to "set aside personal pleasures [i.e., writing artistic but possibly ones not well-received critically or rewarding financially] for socially useful work" (89), a moral virtue inculcated in her from childhood. This, however, seems much less important than the way Alcott made the increasing tension between "artist" and "professional writer," an American cultural struggle, also an intensely personal one, or as she frequently defined it, her own struggle with the issues of "talent" and "genius."

Frequently, in both her private and public writings, Alcott discusses the difference between the two terms, claiming the first for herself, but not the second. For example, in a letter to her publisher James Redpath, she wrote, "people mustn't talk about genius, for I drove that idea away years ago. . . . The inspiration of necessity is all I've had" (rpt. in Stern, "Self-Criticism" 363). Questions of genius often come under consideration in Alcott's work. For example, in *Little Women,* when Laurie asks Amy why she has abandoned her dream of becoming the next Raphael, she replies, "Because talent isn't genius, and no amount of energy can make it so" (405); Laurie himself uses this criterion when he gives up his own dreams of becoming a famous musician. It may, finally, have been the criterion she herself used when she wrote, "I can't be a C.B., but I may do a little something yet." Despite these frequent disclaimers, evidence suggests that Alcott may have been more ambivalent, or perhaps reluctant to "settle" for fame and fortune and abandon "genius" than she would like to have believed.

For example, there are indications that she may have looked upon at least her adult novels with even more artistic yearnings during the post-1870 portion of her career. For one thing, she did something with these novels that she did seldom in her writing career—she worked on them over long periods of time and revised them. Alcott struggled with *Work* for over a decade before finally publishing it in 1872. She received back the copyright from *Moods*, which had originally been published in 1864, and rewrote it for publication in 1882, changing major portions, including the ending.

Upon sending *A Modern Mephistopheles* to her publisher in 1877, she commented, "Enjoyed doing it, being tired of providing moral pap for the young." The entry continues, "Long to write a novel, but cannot get time enough" (*Journals* 204; January, February 1877). Here Alcott makes new distinctions in her work, not only between her children's books and her novels, but also between the novel-length work she had just written for Roberts Brothers and something else she had in mind as a "novel," possibly something more artistic. Considering the entry as a whole suggests that she was doing more than complaining about being "trapped" in the world of children's fiction, which is how the quote is frequently read; she may also have been grappling with the larger question of artistic ambition.

In any case, Alcott's claim that she had no time is arguable, for by this point in her life, the security of her financial status (for four years, she had been recording investments made, as well as income, in her ledgers) should have allowed her to retreat at least temporarily from the demands of her family and her public. The book she "Enjoyed doing" for Roberts Brothers provides another insight into her inability to retreat long enough to write that novel. Early in the book, the young heroine Gladys defuses the boast of the Faust character Felix that his next book will surpass the first by so much "that this first attempt will be forgotten," when she warns him:

> You will never do better; for this came from your heart, without a thought of what the world would say. Hereafter all you write may be more perfect in form but less true in spirit, because you will have the fear of the world and the loss of fame before your eyes. (*AMM* 24–25)

Possibly by this point in her career, when she might finally have been able to take the time to nurture a more artistic novel, the specter of not being able to produce a novel greater than *Little Women,* a true work of genius, intimidated her as much as the *Atlantic's* rejections. Her journals suggest that the question of genius was never settled in her own mind, for she was at work on a never-finished book she called "Genius" in the last years of her life (*Journals* 238; February 1883). The *Modern Mephistopheles* tale, in fact, is based on a story she had published anonymously in 1866 entitled "The Freak of a Genius." At the same time that her own development as a writer and the cultural climate around her might have been encouraging her to reconsider her own position as an artist, then, it is possible that by 1877 she feared that *Little Women,* her most acclaimed work but a children's novel, was only a freak of her genius, a work in which things came together as they never would again, certainly never for an adult work, however much time she might take. She may have been anxious lest the world that lionized her as a professional writer might not be so kind if she claimed to be an artist; it might say of her that her talent was not genius.

Unlike Alcott, Charlotte Brontë seems to have been determined to be considered a serious artist from the outset, though also anxious to escape disapproval as a woman; at any rate, her career was too short to trace such variations in her society and in her artistic attitudes as are evident in Louisa May Alcott's work. However, it is possible to find, in Alcott's lengthy career, many links to the art of Charlotte Brontë; in fact, Gladys's comments to Felix quoted above are exactly what Louisa Alcott, in her last direct reference to Brontë in her writing, claims as the greatness of Brontë's work: it has "heart" (*JB* 290). The connection that the twenty-four-year-old fledgling author had recognized between herself and Charlotte Brontë and the mature writer reiterated— the shared idea that great writing deals with even the largest issues at a deeply human, personal level, the level of the heart— had some of its roots in parallels in their personal lives. By themselves, the biographical parallels between them that Alcott herself acknowledged, along with the autobiographical elements that characterized the work of both, only suggest that literary parallels might also exist. Some of the differences in their personal lives, their cultural situations as American and British women, and their attitudes toward their art caution against any assumption that Alcott's art would mirror Brontë's, however. In Robert Weisbuch's study of the relationships between nineteenth-century American male writers and their British counterparts, he suggests that if his work were extended to include women and minority writers, these writers might encounter a "double bind," in which they "identified themselves as members of an oppressed group" but at the same time would still "join in the American attempt to defend New World possibilities against British taunts" (xx). By turning now to a closer examination of some of the specific echoes of the much-admired author that resonated throughout Louisa May Alcott's efforts to "do a little something yet," then exploring their thematic connections as well, some of the dimensions of this "double bind" will become evident. Tracing the certain identification with Charlotte Brontë evident in Alcott's writing but also noticing the areas of resistance will make it possible to set Alcott more clearly among American writers of the nineteenth century: she responds to Brontë's woman's "heart" but resists her British soul.

CHAPTER 2

Adoption and Adaptation

Writing under the Influence

As equivocal as Louisa May Alcott's disclaimers about matching her talents to the genius of Charlotte Brontë may have been, there is no indication that her artistic efforts were in any sense an attempt to copy Brontë's. Rather, her remarks reveal an understandable mixture of hope and intimidation in a young artist considering the career of an admired forerunner as she embarks upon her own efforts, as she put them, to "do a little something yet" (*Journals* 85; June 1857)—perhaps a bit of Bloom's "anxiety of influence" replaces Brontë's "anxiety of authorship," but one devoid of the male need to destroy the precursor, in part because she saw Charlotte Brontë as a role model, not a competitor. Alcott's writing talent was considerable but different from that of her English counterpart. Even the genres of the published works for which they were most known, Brontë for her Romantic and Victorian novels and Alcott for children's fiction, are far removed from one another. However, the republication of Alcott's novels and sensation fiction and publication of her journals, letters, and two previously unpublished novels (*A Long Fatal Love Chase* and *The Inheritance*) make more evident the extent to which Alcott drew upon her reading of Brontë as she created the heroines, heroes, and plots of her own texts. Tracing the fullness of Alcott and Brontë's literary connections in terms of such fundamental elements as character and plot provides a crucial framework from which to consider thematic connections between the two. Louisa May Alcott and Charlotte Brontë were not merely women who coincidentally wrote at approximately the same period in time; fleshing out the literary connections between them shows conclusively that Alcott frequently and consciously used Brontë as a model, and sometimes as an anti-model, for her own writing. Further, the tension in Alcott between her personal and professional empathy with Brontë as a nineteenth-century woman writer and her American optimist's rejection of Brontë's British world of diminished possibilities—a crucial issue in the thematic relationships between their work—is also evident when one explores the connections between them in such fundamental elements of their fiction as their use of character and plot. Finally, because of the way Alcott's *adoption* of Brontëan elements changes gradually to a more accomplished *adaptation,* to trace the ways in which Alcott manipulates her allusions to Charlotte Brontë is to trace Alcott's own development as an American woman writer of increasingly independent power and ultimately to place her more accurately within her own literary tradition.

In her early novels, *The Inheritance, Moods,* and *Work,* Alcott takes issue with some of Brontë's assumptions even while adopting some of her plots and characters; the resulting lack of cohesion in these books reveals the difficulties of a developing writer not sure enough of her craft to accomplish her goals within it. Alcott's dissatisfaction with the 1864 version of *Moods* and her inability to finish *Work* demonstrate her own awareness of these problems. During the mid-1860s, Alcott delved more energetically into the world of sensation literature, the "potboilers" she published anonymously or pseudonymously that were fruitful both financially and artistically. While mostly formulated along the lines of English sensation fiction, these stories also allude frequently to Brontë. In them, Alcott gradually makes clearer the distinctions between herself and Brontë; she adapts her literary borrowings with more assurance into an increasingly American context as the decade proceeds.

By the time she writes *Little Women* (1868–69), Alcott is adept at writing her own story, making use of whatever Brontëan techniques she finds useful but in more subtle ways, blending her resources of literature and imagination into a voice all her own. This ability to fuse rather than simply to mix elements of plot and character gave Alcott's mature writing a complexity that David Reynolds acknowledges when he ranks Alcott among the principal figures of the American Women's Renaissance (397). With *Little Women*, Alcott "found [her] style at last" (*LW* 436), as Mr. March acknowledges to her alter ego Jo, and was then able, despite her declining health, to proceed with enough confidence to finish *Work*, re-write *Moods*, and complete seven more children's novels and *A Modern Mephistopheles* (among a large body of other, shorter pieces) in the voice she had finally found. But Alcott never entirely abandons the connection to Charlotte Brontë evident in her earliest writing. In the last volume of the March trilogy, *Jo's Boys*, published a little over a year before her death, Louisa May Alcott refers to Brontë as one of Mrs. Jo's favorite writers. This chapter explores Alcott's specific references to Brontë and examines why and how an increasingly competent Louisa May Alcott adapted this particular source to her own purposes.

Although the particular interest here is Louisa May Alcott as a writer, it should be noted that, as a reader, she was certainly not alone in her fascination with Charlotte Brontë; Brontë was a literary and cultural phenomenon on both sides of the Atlantic from the time *Jane Eyre* appeared in 1847, and only became more so after her death and the subsequent publication of Gaskell's biography. Barker notes that, when it appeared in England, "demand for *Jane Eyre* was almost unprecedented"; the first edition sold out within three months, and two more editions were printed and sold out six months later (537). On Alcott's side of the Atlantic, the *North American Review* reported that "a distressing mental epidemic, passing under the name of 'Jane Eyre fever,'" had gripped New England for several months in 1848, to the extent that "every family soon had a copy" of the book ("Novels of the Season" 355). In a lengthy review recapping Brontë's career when the Gaskell biography appeared, this same periodical declared, "Like a meteor, [*Jane Eyre*] swept across the literary heavens," and pronounced it "universally read" ("Charlotte Brontë and the Brontë Novels" 317). Lydia Maria Child, the abolitionist writer who was a "close friend of Mrs. Alcott" and known "very well" to her daughters (Cheney 41), wrote to a friend in 1848, "I was perfectly carried away with [Jane Eyre]. I sat up all night long to finish it" (Meltzer and Holland 238).

Alcott seems especially to have been fascinated by Brontë's female characters, for many Janes and Lucys appear throughout her own stories in seeming echo of the heroines of *Jane Eyre* and *Villette*. Again, this particular fascination as a reader reflects an interest of the time. According to Nina Baym, American audiences and reviewers from 1840 to 1860 became increasingly interested in character development, and particularly in the "inner life as the field of action" (*Novels* 94); at least one reviewer credited this new phenomenon specifically to the influence of Charlotte Brontë, who "initiated a new mode in fiction, in those wonderful narratives wherein she exposed to view the inward workings of a restless and fiery nature" (*Southern Literary Messenger* June 1855; qtd. in Baym, *Novels* 94).

In addition to the general appeal of Brontë's works and characters encouraged by popular taste, Alcott's personal interest may have been piqued by the fact that both Jane Eyre and Lucy Snowe, like Charlotte Brontë and Louisa May Alcott, were women struggling to support themselves in societies where there were few opportunities to do so. Both Jane and Lucy work hard and persistently in the face of great obstacles to achieve their aims. Both find work in many of the same places Brontë and Alcott did: as companions, governesses, and teachers. As both Brontë and Alcott freely acknowledged, they frequently drew upon and reshaped personal experiences as part of their artistic method. But despite these inducements for Alcott to identify with Brontë's female characters, Alcott's characters seldom mirror Brontë's. Alcott generally respects the strength, the morality, the fortitude of Jane Eyre and Lucy Snowe, but often chafes against their acceptance of fate.

In this respect, Alcott joins her American counterparts, male and female. According to Nina Baym, a popular form that she calls "woman's fiction"[1] had gradually developed from the 1820s format, which she calls "plots of necessity"—that is, story structures in which the heroine is thrust into a position of having to prove herself—into a more active heroism, wherein "a woman might *wish* to struggle and survive, [and] might find the protected and pampered ideal life . . . frustrating and dull" (*Woman's Fiction* 277). Mid-nineteenth-century feminists looked for writers whose heroines could "stand on their own feet, well planted, and maintain their poise, whatever wind may blow," according to one of them, Emily E. Ford (*The Revolution*, 4 Aug. 1870; qtd. in Reynolds 340–41); they especially criticized writers such as Cooper, whose heroines seemed to be transported (rather than translated) British heroines. On the other side of the Atlantic, as Margaret Dalzeil found in her study of popular British fiction of the period, "it was taken for granted [in stories in the periodicals] that women were inferior to men in all really important . . . qualities" (87), and that "when in penny periodicals we occasionally do find a heroine living by her own exertions and getting along tolerably well, the story is almost invariably of American origin" (90). Further, according to Robert Weisbuch, the American [male] authors in his study asserted that "English literature constitutes a failure of nerve" and "too-readily accommodates itself to a fallen world" (22). That is, the English novelists might enumerate societal problems in great detail, but then place their heroes in positions where they must accommodate themselves to life as it is, whereas the American response would be more of a call to action (although it may sometimes prove futile) against it. That Alcott's work captured this aspect of the American literary consciousness is evident in a remark by Lavinia Russ, who said she loved Jo March and her family because they were "rebels who looked at the world as it was, saw the poverty, the inequality, the ignorance, the fear, and said, 'It isn't good enough' and went to work to change it" (525).

Whether or not the charges of accommodation and lack of courage are justified in regard to Victorian writers and their literature in general, Charlotte Brontë herself exhibits the attitude to which Weisbuch refers. In her first letter to Elizabeth Gaskell, who was later to become her close friend and biographer, she refers to a magazine article that seems to have been an attempt to arouse women on behalf of their own rights, and comments:

> They say . . . that the amelioration of our condition depends on ourselves. Certainly there are evils which our own efforts will best reach; but as certainly there are other evils—deep rooted in

the foundations of the social system—which no efforts of ours can touch; of which we cannot complain; of which it is advisable not too often to think. (Gaskell 309; 27 August 1850)

One can see this attitude reflected in the heroines Brontë creates; with the double restrictions of culture and gender hindering their action, endurance itself becomes a measure of success. One needn't waste time hoping, much less acting, for significant change. Recall, for instance, Jane Eyre's thoughts as she prepares to leave Lowood:

I desired liberty; for liberty I gasped; for liberty I uttered a prayer; it seemed scattered on the wind then faintly blowing. I abandoned it, and framed a humbler supplication; for change, stimulus: that petition, too, seemed swept off into vague space; 'Then,' I cried half desperate, 'Grant me at least a new servitude!' (86)

This is hardly "Give me liberty or give me death!" Jane goes on to muse that servitude seems more of a possibility for her because "It does not sound too sweet . . . like . . . Liberty, Excitement, Enjoyment. . . . But Servitude: That must be matter of fact. Any one may serve" (86).

This is not say that Jane Eyre is a passive heroine. She does seek and find her "new servitude" at Thornfield, and strives to maintain financial independence through her own efforts; she adheres to her moral code even when that involves leaving the man she loves. Nor should one forget how even these limited assertions of selfhood pushed the limits of English Victorian respectability; an early review of *Jane Eyre* called the novel "pre-eminently an anti-Christian composition" for, among other transgressions, its "proud and perpetual assertion of the rights of man" in opposition to "God's appointment" (Rigby 174). But what is important from an American perspective is that Jane never feels the power to control any but her own small piece of existence; she never dares presume that her own actions might bring about great change in her circumstances. In the opening words of the novel: "There was no possibility" (7).[2]

In the world Brontë creates in *Villette*, Lucy Snowe's perseverance becomes an even more touted virtue as the efficacy of action diminishes. Lucy is an extreme exemplar of re-pressed emotion in a society where more energy is expended in containing passionate thought (much less action) than in any other aspect of existence. As if the strict regimen imposed by Mr. Brocklehurst at the Lowood school in *Jane Eyre* wasn't repressive enough, Brontë ascribes even more confinement and containment to the Belgian girls' school in this novel. The teachers at Madame Beck's school, for instance, are warned against taxing their students with any "heavy demand on the memory, the reason, the attention" (146), while the directress devotes *her* memory, reason, and attention to managing a network of spies within the school in order to ensure that her young charges commit no offenses against propriety. In fact, a major symbol in the novel is that of a nun who was supposedly buried alive in the school's garden during the middle ages "for some sin against her vow" (172), and who now haunts the premises. Tony Tanner comments on the minimizing of action in *Villette*: "The two main physical acts of direct contact in the book are Paul's blow to the face of Madame Beck, and his kissing Lucy, but . . . these two most intimate acts . . . are not really seen, indeed hardly described—we infer them from gaps in the text" (25).

Heroine Lucy Snowe prides herself on her ability to keep her emotions under control, and specifically on her ability to keep hope out of her vocabulary and out of her life. The first time she introduces herself to the reader, in fact, she "plead[s] guiltless of that curse, an overheated and discursive imagination" (69). She consistently congratulates herself for not allowing herself to hope for any life better than what she has. Of course, one of Brontë's points is that, in contrast to Jane's search for a *balance* between passion and reason, Lucy's total repression of feeling is not normal or healthy, and it leads to mental instability. Thus we see Lucy Snowe slipping many times from her determined pursuit of rationality. As she sails for Europe, for instance:

> I saw the continent of Europe, like a wide dream-land, far away. Sunshine lay on it, making the long coast one line of gold. . . . For background, spread a sky, solemn and dark-blue, and—grand with

imperial promise, soft with tints of enchantment—strode from
north to south a God-bent bow, an arch of hope. (117)

However, Lucy as narrator immediately urges the reader to
"Cancel the whole of that" passage and substitute a more Lucy-
like sentiment—"Day-dreams are delusions of the demon."
Almost as a further commentary on her lapse into hope, she
then becomes violently sea-sick (117–18).

To foreground Brontë's commitment to emotional control
in these novels is not to deny that both Jane and Lucy have
moments of activity and passion. Jane, in fact, begins her heroic
journey as a passionate child, but Brontë uses the developing
control of her passions as a measure of Jane's developing ma-
turity, somewhat in the manner of Jo March controlling her
temper. Emotion erupts in Brontë's novels when romantic relationships are threatened, as when Rochester tries to persuade
Jane to run away with him to his villa in the south of France
since they cannot legally marry in England and when Lucy fears
that Madame Beck will separate her from M. Paul permanently.
Alcott's heroines often echo Brontë's at such times, even when
they have otherwise been cast more in opposition to Brontë's
characters, as will be seen in greater detail shortly. However, it is
interesting to note that Shirley Keeldar, Brontë's heroine most
actively engaged with the outside world, seems to have held
little interest for Alcott in casting her own characters. Possibly
Shirley's wealth and position as an English heiress (she is Brontë's
most privileged protagonist) and her lack of real struggle other
than where the question of marriage is concerned make her
less a character with whom Alcott could identify, one she was
less inclined to reshape for her own purposes.

Alcott seems also to have been interested in Brontë's male
characters, but she clearly has an idea of heroism that differs
from that of her English counterpart, and perhaps from many
more romantic or sentimental American readers as well. The
North American reviewer, after identifying Rochester as the hero
of *Jane Eyre*, states that he

became a great favorite in the boarding-schools and in the wor-
shipful society of governesses. That portion of Young America known

as ladies' men began to swagger and swear in the presence of the gentler sex, and to allude darkly to events in their lives which excused impudence and profanity. ("Novels of the Season" 356)

Contrary to such Rochester-worship, in one of Alcott's most famous glosses on *Jane Eyre*, *Work*'s Christie Devon exclaims, "I like Jane, but never can forgive her marrying that man [Rochester], as I haven't much faith in the saints such sinners make" (80). Christie goes on to argue with Philip Fletcher, who has suggested that a good woman might be a man's "salvation," that "a man should have energy enough to save himself, and not expect the 'weaker sex,' as he calls her, to do it for him" (81). As with her heroines, Alcott prefers her heroes to act and not merely to endure. Further, she unequivocally rejects the notion that women are inferior to men and works, in her own fiction, toward an ideal of gender equality. Thus, those male characters of Brontë's who possess wealth and superior attitudes hold little interest for Alcott except, in the case of Rochester, as someone against whom to argue. Active working men, such as *Villette*'s Dr. John and Paul Emanuel, provide more positive models for her, although the question of equality frequently leads Alcott to translate even these sources. Positively or negatively, the characters of Charlotte Brontë's novels often provided Alcott with personalities that she often reshaped or subverted, but nevertheless drew upon, as she developed her talents as an American writer.

NOVELS

The Inheritance, Alcott's first attempt at the novel form at seventeen,[3] demonstrates her use of Brontë as a model from an early age. On an English country estate, the orphan Edith Adelon is governess to Amy, youngest daughter of the Hamilton family. The novel includes a Blanche Ingram–type character in Lady Ida Clare, a "highborn and lovely" (13) but proud woman who seeks to marry for money and who becomes Edith's rival. In coincidental plot developments that echo without exactly replicating *Jane Eyre*, Edith discovers that she is a blood relative to the family she loves, and the fortune she inherits makes her the societal equal of the man she loves and ultimately marries. Edith as a heroine is both excessively demure, unlike Jane Eyre—"With an angel's calm and almost holy beauty, . . . as holy and as pure a heart—gentle, true, and tender" (14)—and at times unexpectedly active, like some of Alcott's later heroines. She climbs down a cliff to rescue her charge Amy when she falls on an outing (while Amy's older brother can only "wr[i]ng his hands in helpless grief" [33]), and later she manages to control her high-spirited mount after Ida spitefully frightens it. Even in this slight juvenile piece, then, Alcott was already imitating her English model in some respects but seeking to articulate a unique—and uniquely American—story in others.

Alcott's experiences with other early novels, *Moods* and *Work*, show clearer signs of authorial struggles as she sought to develop her craft. Although she wrote the first draft of *Moods* in a short period in 1860 when "Genius burned so fiercely that for four weeks I wrote all day and planned nearly all night" (*Journals* 99; August 1860), Alcott "remodelled" it during a three-week period in 1861 (*Journals* 103; February 1861). Publishers' refusals to consider it without major revisions to shorten the manuscript kept it out of print until she undertook another revision that entailed the omission of "ten chapters & . . . many of my favorite things" (*Journals* 132; October 1864). Even when the book finally appeared in 1865, Alcott was not satisfied with it. She wrote: "'Moods' is not what I meant to have it, for I followed bad advice & took out many things which explained my idea & made the characters more natural & consistent" (*Letters* 108; 18 February 1865).

Contemporary reviewers generally agreed with Alcott's assessment; while they applauded the "freshness and self-reliance" (*Harper's* 35) of *Moods* and especially of its heroine, Sylvia Yule, most also acknowledged an unevenness of quality, as though the author had a fine idea but couldn't quite carry it through. One reviewer, sounding a bit like American writers criticizing the British, noted that

> [o]ur writers, being reluctant to enter upon paths which lead over stone walls and through swamps to doubtful lands, have contented themselves with portraying and analysing the characters

formed amid the trials and passions generated by the imperfect but disciplinary conditions of society and its institutions themselves; and though [Alcott] cannot be denied a partial success, it must be confessed that she faints at last, and leaves society with its old frontiers. (*Reader* 422)

Henry James cited a related problem with Alcott's novel in alluding to the melodrama to which she resorted at several points in *Moods*, commenting that "Miss Alcott doubtless knows men and women well enough to deal successfully with their every-day virtues and temptations, but not well enough to handle great dramatic passions" (280), suggesting that Alcott's "fainting" resulted not from a "failure of nerve," but a lack of expertise. In fact, some of the problems of this early edition of *Moods* may be attributed to Alcott's inexpert adaptation of British forms in what is essentially a book steeped in American consciousness.

Moods takes its name and epigraph from Emerson's essay "Experience"; Sarah Elbert's introduction to the 1991 reprinting of the novel argues convincingly for its Americanness, including Alcott's "virtual invention of the American girl . . . temporally and geographically specific" (xxix) in Sylvia Yule, and the Golden Wedding depicted in chapter 5 as "an American version of Jean Paul Richter's *Jubelsnoir*" (xxxiii). Nevertheless, as even James recognized, *Moods*'s dark, brooding Adam Warwick is a Rochester-like hero. The 1865 version of *Moods* opens with a chapter depicting a melodramatic scene between Warwick and his Cuban fiancée, Ottila, which recalls in general the nineteenth-century characterization of the "dark" island woman as passionate and unchaste, and Rochester's story of his own marriage in particular. In a tone repeatedly characterized by the narrator as satirical, Warwick deems Ottila "a woman of strong passions and weak principles; hungry for power and intent on pleasure; accomplished in deceit and reckless in trampling on the nobler instincts" (9), just as Rochester bitterly characterizes his West Indian Creole wife's nature as "wholly alien to mine . . . her cast of mind common, low, narrow, and singularly incapable of being led to anything higher. . . . at once intemperate and unchaste" (*JE* 310).

Then, in a strange reversal of roles, Ottila begs Adam to stay and "save me from myself" (11), much as Rochester pleads with Jane to "be my comforter, my rescuer" (JE 323). For Adam, as for Jane, this is the argument that comes closest to making him relent. Ottila's cry goes "Straight through the one vulnerable point in the man's pride . . . to the man's pity" (11); Jane's "Conscience and Reason turn[ed] traitors . . . and charged me with crime in resisting him. . . . Feeling . . . clamoured wildly. . . . 'Save him; love him'" (JE 321). For Adam, as for Jane, final refusal of the plea rests upon one thing: "Self-respect" (6) is Adam's ultimate reason for leaving Ottila, just as Jane's is "I will respect myself" (JE 321).

But as is clear from the almost immediate reversals of *Jane Eyre* roles in the opening pages of *Moods*, in which Rochester becomes embodied in the weaker of the two lovers, Alcott could hardly be comfortable with this Brontëan hero for even a few paragraphs. Unlike Rochester, who marries his island beauty and regrets it later, Adam Warwick abandons Ottila as the narrator applauds his steadfastness in the struggle between them, "a war which fills the world with unmated pairs and the long train of evils arising from marriages made from impulse, and not principle" (12). Although Adam cannot humiliate himself or Ottila by breaking off their newly made engagement, he leaves with an agreement that if he has not changed his mind in a year, they will not marry. Like Rochester returning to England from the "dripping orange-trees, . . . drenched pomegranates . . . and the refulgent dawn of the tropics" (JE 312) in an attempt to salvage his life after Bertha's madness manifests itself, Adam resolves to go "Straight to the North," because "This luxurious life enervates me" (12). Once Adam returns to New England, however, he becomes a much less melodramatic and more active hero, modeled, as both Sarah Elbert ("Introduction" 30) and Mary Oleson Urbanski have noted, on Henry David Thoreau. Like her hero, Alcott tries to distance herself from the melodrama she almost immediately seems to recognize as unfitting and turns to her own New England roots for a solution. At this point in her writing career, however, she is only able to do this in overt rather than subtle ways, turning her hero modeled on Rochester to one modeled on Thoreau.

Elbert suggests further parallels to *Jane Eyre* in *Moods* in that Sylvia seeks consolation from her eventual husband, Geoffrey

Moor, after Adam's betrayal (she thinks he has returned to Cuba to marry Ottila) just as Jane seeks refuge at Moor House, the home of St. John, Diana, and Mary Rivers, after she learns the truth about Rochester's marriage ("Introduction" 29). However, in most respects, Sylvia's situation does not really parallel Jane's.[4] In fact, if there are further Brontëan allusions in this novel, they are not to Moor House, but to Robert and Louis Moore, the love interests in Brontë's *Shirley*,[5] whose eventual marriages to Shirley and her quiet friend Caroline Helstone take place in a double wedding similar to that of Sylvia and Moor and Sylvia's brother Mark to his "adoringly submissive" (108) Jessie. Like Shirley, whom Brontë describes as "fettered," "conquered," "vanquished," and "restricted" (*S* 637) as she awaits her wedding, and who refuses to make any preparations for the day, Sylvia refuses to set a date for her own wedding after she has agreed to the engagement. Alcott's description of Sylvia awaiting her wedding seems to echo Brontë's: she is "undemonstrative," "unsentimental," and "unchanged" (*M* 108). Just as Louis Moore eventually takes over the preparations for Shirley's wedding, Sylvia's sister Prue takes over hers. In both cases, the brothers' weddings—Louis's brother Robert's to Caroline and Sylvia's brother Mark's to Jessie—eventually force Shirley and Sylvia to proceed with their own weddings, as double ceremonies. If Alcott was taking inspiration from Brontë, it was to recreate the atmosphere of tension surrounding the wedding of what she considered another set of "unmated pairs."

Even here, there is a major difference between Alcott and Brontë in Alcott's attempt to move beyond the traditional marriage plot, "writing beyond the ending," as Rachel Blau du Plessis puts it. Shirley's marriage takes place on the next-to-last page of the novel; the closing paragraphs then focus on the "mighty mill" Robert and Louis build that has forever altered "a bonnie spot—full of oak trees and nut trees" (*S* 645–46). Sylvia's marriage, however, like virtually all marriages in Alcott stories, is but one step along a heroine's path.[6] In this case, it takes place almost exactly at the center of the novel. Alcott not only insists that life continues after the wedding, but that the way in which it continues is worth exploring.

Probably she reasoned that Sylvia would be unhappy and eventually confess her love for Warwick to her husband, but despite a daring discussion in which all the principals except Moor (including the novel's "voice of wisdom," Faith Dane) agree that divorce should sometimes be an option for unhappy couples, she could not quite propose this solution for her heroine. Left with no clear direction, Alcott lapses into melodrama in a denouement which has Sylvia summoning Moor back from Europe not because she loves him but because she is dying; he and Warwick (who has accompanied him) are shipwrecked in sight of land, á la Margaret Fuller, and Adam drowns saving him; Moor returns to Sylvia to tend her lovingly until her death a few months later. In this early novel, Alcott begins by using Brontëan characters, but already realizes clear differences between herself and her literary model. They appear not only in plot and character, but also in the stylistic ways in which the plots and characters are presented. While Sylvia's inner life, the strongest focus of a Brontëan heroine, is important to Alcott, she expresses the inner life through external, not internal, dialogue. Possibly Alcott's interest in the theater gave her an ear for the power of conversation to reveal character; in any case, the use of dialogue, and particularly the American vernacular, that characterizes Alcott at her best is already evident in this early novel. Nevertheless, in this first version of *Moods*, melodramatic speech mingles uncomfortably with believable dialogue just as Rochester finds his way into the character of Adam Warwick. At this point Alcott's own art was not yet formed enough to go confidently in a new own direction, even though she instinctively began to abandon the old.

The other major enterprise upon which Alcott was working at this time demonstrates some of the same problems as *Moods*: specifically, the determination to move in a new direction coupled with the uncertainty of exactly where that would lead. Alcott began the project, which at this time she called "Success" or "Christie," with great enthusiasm. She offered a look at the portion of it that she had completed to James Redpath (publisher of her first successful book, *Hospital Sketches*, the marginally fictionalized account of her experiences as a

Civil War nurse), asserting that, though unfinished, it was "better written and more interesting" (*Letters* 87; July 1863) than another piece she was sending him. She answered another of Redpath's requests for more stories with "I'll work with all my might at Success & let you have it as soon as possible, for I want that to come first" (*Letters* 97; 2 December 1863). She apparently encountered some sort of a block shortly thereafter, for she wrote Redpath in January 1864, "'Success' is just where I left it for though I have tried a dozen times I cannot get on with it" (*Letters* 101), and only nine days later, "'Success' still remains in a muddle" (*Letters* 104). She notes in her journal later in the year that she "Wrote several chapters of Christie & was getting on finely" (*Journals* 132; October 1864) when it became clear to her how she might revise *Moods* for publication; at that point the unfinished "Success" seems to have been laid aside for eight years.

While no clear evidence exists to determine exactly how much of the novel was written when Alcott abandoned it in 1864, she had described the plan of it to Redpath in her first letter concerning the work:

> This one was begun with the design of putting some [of] my own experiences into a story illustrating the trials of young women who want employment & find it hard to get. . . . The story is made up of various essays this girl makes, her failures & successes told in chapters merry or sad, & various characters all more or less from life are introduced to help or hinder her. (*Letters* 87; July 1863)

The many allusions to Brontë's *Jane Eyre*[7] and *Villette*, especially in the early chapters of the novel, and the allusions to one of Alcott's favorite works, *Pilgrim's Progress*,[8] in all three novels, suggests that Alcott conceived her work-in-progress as a female *bildungsroman* at least somewhat in the spirit of two of Charlotte Brontë's powerful novels with autobiographical aspects like her own. Further parallels may have suggested themselves since both women had shared many of the same work experiences—governess, companion, teacher—en route to writing careers.

But there is no doubt, from the first line of Alcott's novel, that she has Brontë's tales in mind as models only to a certain point, after which they are almost anti-models. David Reynolds's comment that "the combined forces of Protestantism and democracy enabled American women to be more independent and morally self-controlling" (341) than their foreign counterparts, both in fact and fiction, is useful in clarifying a point of division between Brontë and Alcott. Brontë's heroines share with Alcott's both the moral force and the work ethic associated with Protestantism, but the rigid class structure of England precludes from Brontë's striving heroines the optimism that their assertiveness can make a real difference in their lives.

This optimism manifests itself in the exuberant, semi-mocking tone that Alcott utilizes in the early chapters of "Success." This voice, in one sense, aligns her with other American writers of her time, whose "troubled refusal" of the Romantics eventually gave way to an impulse for "undoing [the Victorians] by parody" (Weisbuch 20). Alcott's tone, however, is never mean-spirited. In fact, the sprightly voice she employs in "Success" is one that previously had served Alcott well as Nurse Tribulation Periwinkle in *Hospital Sketches* and would do so again in a short piece on the utopian experiment at Fruitlands in which her family had participated, called "Transcendental Wild Oats." The tone is satirical in that it holds a mirror up to reality in the hope of effecting change. Alcott uses this tone when taking a realistic look at serious problems: the Civil War hospital, the idealistic notions of the transcendentalists, and in this case the conditions of working women. However, Alcott's treatment of social problems in the early episodes of Christie's story has none of the bitter edge that sometimes characterizes satire: her satire is much more Horatian than Juvenalian. It tends to resemble the humorous tone of her countryman Ben Franklin's satirical essays, although Alcott is never as earthy as Franklin.

Levity may seem an odd approach to Christie's story. Like Jane Eyre, Christie Devon is an orphan whose mother commits the unpardonable sin, in her family's eyes, of marrying a poor man for love; both her parents die within a short time of one another, leaving their young daughter in the care of relatives. Though Alcott grants her heroine an understanding Aunt Betsey, her mother's brother, Uncle Enos, is a match for Jane Eyre's

Aunt Reed; totally unsympathetic to his young niece, he deems her "Jest like her mother, full of hifalutin notions, discontented, and sot in her own idees" (*Work* 9), thus reversing the aunt/uncle sympathies in *Jane Eyre*. Another important Brontë heroine, *Villette's* Lucy Snowe, is also an orphan living with relatives, but she doesn't choose to reveal the specific circumstances, and in fact rather perversely conceals them.

Both Jane and Lucy, however, are forced out of their adoptive homes, Jane when she is sent to school at Lowood and Lucy when "there remained no possibility of dependence on others" (*V* 95). Contrast these situations with Christie Devon's first words: "Aunt Betsey, there's going to be a new Declaration of Independence" (*W* 1). With an allusion to the Seneca Falls Convention of 1848, which had drafted a new Declaration of Independence that asserted that all men *and* women were created equal, Alcott's American heroine leaves a home that is stable and at least partially loving because "I'm old enough to take care of myself," adding, "and if I'd been a boy, I should have been told to do so long ago" (2). As Elaine Showalter observes, the opening alone demonstrates "how much more radical [than British] American thinking was on the woman question by this time " (Introduction, *Alternative Alcott* xxxi).

Once Christie's journey toward self-sufficiency is underway, Alcott repeatedly makes references to Brontë, but her lighter tone suggests that, unlike the creator of Jane Eyre and Lucy Snowe, she has confidence that her character's efforts will bring about a brighter future. That is, her more optimistic attitude toward her subject matter dictates a style that corresponds to it. Further, Christie looks upon the various passages in her journey as new adventures, not new servitude; like her character's attitude, Alcott's prose proceeds more through detailed depictions of outward events rather than the internal thought processes that Brontë shares with her readers.

Unlike Jane or even Lucy, Christie feels she is not educated enough to be a governess, so she cheerfully accepts her first job as a household servant; her employer, Mrs. Stuart, almost immediately decides Christie's name is too long and that "I should prefer to call you Jane" (19). Christie keeps this job for one year, until she accidentally sets fire to the Stuarts' attic when she falls asleep reading. The Stuarts, returning from a social evening, frantically rescue their servant and their house, but the sight of Mr. Stuart "skipping among the fragments with an agility which contrasted with his stout figure in full evening costume, and his besmirched face," and Mrs. Stuart, "in her most regal array" but with her "tiara all askew" (32), strike Christie as so ludicrous that she breaks into a "hysterical . . . peal of laughter" (32), at which Mrs. Stuart declares that "She has been at the wine, or lost her wits" (32) and fires her, although "Mr. Stuart would have pardoned her on the spot" (33).

Alcott's language in this passage recalls the dramatic fire at Thornfield set by the madwoman in Rochester's attic, his wife Bertha, the hysterical laughter Jane often hears coming from the upper rooms of the mansion, Mrs. Poole's propensity for drink that allows the woman she is supposed to be guarding to escape and set the fire, Rochester's attempt to save her and the servants from the fire, and finally, Jane's later aside to the reader that "I forgave him [Rochester] . . . on the spot" (JE 302). Alcott transforms some of the most dramatic moments of *Jane Eyre*—the fire that maims Rochester but also frees him from his marriage, and possibly more importantly, Jane's immediate forgiveness of his treachery—into an exciting but eventually minor incident in Christie Devon's life. These events, placed well toward the end of Brontë's book, after her heroine has struggled to attain much personal growth and development, help to bring about Jane's fairy tale ending; however, they are but the first step in Christie's journey. The "twinkle" in Mr. Stuart's eye as he lets Christie go the next morning may well be in the eye of Louisa May Alcott as well. A convenient fire is not enough to bring about a happy ending for her heroine, for most of her adventures still lie before her.

Christie's next exploit takes her into the world of the theater; it alludes to Brontë's *Villette*, beginning with the young woman who persuades her to try acting, Miss Lucy Black. Although Christie works professionally as an actress and Lucy's experience in *Villette* is limited to one performance, Lucy Snowe's performance resembles Christie's last appearance on the stage. Christie's show is a "benefit," a special performance meant to showcase her as an actress; Lucy's is a last-minute substitution in an amateur production for her employer's fete; in both cases, the heroines act opposite friends in a love triangle and discover previously untapped power within themselves.

Although Christie's diligence at her craft has shown her to be a competent if not brilliant actress, her performance at the benefit "surprised even those who knew her best" (53). The emotional power of her friend Lucy's performance further enhances Christie's acting; onstage, Christie realizes that Lucy's fear that Christie is plotting to win the actor whom she loves, St. George, has given "sudden power and passion" to the girl's performance. Christie responds by using the words of the play they are performing to reassure Lucy she will "restore the stolen treasure" (54). Lucy understands and completes the play, "comforted without knowing why" (54). Brontë's Lucy, *Villette*'s Lucy Snowe, plays a man in her performance; she is one of two rivals for the affections of the character played by her friend Ginevra Fanshawe. After a difficult start, Lucy feels "the right power come—the spring demanded rise and gush inwardly" (210). As she becomes more comfortable on stage, she begins to realize that Ginevra is playing her role, not to the stage actors, but to her real-life secret beau in the audience. Lucy herself is in love with this man, and displaces her passion onto Ginevra as the part requires her to try to win Ginevra's character back to herself, while Ginevra responds as did Christie's friend Lucy: "I acted as if wishful and resolute to win and conquer. Ginevra seconded me; between us we half-changed the nature of the *role*, gilding it from top to toe. Between the acts M. Paul told us he knew not what possessed us" (210).

While Christie uses the talent that emerges in this performance to help her woman friend, Lucy Snowe uses hers to tease the man she admires by showing him that his love can, in fact, be won away from him. Further, although both women discover this unusual power in what prove to be their final stage performances, Alcott's attitude in moving Christie away from the theater is very different from Brontë's. Christie had already begun to realize that three years as an actress had had its satisfactions, but was turning her into a woman with "no care for anyone but herself" (49); she regards herself as "a child who knows it is astray, yet cannot see the right path" (52) and resolves to leave the profession after her benefit. A piece of stage machinery that falls and injures her at the end of the performance merely confirms her decision.

Lucy Snowe, on the other hand, is at first delighted with her on-stage accomplishment, but then decides that "to cherish and exercise this new-found faculty might gift me with a world of delight, but it would not do for a mere looker-on at life," and so makes a deliberate decision to "put by" her artistic ambitions (211). While Christie thoroughly examines this career and decides it is not something that will ultimately bring her happiness, Lucy seems to abjure it precisely because she thinks it might. Here again, Alcott seems specifically to be comparing her active heroine's hopeful progress with Brontë's heroine's urge to repress both activity and hope.

In Christie's next career, that of governess (she had "increased her knowledge of music, and learned French enough to venture teaching it to very young pupils" [59] by this time), Alcott returns to the world of *Jane Eyre* and amplifies her earlier allusion to Jane's pardoning of Rochester. After Christie takes a job as governess to two young children (whose mother's name happens to be Charlotte), her employer's wealthy brother begins to take an interest in her. It is crucial to the core of humor with which Alcott imbues this episode that Philip Fletcher is never portrayed as a villain, but as a selfish man, spoiled by "thirty-five years of ease and pleasure" (62), whose idea of a wife is "a good-tempered, faithful soul to take care of me" (76). He approaches Christie to propose with a "mixture of tender, selfish, and regretful thoughts in his mind" (77)—and finds her reading *Jane Eyre*.

After Christie voices her negative opinion of Rochester to Fletcher, a discussion ensues in which Christie declares it is no "fair bargain" (81) for a man to expect a woman to "save" him—exactly what Rochester asked of Jane, and what Philip does, in fact, expect of Christie. The condescension with which he treats her in offering to "forgive" her poverty and her acting career if she will but obey his command to "smile, and say, 'Yes, Philip,' like a sweet soul" (83) only enrages Christie. When he protests that she should be "grateful for the sacrifice I made," she answers:

The sacrifice would not have been *all* yours, for it is what *we are*, not what *we have*, that makes one human being superior to another. I am as well-born as you in spite of my poverty; my life, I think, has been a better one than yours; my heart, I know, is fresher, and my memory has fewer faults and follies to reproach me with. What can you give me but money and position in return for the youth and freedom I should sacrifice in marrying you? (87)

The scene recalls Jane's speech to Rochester in which she asserts her equality with him:

Do you think, because I am poor, obscure, plain, and little, I am soulless and heartless?—You think wrong!—I have as much soul as you,—and full as much heart! And if God had gifted me with some beauty, and much wealth, I should have made it as hard for you to leave me, as it is now for me to leave you. . . . —it is my spirit that addresses your spirit; just as if both had passed through the grave, and we stood at God's feet, equal,—as we are! (255–56)

And Rochester assents: "As we are!" (256). But this scene takes place when Rochester is still withholding the secret of his marriage, so the spiritual equality to which the two attest is not supported by the facts of the situation: Rochester is still very much in control, even though he complains, "You master me" (263). Even when Jane's inheritance and Rochester's misfortunes have ostensibly made them more equal (Gilbert and Gubar 368–69), the language of the text speaks to this issue equivocally. Jane persists in calling Rochester "Master" or "Mr. Rochester," yet is touched by "his dependence" (444) on her.

After their marriage, Jane claims, "I am my husband's life as fully as he is mine" (456), yet the life she describes is one where she is his willing servant, waiting on him, reading to him, and leading him where he wishes to go. While in Brontë's eyes the love they share makes them the spiritual equals they had declared themselves to be earlier (and even Alcott has Christie declare in the first chapter of *Work* that love makes dependence bearable [9]), a life of service to a semi-invalid (as are both Rochester and Fletcher) is clearly not the sort of · marriage Alcott has in mind for her own heroine. Thus Alcott's heroine specifically repudiates the caretaker marriage Jane Eyre effects with Rochester and asserts that there is more to equality in marriage than wealth and social class. Christie manages once again to find some humor in her situation; she greatly enjoys her employer's chagrin when she discovers that her brother has proposed to the governess and goes on her way to another adventure that allows Alcott to make even more comments on the reasons people marry in *Jane Eyre*.

Having refused a position as the wife of an invalid, Christie next takes a job as companion to an invalid, Helen Carrol. Alcott's tone in the novel becomes much more serious from this point on; it soon becomes clear that Helen suffers from a form of hereditary madness. This particular plot device was not uncommon in gothic or sensation literature; some of the details may well stem from Alcott's "experience in caring for a young friend during a temporary fit of insanity" (Cheney 111) during the summer of 1860, her sister Anna's experiences in teaching art at an asylum in Syracuse shortly after that, or, if this chapter was added to the book at a later date,[9] Alcott's experiences in caring for the invalid Anna Weld during her first trip to Europe in 1865. However, the many names and plot similarities in this episode that match those in *Jane Eyre*, and its placement in a part of the novel that contains so many allusions to Brontë, suggest that Alcott was again shaping her own narrative in ways that comment more seriously on Brontë's and that further her own purposes as well.

Alcott deals with two generations of madness here; Mrs. Carrol had married Mr. Carrol because "He was rich, she poor and proud" (109) and had four children with him, although she knew of the hereditary madness in his family.[10] Both parents had kept the secret from their children until Mr. Carrol revealed it to his oldest son on his deathbed. The great suffering that ensues, however, is not so much that of the married couple—Mr. Carrol dies without contracting the disease and his wife is left a rich widow—but upon their children. Helen (the name of Jane Eyre's young friend who dies at Lowood) is engaged to Edward (Rochester's first name) when her brother finally tells her the truth about her heritage; despite their love, they break off the engagement and Edward leaves for India. Helen then attempts suicide and is locked up in an attic room for a year to hide the family's embarrassment, until Christie arrives to stay with her.

By appropriating details from *Jane Eyre* but blending them with her own imaginative process as she does here, Alcott demonstrates the way in which her mature work was to allude to Brontë in more oblique and subtle ways as she developed in artistic power. Brontë brings the idea of marrying for money into *Jane Eyre* in a negative light in the person of Blanche Ingram, and makes it clear through her depiction of the relation between Jane and Rochester that spiritual compatibility is a much more valid and important reason for marriage than money. She even gives Jane an inheritance before her return to Thornfield so she does not need Rochester's money, but instead is free to marry him for love. Alcott's purpose is far different, as is her emphasis; she wishes to foreground the pernicious effects, not on the would-be spouses, but on the children of the "unmated pairs," as she calls them. So, while Mr. and Mrs. Carrol do marry for money, the more deleterious effects are visited upon the children of their union; Helen Carrol eventually succumbs to the family madness and commits suicide. Thus the match between the two novels is much less exact in this chapter of *Work* than in the earlier ones, but this is precisely the point. While Alcott may have been moved by *Jane Eyre* and by Brontë's insights on love and equality as the proper basis for marriage, her own agenda was far different from Brontë's, and the more power she gained as a writer, the more she was able to articulate her own purposes in her writing. Alcott's marriage discussion, in this case, probably reflects her own observations of romance in America, and particularly her experience as the child of an "unmatched pair" as much as Brontë's reflects her observations of British society and culture.

Unmarried herself and no longer needed as a nurse/companion after Helen's death, Christie's fortunes deteriorate after leaving the Carrols; she loses her job at a sewing factory when she stands up for a woman she has befriended because the supervisors have discovered her past as a "fallen woman" (although, in a fashion typical of Alcott's active approach to life, Christie quits; she is not fired) and nearly starves, emotionally as well as physically, trying to make her living by taking in sewing in her lonely room. Christie wanders out in a fit of fever and despair, as did Jane after leaving Rochester, as did Lucy Snowe during her lonely school vacation.

As Jane is reborn at Moor-House and Lucy at the Brettons', Christie too is nursed back to health, but in the much more humble home of the washerwoman Cinthy Wilkins. After recovering, Christie goes to work as companion and housekeeper for a Quaker woman, fantasizing Mrs. Sterling's son David into heroic proportions after she is told that he "had a great trouble some years ago and suffered much" (216–17). In one more allusion to Brontë, Alcott has Christie "set out to find her master" (225) when Mrs. Sterling asks her to call David in to dinner. Even though what she finds is a "workman scraping the mould off his boots," with "nothing interesting, romantic, pensive, or even stern" (226) about him, Christie persists in attempting to make him into a Byronic hero. She can't help thinking, "I'd rather he'd be masterful, and order me about" (236). Christie's struggles with her perceptions of David may well mirror Alcott's own frustrations: having directly eschewed Rochester as a model earlier on in her story, she now struggles to create an alternative to him.

It is unknown where in the "muddle" of this novel Alcott stopped in 1864, but it seems safe to assume that some consternation may have developed at this point, for Alcott had never yet created a *happy* wedding for any of her heroines; one can imagine that marriage may have seemed an unsatisfactory conclusion considering the adventurous heroine she had in Christie and the solitary pilgrimage upon which she had set out. At any rate, in November of 1872, she "Got out the old manuscript of 'Success,' and called it 'Work'" (*Journals* 183). It began publication in the *Christian Union* less than a month later, and was published as a complete book in June 1873. The later chapters of the novel describe the slow process of Christie and David's developing friendship, romance, and wedding, immediately after which they both march off to the Civil War, he as a soldier and she as a nurse. Alcott provides this relationship, founded upon Christie's abandonment of her romantic notions and the slow development of love between equals who work together, as an alternative to the unfair bargain she saw in *Jane Eyre*.

As in *Moods*, there is life (for the heroine, at least) after marriage. David dies in the war, but Christie lives to give birth to their daughter. The novel takes Christie to age forty, when she is the head of a community of women that includes many of the women she had met upon her adventures; she now enters public life as a mediator between working women and "ladies" who are "rich . . . in generous theories, [but] poor in practical methods of relief" (426). As Brontë does in *Jane Eyre*, Alcott incorporates allusions to *Pilgrim's Progress* in the closing pages of *Work* when Christie receives a painting of Mr. Greatheart leading the way from the City of Destruction. This shared allusion highlights another difference of style and purpose between Brontë and Alcott. Brontë compares St. John Rivers to Greatheart in a symbolic way to explain his character more fully as it appears to Jane at the end of the novel. Alcott works more allegorically than symbolically; Christie's character is defined well enough for the reader to perceive her as an individual, yet Alcott presents her as a secularized version of the allegorical Christiana in *Pilgrim's Progress*. Early in *Work*, Christie is described as "one of that large class of women who, moderately endowed with talents, earnest and true-hearted, are driven by necessity, temperament, or principle out into the world to find support, happiness, and homes for themselves" (11). If Alcott's "translation" lacks the lush imagery of Brontë's gothic romance, it also holds out the possibility for others to participate in her adventure and her triumph. Christie Devon's determined heroism brings her a "happy ending" marked by more possibility and more community than does that of Jane Eyre, alone with her child and her husband at Ferndean. Both authors give their heroines their due reward, but Jane's triumph, though true to Jane's quest for love and belonging, clearly is not encompassing enough for Alcott or the goals she sets for her own heroine.

The mid-1860s did not mark the end of Alcott's *Moods* any more than it had *Work*. When her publisher returned the copyright of the novel to her in 1881, she revised it again for republication in 1882, making significant changes in the beginning and end. She eliminated the melodramatic first chapter, in which Adam Warwick confronts Ottila in Cuba, and changed the ending so that Sylvia does not die, but lives to make the best she can of her marriage to Moor, even though he is never the consuming passion of her life. As a result, the 1882 version opens with a chapter titled "Sylvia," in which the reader meets the tomboyish teenager as she is being dragged out of bed in the morning by her more ambitious (and ladylike) sister; it ends with Sylvia the wife trying to live with the consequences of her actions. Thus Alcott removes the emphasis the earlier novel placed on Rochesterian/Thoreauvian hero, Adam Warwick, and places her heroine squarely at the center of the plot, where she dominates the action from beginning to end.

Alcott does not alter the marriage discussion at the novel's center—for the novel does revolve around the marriage plot to a much larger extent than does *Work*—but a slight change to Sylvia's later discussion with Faith Dane is worth noting. In the first version of *Moods*, Sylvia (already married to Moor) asks Faith "to which [of the two men] should you cleave" if she were in her position, and Faith answers, "To neither" (178). She rejects Moor because "Friendship cannot fill love's place," but also rejects Warwick as a mate for Sylvia, because of her own personality flaws. Faith's choice of words is interesting here: "If you were blind, a cripple, or cursed with some incurable infirmity of body, would you not hesitate to bind yourself and your affliction to another?" (179) and Sylvia answers that she would not merely hesitate, but refuse. Faith continues, saying that Sylvia's immature moodiness is an affliction that she should not take the chance of imposing upon another person. This might be seen as a commentary on *Jane Eyre*, for Rochester is both blind and crippled when he and Jane finally marry.

In the 1882 version, Sylvia's question is slightly altered: she asks "which of the two who love me should I have married had fate given me a choice in time" (270).[11] Faith again says "Neither," presumably rejecting Moor as before, and commenting again on Sylvia's "infirmity." However, she then continues to predict that union with Adam would be an "unequal marriage" because his powerful personality would destroy her: "it would be like a wood bird mating with an eagle" (271). The profusion of bird imagery throughout *Jane Eyre*, including Rochester's comment that Jane is like "a wild, frantic bird that is rending its own plumage in its desperation" (256) during his first proposal, his reference to her as "my skylark" in the second (444), and most of all, Jane's comment immediately after that "this avowal of *dependence* [was] just as if a royal eagle . . . should be forced to entreat a sparrow to become its purveyor" (444; emphasis mine) suggest that Alcott was making an even stronger and more direct comment on the Jane-Rochester marriage than she had earlier. Not only was it improper for Jane to run away with Rochester while his wife was still living, but it was wrong, to Alcott at least, in an even more serious way at the end. Alcott's insistence on equality of the power of personality in marriage clearly reveals her American and her personal bias; whereas Brontë had the British class structure to contend with in asserting Jane's equality with Rochester, Alcott need not attend to this problem, at least overtly. She is far more concerned that a union of a strong, Byronic personality—an "eagle"—with a weaker one—a "wood bird"—will eventually result in one overwhelming the other or one being put in the position of needing to "save" the other. In either case, what she most fears is that the price of gaining love is the loss of self.

At the same time that Alcott's revision of *Moods* puts increasing distance between herself and Charlotte Brontë in a general sense, it makes her connections to American ideals even more specific. Her new second chapter recasts Moor as a nature lover, making him, in addition to Warwick, more of a Thoreauvian hero (although Moor is rich!) and ultimately a more suitable match for Sylvia than in the earlier version. More importantly, her revisions emphasize the relationship between her fictional piece and Emerson's essay "Experience," from which she had drawn both her title and epigraph. The original epigraph, quoting Emerson, reads, "Life is a train of moods like a string of beads; and as we pass through them they prove to be many colored lenses, which paint the world their own hue, and each shows us only what lies in its own focus." Indeed, the earlier *Moods* demonstrated the many dangers and problems brought about by a life ruled by temperament. As Emerson also noted in this essay, "We see young men who owe us a new world . . . but they never acquit the debt; they die young and dodge the account" (232), an accurate description of the narrative outcome for both Sylvia and Adam in 1864.

The later version, however, uses Sylvia's experience to exemplify not only the problems of temperament, but Emerson's solution to them as well:

> We should not postpone and refer and wish, but do broad justice where we are, by whomever we deal with, accepting our actual companions and circumstances, however humble or odious, as the mystic officials to whom the universe has delegated its whole pleasures for us. . . . We live amid surfaces, and the true art of life is to skate well on them. (236–37)

Sylvia decides to accept her companion and her circumstances, Moor returns home to "his wife, not the wayward child he wooed, the melancholy girl he married, but a woman" (276), and the two decide to try to make their marriage work. In learning to deal with Moor as her husband and with her life as a woman and not a moody child, Sylvia does begin to "skate well": "to live, not dream, a long and happy life" (*M* 280). It is "a wiser if less romantic fate" (225), as Alcott notes in her new Preface; it is also a more Emersonian, less Brontëan one.[12] Alcott, too, was learning to "skate well" in her early novels; her experiments with parody and allegory in them may represent an attempt to bring the passionate "heart" of Brontë's fiction into her own without lapsing into melodrama or sentimentality. In her early novels, Alcott draws heavily upon her reading of Brontë, if sometimes only to argue with her, as she creates her plots and characters. As she revises *Moods* and completes *Work* later, however, Alcott assimilates her reading of Brontë into a context increasingly American and increasingly her own, though she never abandons the connection entirely.

SENSATION FICTION

Alcott had written in her preface to the revised edition of *Moods* that thirty years of life experience between this and her first conception of Sylvia's story had taught her "the possibility of finding happiness after disappointment, and making love and duty go hand in hand" (225). This life experience, especially during the 1860s, included professional experiences through which she developed her literary talent. Much of her writing during this period involved, in Emerson's words, learning to skate well on a fascinating new surface, the weekly newspapers that specialized in sensational stories accompanied by graphic illustrations. Alcott considered this work "good drill for fancy and language" (*Journals* 109; June, July, August 1862), felt that she had a "natural ambition . . . for the lurid style" (Pickett 107–8), and acknowledged, "they pay best & I cant afford to starve on praise when sensation stories are written in half the time & keep the family cosy" (*Journals* 139; February 1865). While she continued to practice her craft and to keep the family warm with her efforts in this genre, she also continued to draw upon her reading of Charlotte Brontë, sometimes adopting, sometimes adapting, sometimes resisting the power of Brontë's characters and attitudes.

Alcott's choice to publish anonymously and pseudonymously in the pages of such periodicals as *Frank Leslie's Illustrated Newspaper* seems to have been a conscious decision to indulge what she called her "natural ambition" (Pickett 107), but it is interesting that she chose to write for Frank Leslie (twenty-six of the thirty-three located Alcott thrillers originally published from 1858 to 1870 appeared in Leslie publications), whose periodicals—particularly the *Illustrated Newspaper*—resembled the racier world of English sensation fiction more closely than they did any of the more tame American ones. Leslie's publishing style should not be surprising, since he was an Englishman, trained at the *London Illustrated News*, who changed his name, came to America to escape personal problems, and actually worked for P. T. Barnum for a time before establishing his own periodicals. According to Madeleine Stern,

> Leslie assessed public interest instinctually, and seized upon every incident and narrative that would increase circulation, from prizefights to murders, from scandals to Civil War. He loved sensationalism especially when graphically illustrated, and he served

it to avid subscribers in the form not only of on the spot news reports but of fiction. ("Introduction," *Freaks* 15)

Alcott placed two early "thrillers" in Leslie's paper, but her most vivid and accomplished efforts in the genre were written during and immediately after her trip to Europe in 1865–66, suggesting that she might well have perused English sensation stories while abroad.

Winifred Hughes's study of the English sensation novel—including Mary Elizabeth Braddon's *Lady Audley's Secret*, which Alcott likely had read—suggests several reasons why the form may have attracted Alcott. Hughes characterized the sensation genre as one that exhibited "some of the hidden strain and ambivalence present in mid-Victorian society" (18) through its "violent yoking of romance and realism" (16). For Alcott, who responded strongly to the romanticism of Brontë but whose work was also characterized by the realistic detail of *Hospital Sketches* and her accomplished use of the American vernacular in *Work*, a genre that welcomed the mixing of forms may have seemed the perfect place to experiment with "finding her style."

Further, though Hughes admits that sensation writers were not above using the most sordid details of current social problems in order to make their stories even more lurid and shocking, she argues that "the higher forms of the sensation novel . . . are also in the business of crusading for social or political reform" (34). Thus, the same details that Frank Leslie might have appreciated as a means of selling papers might also have served Louisa May Alcott well as she sought to advance her agenda of social reform.

Finally, sensation novelists specialized in the creation of "mature, sexually aroused women, heroines as well as adventuresses" (Hughes 40); one might find a "conventional wife . . . plotting murder on the side" (45), or a former prostitute married to a nobleman. Although critics condemned these heroines as "a threat to the entire social and moral fabric of Victorian England" (qtd. in Hughes 46), such characters would be extremely useful to a writer like Alcott, who was interested in moving her heroines into adventures beyond hearth and home.

Alcott did, in fact, use her forays into sensation fiction to develop her ability to create exciting and multidimensional female characters, "keeping the family cosy" at the same time. Alcott specialized in these tales through much of the 1860s; thirty-three previously published tales have now been recovered through the efforts of Madeleine Stern and others, and Alcott's journals indicate that many more existed. Among her most successful efforts in the genre are "Behind a Mask," *A Long Fatal Love Chase*, and "A Nurse's Story," all three of which were written within a short period in 1865–66, shortly after her return from a European trip and before the creation of *Little Women*. In terms of plot and character development, these stories represent noticeable growth in Alcott's command of her craft. The settings gradually pull away from England and toward America—and all three tales make frequent allusions to the work of Charlotte Brontë.[13]

In the first of these, "Behind a Mask," the image of the title coincidentally parallels an anecdote related by Elizabeth Gaskell early in her biography of Brontë. Patrick Brontë tells Gaskell about his children "inventing and acting little plays of their own" (36–37), which one day gave him an idea:

> [T]hinking that they knew more than I had yet discovered, in order to make them speak with less timidity, I deemed that if they were put under a sort of cover I might gain my end; and happening to have a mask in the house, I told them all to stand and speak boldly from under cover of the mask. (37)

A Socratic question-and-answer period ensued, in which the children's bold answers to their father's questions apparently convinced Patrick Brontë that he had a group of extremely precocious and talented children—as indeed he had. But whether Gaskell's biography or total coincidence is responsible for the image of this particular title, the subtitle—"A Woman's Power"—is all Alcott. Alcott takes care to keep *Jane Eyre* in the reader's mind as the story proceeds, but Jean Muir is as much a revision of Jane Eyre as is Christie Devon; both Christie and Jean take life into their own hands, but Jean's methods are much more "sensational," as befits the genre.

As Elizabeth Keyser notes (47–48), the initial description of Jean's dress and appearance upon her arrival at the Coventry estate is very like Jane's arrival at Thornfield, and the family's discussion of governesses prior to Jean's appearance reminds one of the Ingram family's similar discussion in *Jane Eyre*. The first Coventry to fall in love with the new governess shares Rochester's given name, Edward; Jean eventually marries Edward's uncle, Lord Coventry, in a ceremony conducted by a Reverend Fairfax (Rochester's middle name). Jean nurses Gerald Coventry, as Jane nurses Mason, when each man is stabbed by his sibling in a fit of passionate rage. In both stories, tableaux enacted as entertainment pit governess against fiancée for the attentions of the lord of the manor, although, as in *Work*, Alcott's use of acting *reveals* to Gerald Coventry his own awakening feelings for Jean; it is neither false nor is it used to conceal.

By the end of the first chapter, it is clear that Jean is no Jane Eyre, come to eke out a meager living as a governess with no goal higher than self-support. She is a thirty-year-old, divorced former actress whose clear intent is to play her role well enough to secure her livelihood permanently by marrying into the family; the character as Alcott casts her is more like Becky Sharp than Jane Eyre,[14] and the tale itself is more satire than gothic romance. Alcott chooses as her particular target the class system that allows the Coventry family, despite its flaws, to look down on Jean sight unseen because she comes from a different social class, and in a more general sense, Victorian society's expectations for female behavior. Significant to her criticism is a detail from the opening scene that directly contradicts *Jane Eyre*. In Brontë's novel, Mrs. Fairfax sends a carriage to get Jane, and solicitously looks after her comfort when she arrives. "Mask" opens with the family sitting around complaining about the governess who hasn't arrived, even though Gerald Coventry has forgotten to send a carriage to get her. Only Ned, who is cast as a young fool by his family, and Bella (an allusion to the "Bells"?), a child, dare to suggest that someone should "stand by poor little Muir" (98). Despite the rage that Jean later expresses to her friend Hortense about this insult, she only meekly observes at the time, "No apology is needed. I did not expect to be sent for"

(99). Jean must play the expected role if she is to work her way into the family, and she does so.

Jean also realizes that, regardless of her charms, she will never attain her ultimate goal, marriage to Sir John Coventry, unless she is a member of the nobility, just as Jane's recognition and legacy from her wealthy uncle is part of the "equalizing" process in *Jane Eyre* (Gilbert and Gubar 366–69). To effect her own rise in stature, she convinces Sir John that she is the long-lost child of a certain Lady Howard, who, cast off by her family for marrying beneath her, left her daughter in a French school. To Hortense, Jean writes: "It worked like a charm; he told Monsieur [Gerald Coventry, the eldest son], and both felt the most chivalrous compassion for Lady Howard's daughter, though before they had secretly looked down on me, and my real poverty and lowliness" (197). Jean's manipulations continue to the end of the tale, until she is the wife of Lord Coventry; in a return to the tale's initial images, the bell her husband rings to order "Lady Coventry's carriage" assures her that "the game was won" (202). This is a Horatio Alger story, a fairy tale ending: the young woman who had to find her way to the Coventry home and ring the bell for herself when no carriage was sent for her, now has a carriage of her own.

But to focus only on Jean's machinations in this tale is to understand only the negative implications of "a woman's power," the sexual "power which a woman possesses and knows how to use, for the weal or woe of man" (149), as Alcott describes it when Jean is conquering Gerald, or when she, like Jane Eyre, is repeatedly referred to in the tale as a witch. Alcott also understands the positive implications of female power. Jean exerts an American work ethic grounded in unbounded possibility (that is, the belief that hard work makes any goal attainable) and an indifference to class—self-serving though it may be—that joyfully inverts the world of her indolent English employers. Under Jean's influence, the family that seems almost asleep upon her arrival comes to life. She encourages Gerald to obtain a commission for his brother Ned, who, as the younger male, seems to have little to do. Gerald is so idle in the beginning that "the family had given him [Lucia] for his future mate, as he was too lazy to choose for himself"

(124). In order to please Jean, he decides to "ride over the whole estate, and attend to things as a master should . . . and endeavor to be all that my father was in his time" (165–66). His first day of real work leaves him "exhilarated" and "talking animatedly" (166), to the amazement of his family. Wherever Jean is, there are "bursts of laughter" and "animated conversation" (118). The narrator comments, "The very servants liked her; and instead of being, what most governesses are, a forlorn creature hovering between superiors and inferiors, Jean Muir was the life of the house" (120). This last point is especially important because of the way Jean is able to cross class barriers in both directions and to win the affections of the whole household.

Alcott uses the Brontëan model of focusing on the "interior life" of characters to develop Jean as a complex human being. She never allows the reader to forget that Jean's activities are calculated to further her own purposes (she sees Ned's commission as a means of getting him out of the way to clear her path to his older brother and uncle, for example); on the other hand, she never allows us to forget Jean's humanity, either. Although we see her drinking and removing a large amount of actress's make-up at the close of the first chapter, we also see her crying in that scene. In the letter to Hortense, she writes, "I was very miserable that night when I got alone. Something in the atmosphere of this happy home made me wish I was anything but what I am" (196). For every deceitful scene in the story, Alcott also lets us see scenes in which Jean feels "genuine remorse" (178) or "tears of real feeling" (181). Although even Jean's marriage comes about as a result of deception, she tells Sir John at the time, "I will be true as steel to you, and make your life as happy as it deserves to be"; and the narrator adds that what she promised "she faithfully performed in afteryears" (180). She extends her hand to Ned and Bella, the two who were kind to her from the start, saying, "To you I will acknowledge that I am not worthy to be this good man's wife, and to you I will solemnly promise to devote my life to his happiness. For his sake forgive me, and let there be peace between us" (210).

With this tale, Alcott contributed to the story papers an

adventuress/heroine who is indeed a formidable "threat to the social and moral fabric of Victorian England," a threat that has as much to do with her American idealism as with her treachery. By alluding to *Jane Eyre* while changing important details, Alcott manages not only to create "sensation," but to re-create Brontë's atmosphere of social criticism as well; her revision of Brontë emphasizes the deleterious effects (on both upper and lower classes) of impregnable class divisions that enable the wealthy to live lives of utter laziness while scorning those who live the best they can with limited options. It is also a severe critique of nineteenth-century social expectations for women. All the overt actions through which Jean endears herself to the household—making and serving perfect tea, teaching French to a young woman, nursing, singing, playing the piano—make her a veritable model of Victorian womanhood. The household is deceived because it never considers that the "perfect woman" could be just a role like any other. More positively, the story attests to the value—but unlike Brontë, also the possibility—of moving beyond accepted social structures to let all people achieve their full potential. Alcott's heroine, though cast as an Englishwoman, exudes a nineteenth-century American reformer's hope that "woman's power" can effect positive change, not only in the individual but in the society in which she finds herself. Alcott's accomplishment in this tale, then, goes far beyond David Reynolds's approbation of her "marvelously two-faced heroine" (409); the more important, and more original "fusion of opposite elements" (Reynolds 409), is not the creation of a woman who can *act* angelic and *be* demonic, but one who can wield power that is at once both frightening and benevolent.

In Rosamond Vivian,[15] the heroine of another sensation tale written about the same time as "Behind a Mask" (but never published until 1995), Alcott presents, in European settings, an American "type" that David Reynolds would recognize as an "adventure feminist"—a "moral exemplar" who was also "notably spunky and active, especially when compared with her counterparts in British and Continental fiction" (339). It appears that Alcott, in creating her own "lurid" tales, was able to combine the "racier" plot of the English models with the "spunkier" American heroine. While *A Long Fatal Love Chase* maintains links to Europe with its Faustian and Brontëan allusions and its chase all over the continent, it begins and ends on an island off the coast of England, possibly a metaphorical indication that Alcott's imagination is moving away from England and toward America.

As the novel-length tale opens, Rosamond reminds us of Jane Eyre, gazing out a window to forget the life inside the house in which she lives. Like Jane, she is an eighteen-year-old orphan (Jane Eyre is eighteen when she meets Rochester) living with family but without love; Rosamond resides with and takes care of her invalid grandfather, who gives her a home but no affection because he nurses a grudge against her father who married a woman of whom he did not approve. Rosamond's opening lines clearly recall the Faust legend—"I'd gladly sell my soul to Satan for a year of freedom"—but her demeanor could as easily describe Jane Eyre (or her demonic double, Bertha Rochester): Rosamond was "like a caged creature on the point of breaking loose" (3).

The Mephistopheles (Alcott's original title for the work was "A Modern Mephistophiles" [sic], a name she eventually used for another book much later in her career) who promptly knocks on her grandfather's door, despite the name Philip Tempest, appears to be as much Rochester as Satan: he is over thirty, powerfully built, with striking eyes. Like Rochester, he is also a wealthy man who is unhappily married but not divorced (Tempest and his estranged wife are fighting over custody of their son). Tempest's wife, Marian, has no inconvenient brother around to impede the courtship; he and Rosamond are married in a little over a month. Several of the conversations between Rosamond and Tempest during the early part of the story echo those between Jane and Rochester.

In their proposal scene, for example, Tempest, like Rochester, "teases" his future wife to the point of tears with the implication that he means to send her to work far away from him. He tells Rosamond that he has to leave, but has found her a position that will free her from the island and her grandfather—that of companion to someone in England; only when Rosamond is bidding him a tearful goodbye does he admit that he wants her to be *his* companion. Once she is aboard his yacht, he urges her to "defy public opinion" (41) and go off with him to his European villa (again like Rochester) without the benefit of marriage. Rosamond refuses, however, and Tempest produces a cleric he pays to conduct a sham marriage ceremony.

A conversation the two have after a year of marriage recalls *Jane Eyre* once again. When Tempest suddenly remarks that love makes "fools of men and slaves of women" (45), she denies that she is a slave. Further, she says that while she would "do anything that was right, make any sacrifice except of principle, and defend you against anyone who wrongfully accused you" (45), and even stand by him if he had done wrong and repented, she would certainly leave him if he proved false to her. When Tempest suggests that she would go away to die of longing for him, she corrects him: "No, live and forget you" (46). This passage parallels several in *Jane Eyre*. When Mason turns up unexpectedly during Rochester's charade as the gypsy fortune teller, Rochester asks Jane whether, if all his associates turned their backs on him, she would "dare censure for my sake," and she answers, "I could dare it for the sake of any friend who deserved my adherence; as you, I am sure do" (207). When Rochester sings his then-fiancée Jane a song about a lover who "has sworn . . ./With me to live—to die," however, Jane quickly asks "whom he was going to marry," since she "had no intention of dying with him" (275).

In all these scenes, echoes of lines from *Jane Eyre* serve as intertextual warnings that, like Jane's, Rosamond's principles will be tested when she eventually discovers that her honest fidelity is not returned. In addition to dialogue from *Jane Eyre*, Alcott reprises the blasted chestnut tree that is split by lightning on the night Rochester proposes to Jane with a cedar tree destroyed in a storm on the night of Tempest's arrival. Although the "blasted oak" motif abounds in Romantic literature, the many other echoes of *Jane Eyre* suggest Brontë's novel as its particular source here. Also, Tempest's wife appears at his and Rosamond's home, and in an argument with him in the "red room," she tells him she is going to warn Rosamond about him. Again, the overtones of the "red room" at Gateshead and Bertha Rochester as a warning figure for Jane resonate in Alcott's story. Like Jane, Rosamond finds it necessary to leave the man with whom she is still in love. Alcott even uses Brontë's moon-mother admonition to Jane to "Flee temptation" (324) as a chapter title in her own work, and puts the phrase in quotes within the chapter in clear indication of the consciousness of her allusion.

Ultimately, however, this story is not a reprise of *Jane Eyre* but an argument against it because, despite the many connections at external levels, Alcott cannot believe in Rochester/Philip as a romantic hero. As Christie Devon says in *Work*, "I haven't much faith in the saints such sinners make" (80).[16] Although Jane, reading his character phrenologically, decides that Rochester is not philanthropic, he points out some other bumps on his head, asserting, "but I bear a conscience" (133), and Brontë does make him a heroic character. While Tempest, like Rochester, embodies traits of a Byronic hero, neither he nor Rochester is a hero to Louisa May Alcott. Her characterization of Philip Tempest as Mephistopheles makes it clear that she does not believe in devils with hearts of gold. Tempest has no conscience, no sense of remorse. He chases Rosamond all over Europe, lying to people about her, bribing priests, even having her committed to a madhouse, not because he loves her, but to punish her for daring to defy him. Toward the end of the story, he forces his way into the home where she is staying with his wife, Marian, their son, and a priest who has assisted her; after bullying everyone present, he leaves, "solacing himself with the thought that he had made them all as unhappy as was possible in so short a time" (233). In the last chapter, when Tempest tries to kill Ignatius by ramming his boat, he kills Rosamond instead. He stabs himself over her body, declaring, "Mine first—mine last—mine even in the grave!" (242). His character has all the fire of Rochester, but none of the redeeming qualities Brontë believes, but Alcott doubts, that Rochester possesses.

As much as Tempest is Alcott's re-vision of Rochester, Rosamond is a new Jane; she is Jane "translated" into an American heroine. She has what Barrett Wendell, writing of the characters in *Little Women*, disparagingly called "that rude self-assertion which has generally tainted the lower middle class of English-speaking countries" (337)—what a more sympathetic reader might have called independence. In truth, Rosamond more strongly resembles *Little Women*'s Jo March, with her determination and her tomboyish behavior, than she does Jane Eyre. The first time she meets Tempest, she both frightens and intrigues him by walking out on a ledge outside her grandfather's house, which sits high up on a cliff. She swings down from her second-story bedroom to eavesdrop when Tempest argues with Marian after she arrives unexpectedly at their villa. When Rosamond learns that Tempest has betrayed her, she uses all her resourcefulness to get away from him: she climbs across Parisian rooftops, has herself transported in a wicker basket, cuts her hair to disguise herself as a boy, and even joins a Catholic convent although she is a Protestant. While Rosamond and Jane both make determined moral choices to leave men they love on grounds of principle, one can hardly imagine Brontë's heroine climbing down drainpipes in her Quakerish gowns! Despite the melodramatic ending of this tale, Alcott was clearly on her way to formulating the heroine that Madelon Bedell called "the American female myth" ("Introduction" xi): Jo March. In *A Long Fatal Love Chase*, she continues to allude to Charlotte Brontë but works as much against as with her, and begins to put distance, both geographical and aesthetic, between herself and her English counterpart.

In probably the best-written "thriller" from the mid-1860s, Alcott moves the setting from England all the way to America, while still referring through some of its details to both *Jane Eyre* and *Villette*. In "A Nurse's Story," published in six installments in *Frank Leslie's Chimney Corner* (a paper that printed tales of mystery and intrigue, but was less sensational than his *Illustrated Newspaper*) in late 1865 and early 1866, Alcott creates (or revises) the "companion to a mad woman" plot that she uses in almost identical form as the "Companion" chapter of *Work*. This story boasts an additional plot whose complex structure and accompanying character development showcase the extraordinary writing talent Alcott was evolving.

The first plot, which deals with hereditary madness, makes

direct allusions to *Jane Eyre* to comment on the consequences of valuing money and social position above honesty. In a parallel plot, Alcott alludes to Brontë in the much more subtle way characteristic of her later writing, by transforming Brontëan situations and characters to her own purposes in order to express her own themes. The madness plot as Alcott reused it in *Work* has already been discussed above, and plays itself out here with only slight variations. The young woman's name is Elinor, not Helen, the family name is Carruth, not Carrol, and the uninformed younger sister and her husband-to-be are treated with far less sympathy than in the later version. According to Robert Steele, who mysteriously controls the family, the sister's fiancé Fred's knowledge of the madness of the family into which he intends to marry "would not influence [him]; he cares only for money" (72). One other scene is absent from this portion of the tale when it appears in *Work*, certainly due to its more "sensational" nature, but is worth noting for its relation to *Jane Eyre*. The "mad sister" Elinor puts on the gown she was to wear at her aborted wedding and appears at her sister's wedding in warning, much as the mad Bertha Rochester appears in the midst of Jane's wedding finery in a robe "white and straight" (*JE* 286) as a kind of spectral warning to Jane against marrying Rochester. Although it is a fine, if melodramatic, moment that reinforces the story's connection to Brontë, one can easily see why Alcott would have excised it from *Work*, not only because the novel's heroine is a young woman who steadfastly tries to overcome her penchant for romance and to look at life realistically, but because the novel itself was clearly meant for a wider and probably more conservative audience than the one that read Leslie's newspapers.

The other plot of "A Nurse's Story" alludes to Brontë more subtly, again developing complex characters through psychological exposition. The heroine of the story in this case is Kate Snow, a character whom Alcott imbues with elements of Lucy Snowe's character that are useful to her purposes even as she adds to them a more active, assertive personality. Kate Snow is an orphaned governess-companion, recently arrived in America from England (significantly, unlike Lucy, Kate travels west to the New World, not east to the old, to "earn [her] bread by any honest work" [31]). The letter she carries with her from a former employer, "L. S." Hamilton, is a further reminder of Brontë's Lucy Snowe. At any rate, Kate's most conspicuous quality—her power of observation—surely reminds the reader of Brontë's heroine, as does Alcott's first-person narrative point of view, made fashionable for a period beginning in the 1850s and attributable to Brontë's influence, according to Baym (*Novels* 146), but unusual though not unheard-of in Alcott.[17] As Kate meets each member of the Carruth family, she reports to the reader as a disinterested observer who remains purposefully tranquil amid the madness and mystery about her, much as Lucy reports the perturbation of each member of the Bretton household when Mr. Bretton leaves Polly with them and determinedly comments, "I, Lucy Snowe, was calm" (*V* 79). In Kate's first interview with Mrs. Carruth, she

> observed her with redoubled interest. . . . I am quick at reading faces, and her's was the most tragical I ever saw. Such anxious eyes, such melancholy lines about the mouth, such a hopeless undertone in the steady voice, and an indescribable expression of unsubmissive sorrow!—all proved that life had brought some heavy cross, from which her wealth could purchase no release, for which her pride could find no effectual screen. (30)

Mrs. Carruth's "heavy cross" is even more burdensome than Kate first realizes. In addition to the family curse of madness, which seems to be visiting itself upon her eldest daughter, her husband's first wife and their son have appeared, threatening to expose both Kate's employer and her children as illegitimate. The resurrected son lives in her household to prevent any of them from revealing the secret before he and his mother (the first, supposedly deceased Mrs. Carruth) negotiate their revenge. Kate knows nothing of this other situation, only that the man known as Robert Steele has unusual power in the household. The first time she has the opportunity to meet with him, she reports:

> I resolved to observe this man as closely as he did me, for a curious feeling of antagonism had sprung up within me. I liked to

study character, and fancied that I had some skill in understanding both faces and the natures of which they are the index. . . . [W]hile tranquilly eating bread and butter, I looked and listened with all my senses alert. (49)

This second scene, while serving as an example of Kate's discernment, also indicates the more interesting conflict in this intriguing second plot, the struggle that ensues between Kate Snow and Robert Steele. While they are a bit like Rosamond and Philip in *A Long Fatal Love Chase*, Alcott here endows both characters with much more psychological dimension than in the longer story written around the same time. Kate, like Rosamond, thrives on the adventure in which she finds herself immersed; it leaves her "in a fever of excitement" (87). But unlike Rosamond, she wrestles with her conscience over the deception she must ultimately use to thwart Robert, who by this time she knows is in love with her. This complication ensues because Steele himself is far more psychologically complex than the Mephistophelian Philip Tempest. He is part fiend, no doubt; Harry Carruth refers to him as "Satan" (56), and Kate tells him he is "as proud as Lucifer" (91). Steele is literally hell-bent upon revenge; he tells Kate that "If a word from me could save them all from the disgrace in store for them, I would not utter it, though I confirmed my damnation by the silence" (74). As Kate realizes, however, "He has got a conscience . . . in spite of the evil spirit that possesses him" (56). As it turns out, even having a conscience, as does Rochester, is not enough to make Robert Steele a good marriage prospect to Alcott. Nevertheless, the frank recognition of the capacity for harm within Kate and good within Robert makes passion ever-present in the encounters between the aptly named Snow and Steele and makes Alcott's use of psychological characterization in this tale one of her finest efforts ever.

The conflict between these characters makes for interesting comparisons with the encounters between the icy Lucy Snowe and the fiery Paul Emanuel, and between Jane and Rochester, in Brontë's novels in which fire and ice are also recurring motifs. Kate even repeats Jane's words to Rochester at one point; when she has asked him to let the family reveal their secret to Amy's fiancé and he replies that it wouldn't make any difference, he asks:

"Will you believe a half-insane girl before me?"
"Yes."
"Have you no faith in me?"
"Not a whit." (72)

The last two lines are exactly the exchange between Jane and Rochester that follow when he declares her to be "my equal . . . and my likeness" (JE 257) and asks her to marry him. Robert, too, eventually declares his love to Kate, but the deceptions between them keep them from ever being real equals, and keep them from being lovers. Robert Steele decides to reform in the hope that it will bring him Kate's love. But when he realizes that the impact of the confession that ruins him has been negated by Kate's intrigues, which would have saved the family even without it, he rages at her: "You have destroyed my faith in truth, my desire for virtue, my power of loving nobly, and sent me out into the world a desperate man. God may forgive you—I never will!" (106).

Years later, Kate encounters the ruined Steele (as Jane finds the ruined Rochester) in an asylum where he has been afflicted by bouts of the family madness. They are reconciled, and Kate takes him to her home—but to nurse him, not to marry him—until his death a short time later. The marked difference in the conclusion of the romance in "A Nurse's Story" in comparison with Jane Eyre, despite Alcott's allusions to Brontë in her own story, points up important differences between their outlooks and purposes. The deception that bothers Alcott so much when Rochester dresses as the gypsy fortune-teller and again when he first proposes to Jane is not a major issue to Brontë, even though Jane admonishes him in the first instance, saying, "I shall try to forgive you: but it was not right" (JE 204). Brontë posits that the perceived inequity between Jane and Rochester in her novel is inequity on a financial and social level and can be remedied; their spiritual equality is more important than any other issue, and once recognized, sets the stage for their eventual happiness. In Alcott's tale, as in Brontë's, the passion between hero and heroine is undeniable, but the deceit upon which the Kate/Robert relationship rests creates an inequity that has nothing to do with their relative social positions and thus is not repairable.

This tale, then, while putting more artistic distance between herself and Charlotte Brontë, also showcases Alcott's development as an artist in her ability to express an original theme and to manage a gripping double plot and complex character development. Moreover, the increasing subtlety with which Alcott uses Brontë in the sensation tales, imaginatively blending Brontëan allusions into the rapidly expanding repertoire of her own artistry, indicates the direction in which she continued to move in the fiction that followed her forays into the anonymous world of sensation literature. Her use of Brontë becomes more implied than overt, her fiction more assuredly American, as she creates the tales for which she became and has remained most remembered: her children's novels.

CHILDREN'S NOVELS

Not only were many of Alcott's works from 1868 on expressly books written for children, but they were also books whose evocation of distinctly American landscapes and characters would be noted by reviewer after reviewer. Only in the first (*Little Women*, 1868) and the last (*Jo's Boys*, 1886) of Alcott's eight children's novels does the Brontëan connection appear in any important sense; in the first, interesting parallels to Brontë exist that serve mostly to distinguish her work from Brontë's, and in the last a direct reference to Brontë signals the crux of Alcott's American admiration of the British writer, despite their many philosophical and cultural differences.

Little Women as originally published in 1868 was only the first half (twenty-three chapters) of what we know as this novel today. It ends neither in death nor in an epidemic of marriages; Alcott left Beth ill from the effects of scarlet fever but recovering, Meg agreeing to marry John, but only after a three-year engagement, and Jo vowing to continue her writing, to remain a friend to Laurie, and never to marry. The widespread popularity of *Little Women* prompted her publisher to ask for an immediate sequel, but despite her pleasure at the novel's success, Alcott had misgivings about the future of her March family, particularly with respect to the Jo/Laurie relationship. She wrote to her uncle, Samuel May:

> I [d]ont like sequels, & I dont think No 2 will be as popular as No 1, but publishers are very *perwerse* [sic] and wont let authors have thier [sic] way so my little women must grow up & be married off in a very stupid style. (*Letters* 121–22; 22 January 1869)

When she had begun "No 2," she rejoiced that "As I can launch into the future, my fancy has more play," but also confided that fancy might have its constraints: "Girls write to ask who the little women will marry, as if that was the only end and sum of a woman's life. I *wont* marry Jo to Laurie to please any one" (*Journals* 167; 1 November 1868). There were even suggestions, given popular expectations, that the second volume be called "Wedding Marches."

With Beth ill and Meg engaged as volume 1 closed and their real-life counterparts having died and married respectively, their fictional futures were not so much in question as those of the youngest sister Amy and especially Jo. As fans and publisher clamored for mates for Jo and Amy when Louisa and May remained single, Alcott faced a dilemma in resolving the marriage plot similar to one that Charlotte Brontë had encountered in creating the final volume of *Villette*—a dilemma about which Alcott would have read in Gaskell's biography:

> Lucy must not marry Dr. John; . . . he is a 'curled darling' of Nature and Fortune, and must draw a prize in life's lottery. His wife must be young, rich, pretty; he must be made very happy indeed. If Lucy marries anybody, it must be the Professor. . . . The conclusion of this third volume is still a matter of some anxiety. (Gaskell 360; 3 November 1852)

Although Brontë's pressures were largely internal while Alcott's resulted more from a conflict between her own inclinations and public expectations, Alcott was as anxious to find a narrative outcome other than a Jo/Laurie marriage as Brontë was to keep Dr. John from Lucy. The love triangles within which each author resolved the marriage dilemma illuminate some interesting parallels, and also some marked contrasts, between the two novels.

Both *Villette*'s Dr. John Graham Bretton and *Little Women*'s Laurie are handsome, likable, and privileged. For both characters, the privilege granted them by their relative wealth in comparison with Lucy and Jo (though Laurie is much wealthier than Dr. John) accompanies a certain shallowness of character. The sixteen-year-old Graham introduced to the reader at the beginning of *Villette* is, as Lucy describes him, "a spoiled, whimsical boy" (72), too self-absorbed to notice the extent of six-year-old Paulina's attachment to him. He teases her, ignores her when his friends come around, and even kicks her accidentally because he does not notice that she has fallen asleep at his feet. When Graham reappears in Villette ten years later, he is a competent, hard-working doctor who protects and loves his mother dearly, but a certain shallowness still remains. Even Lucy, who is in love with him, admits that "his actual character lacked the depth, height, compass, and endurance it possessed in my creed" (327). Graham's infatuation with the beautiful but flighty Ginevra Fanshawe, despite evidence that she is untrue to him, attests to his attachment to superficialities. His eventual relationship with Paulina adds depth to his own life, but even here, the main qualities that attract him to her are the requirements Brontë herself had set up: she is young, rich, and pretty.

In *Little Women*, Alcott expresses Laurie's weaker qualities not so much in terms of superficiality, but in his lack of industry, a fault Graham Bretton does not possess. Laurie's ambition is "to be a famous musician . . . and all creation is to rush to hear me; and I'm never to be bothered about money or business, but just enjoy myself, and live for what I like" (142). Once in Europe, he does not pursue his music—he "just let himself drift along as comfortably as possible" (400)—until he is brought up short by Amy when he visits her in Nice. She declares him to be "faulty, lazy and miserable" (407), and despite his attempts to brush off her lecture, he carries the sting of her "I despise you" (407) with him as he returns to his grand-father and finally begins to make something of his life.

The women whom these men ultimately marry, though vastly different in economic status, have traits in common as well. Paulina Home is a pampered only child who is repeat-edly referred to, even at age six, as "little woman."[18] Although Amy March is not rich, she is young and pretty and is also pampered by her family. Amy is chosen for a tour of Europe, though Jo is older, because she ingratiates herself with her aunt. Both girls have speech aberrations that seem to rein-force a continuing image of childishness even as they grow into womanhood, Paulina with her lisp, and Amy with her tendency to malapropisms. Nevertheless, each young woman develops a steadiness of character; Paulina's is observable in the increasing grace with which she assumes her social posi-tion as a countess and as her widowed father's hostess, and Amy's in the diligent attention to her art that her extended stay in Europe allows.

As for the heroines, while the fiery, impetuous, impatient Jo March bears little obvious relation to Brontë's long-suffering Lucy Snowe other than the passionate nature the one exudes while the other represses, both Jo and Lucy stand out as emi-nently practical characters in the midst of emotional, turbulent situations. Lucy's outward calm makes her the confidante of virtually every character in *Villette*; Ginevra, for instance, confides in her and calls her "old Diogenes" and "Mother Wisdom" (153) because she always dispenses sensible advice even in the face of Ginevra's most preposterous antics. Jo constantly guards against being "sentimental," and her friendship is especially val-ued by Laurie because she is not a flirt, but a "sensible, straight-forward girl, who can be jolly and kind without making a fool of herself" (326).

But neither Brontë's Dr. John nor Alcott's Laurie are destined to marry "sensible" girls. The presence of the attractive charac-ters Paulina and Amy allow both writers to avoid the marriages they considered untenable as well as to reward their handsome heroes with beautiful women. There are important differences in the way this takes place, however, that point to important cultural differences between Brontë's England and Alcott's

America. First of all, in avoiding the marriage for which the respective novels seem to be heading, Alcott makes it Jo's choice to refuse Laurie; in *Villette*, the choice is in male hands. Lucy, recognizing that Graham will never love her, cannot change that fact and, with her customary forced stoicism, buries the letters he sent her. Alcott proposes the existence of a society where not only may a wealthy man propose to a poor woman—and the extent of Laurie's wealth is part of Alcott's effort to emphasize this point—but where the poor woman may actually refuse the proposal. Alcott's attitude presupposes that an American woman has other options in life, which, at least in comparison with a woman in Brontë's England, she certainly did.

The matches each writer substitutes for the ones their heroines seem headed toward also yield some interesting comparisons between the two novels. While Alcott's early biographer Ednah Cheney claims "no prototype existed" (192) for Jo's eventual husband, Professor Friedrich Bhaer, Madeleine Stern suggests that Louisa "mined from her memories" (184) of Reinhold Solger, a lecturer she had heard at Frank Sanborn's school in Concord, and Dr. Rimmer, her sister's art teacher, for Bhaer's qualities. However, there are no indications from Alcott herself that either of these real-life persons served as a model, whereas she was quick to point out such correspondences where many of her other characters were concerned. A number of matching plot details connect the fourth member of Alcott's "psychologic quadrilateral" (Burlingame 205) in *Little Women* with *Villette's* M. Paul Emanuel (or a combination of M. Paul and his earlier incarnation, William Crimsworth, whom Brontë *called* "The Professor").

One important way in which Friedrich Bhaer resembles M. Paul is that they are both "foreigners" as far as Jo and Lucy are concerned. This gives each of them a touch of the exotic; it somehow makes them more appropriate matches for these two unusual women. Jo's originality is presented in an overtly positive light; but even though Brontë's overall portrait of Lucy Snowe is that of a profoundly disturbed woman, cultural circumstances tend to make her that way. Her innate wisdom, imagination, intelligence, and competence still make her deserving of a mate as original as herself.[19]

Both Jo and Lucy meet their future loves—these "foreigners"—when they themselves are away from home. Jo meets Professor Bhaer when she leaves home for New York and is employed as a governess to the children of Mrs. Kirke, who runs a boardinghouse. Lucy, arriving in Villette after she leaves England, meets M. Paul when Madame Beck hires her as a governess to her children, since she does not speak French well enough to teach at the boarding school Madame Beck runs. Professor Bhaer lives at Mrs. Kirke's boardinghouse and "gives lessons to support himself and two little orphan nephews" (334); M. Paul teaches at Madame Beck's and has a whole group of near-relatives dependent upon his support, including a young girl who is his god-daughter and ward. Friedrich and Jo become close friends when she darns his socks for him and he begins to teach her German. Lucy and Paul are drawn together when he teaches her French, and though he initially rages when she takes up her sewing while he lectures at the school, he is touched when she makes him a watchguard as a gift. Both men give the women books as tokens of their esteem.

Both women are roused to uncharacteristic displays of emotion toward the men when they mistakenly believe their loves are about to take permanent leave of them. Lucy cries, "My heart will break!" (580) when she thinks Madame Beck has come inexorably between herself and M. Paul; Jo dissolves into tears visible even in a rainstorm "Because you are going away" (474). Once the respective couples come to an understanding, the parallels continue further: neither marriage can take place immediately, for Friedrich has accepted a teaching job at a small college in the West, where he must work until he earns enough to secure his nephews' futures; M. Paul undertakes a three-year voyage in order to manage his own family responsibilities. Like Friedrich's "voluminous letters" (481) to Jo, the "full-handed, full-hearted plentitude" (594) of M. Paul's letters to Lucy keeps her content through their long separation.

It should be noted that, to the extent that Alcott draws upon Brontë's hero here, it is a much less overt and more translated use of her source material than the way she used Brontë in her earlier fiction; she utilizes Paul Emanuel's more positive qualities in ways that suit her purposes, while omitting some of the more negative parts of his personality. Thus Friedrich is intelligent, compassionate, responsible, and a good teacher, much like M. Paul, but has none of the more confrontational qualities which M. Paul sometimes exhibits. M. Paul seems to like Lucy more when she makes mistakes so he can berate her; even when he is obviously beginning to care for her, he makes a point of criticizing her to see whether or not she will stand up to him. While he enjoys being contradicted, the ultimate relationship between Paul and Lucy is always that of master and pupil; she refers to him as "Monsieur" and "my king" (587) even after they are engaged, much as Frances Henri continues to call Crimsworth "Monsieur" and Jane Eyre calls Rochester "Master."

Friedrich Bhaer has a much gentler demeanor than Crimsworth or M. Paul, both toward the world in general and toward Jo in particular. He occasionally vents frustration at a pair of especially recalcitrant young ladies to whom he tries to teach German, but generally he seems defined by gentleness, kindness, and patience. He allows the children in the boarding-house to climb all over him and demand stories from him. When he appears in *Jo's Boys* he is a father so loving that Alcott comments, he "opened his arms and embraced his boys like a true German, not ashamed to express by gesture or by word the fatherly emotions an American would have compressed into a slap on the shoulder and a brief 'All right'" (149). He treats Jo with respect as well; even though he is her teacher, he never demeans her as M. Paul does Lucy. Although many critics assert that Friedrich is at best a benevolent dictator, since he "forces" Jo to stop writing, his comments about her writing are directed solely at the "rubbishy" tales which he decries for their possible bad influence on impressionable minds. He likens the writing of such stories, lively and entertaining though they are, to "put[ting] poison in the sugarplum, and let[ting] the small ones eat it" (355). Though Jo unsuccessfully attempts to write other kinds of stories and finally "cork[s] up her inkstand" (357) for the time being after this discussion, she eventually returns to her writing and becomes more famous than she can comfortably handle, as the "Jo's Last Scrape" chapter of *Jo's Boys* demonstrates. Her marriage to Friedrich may not satisfy twentieth-century sensibilities, but it is based upon mutual respect and love. Jo immediately shifts from calling *her* professor "sir" to "Friedrich" when they have declared their love, an incident to which Friedrich calls attention with "grateful delight" and a comment that "It [her calling him by his first name] is more sweet to me than I can tell" (475).

As with the marriages between Laurie and Amy and Dr. John and Paulina, the outcomes of their central protagonists' romances serve to clarify further some of the differences between Brontë and Alcott at this point in Alcott's writing life. Jo and Friedrich begin a school together, a "happy ending" that seems odd for Alcott to conceive for a heroine so much like herself. As noted previously, she disliked the profession as much as Brontë did. Yet this was also the ending Brontë posited for both Lucy Snowe and *The Professor*'s Frances Henri and William Crimsworth. Alcott here alters Brontë's model, however, in that M. Paul sets up a school for Lucy before his departure wherein she considers herself his "faithful steward" (587), but Jo's inheritance after the death of Aunt March, not her husband's machinations, makes the founding of Plumfield school possible. In a reversal of Brontë's outcome, where the husband-to-be provides the home at least initially—M. Paul finds Lucy a set of rooms where she can live and teach, and even recruits her first four students for her—Jo's money and the home she inherits provide both her husband a place to "train and teach in his own way" and her father an opportunity "for trying the Socratic method of education on modern youth" (*LW* 482–83). It seems ironic that at the end of their respective journeys, Jo, who wanted to remain single and independent, is married, while Lucy, who sought love, is single and independent. Nevertheless, Jo's situation reflects Alcott's American optimism; Jo March Bhaer may be the first American literary heroine to "have it all," both love and career.

One further parallel between *Little Women* and *Villette* that is approached radically differently from opposite sides of the Atlantic is the preoccupation with spying and surveillance in Brontë's novel. Virtually everyone in Madame Beck's pensionnat spies on everyone else, mostly to maintain control.[20] Lucy is aware of Madame Beck looking at her and going through her belongings as she supposedly sleeps; M. Paul observes Madame Beck's "private" garden from his own vantage point; *both*

Madame Beck and M. Paul steal Lucy's letters and read them. M. Paul's dependence on his eyeglasses further emphasizes the interest placed on close scrutiny in this novel. In fact, one of the most tense moments between Paul and Lucy occurs when she breaks his spectacles, which "had in them a blank and immutable terror, beyond the mobile wrath of the wearer's own unglazed eyes" (411), and the nearsighted teacher declares that she has rendered him "blind and helpless" (413). Because of the other parallels that exist between the last volume of *Villette* and this portion of *Little Women*, it is interesting to note that Jo obtains her first look at Friedrich Bhaer (whose near-sightedness is repeatedly alluded to) by peeking at him through the curtain that covers the glass door between the nursery and Mrs. Kirke's parlor, where he is giving lessons: "It was dreadfully improper, I know," she writes home, "but I couldn't resist the temptation" (335). The Professor eventually catches her listening, for she develops the habit of opening the door and eavesdropping on his lessons, and observes her in return: "You peep at me, I peep at you" (341). Alcott's "translation" of the habit of surveillance has none of the sinister connotations of that activity as it transpires in *Villette*; in fact, as noted previously, her sensation heroines often thrive due to their astute powers of observation. For Alcott, careful observation indicates useful connection to and interest in the world outside the self. For Brontë, it is a negative trait, a means of repression and control that largely seems to her to be indicative of the flaws within Madame Beck's Catholic religion. Nevertheless, the action, if not the tone, may well have had its source for Alcott in her reading of Charlotte Brontë.

While some elements of the plot of *Little Women*, and at least one of its characters, Professor Bhaer, provide interesting parallels to the work of Charlotte Brontë, Alcott does not, in general, allude to Brontë a great deal during her career as a children's writer. Certainly, in view of Alcott's history of allusions to Brontë, it is tempting to read the March family's servant Hannah, one of the overt discrepancies between the real-life Alcotts and their fictional counterparts, as a translation of the servant of the same name who is practically a member of the Rivers family in *Jane Eyre*. Also, in *Jack and Jill*, the female title character, whose name turns out to be Jane and is of English heritage, is at one point lectured to about the patient fortitude of a young woman named Lucinda Snow. However, Hannah is a common servant's name, and other plot details in *Jack and Jill* do not re-create Jane's or Lucy's story; they would not even be presented as possible references without Alcott's many other allusions to Brontë. And beyond the textual details already discussed, none of Alcott's other children's stories seem to allude to Charlotte Brontë. In fact, while a plethora of literary works drawn from Alcott's own reading experiences, from fairy tales to sentimental novels to Goethe, are mentioned in *Little Women* as the reading of Jo and the other characters (see Crisler), Brontë's name never appears.

There are at least two explanations for the sudden virtual absence of intertextual reference to Brontë. First of all, the difference in genre and, by extension, in audience between children's and adult fiction is so great that the impulse to adopt or adapt may have made no literary sense to Alcott as she wrote these novels. More importantly, however, Alcott, having "found her style at last" in *Little Women*, increasingly asserted herself as an American writer as she continued to practice her art. Her self-assurance as a writer and the goal she now more confidently pursued in her writing—to provide children with stories having "truth to life" (*Journals* 167; October 30, 1868) and not just morality tales—now moved her writing into a stage that had little direct connection to Charlotte Brontë. The sophistication with which she adapts the general situations of *Villette* to her own purposes in *Little Women* certainly suggests that she was coming into her own, and very successfully.

In the pages of her last full-length work, *Jo's Boys* (1886), published less than two years before her death, Alcott makes an overt reference to Brontë with no inclination toward allusion. In *Jo's Boys*, Alcott puts into words a tribute that explains why, despite her many differences with Charlotte Brontë regarding the more active and hopeful life she expected her own heroes to lead, she still remained fascinated by this writer. When one of the girls at Plumfield announces, "My ambition is to be a George Eliot, and thrill the world!" Mrs. Jo replies that Eliot's novels "don't thrill me as little Charlotte Brontë's books do. The brain is there, but the heart seems left out" (290).

The woman's heart in Brontë's novels drew a life-long response from Alcott as a woman whose culture and circumstances had shaped her, and sometimes restricted her, in many of the same ways as Brontë's world had shaped and constricted her. Alcott seemed particularly attracted to the strength of Brontë's heroines, especially Jane Eyre and Lucy Snowe. At the same time, Alcott's response to her predecessor and model is never simple admiration; it is always complicated by the tensions between identification with her as a woman writer and as a nineteenth-century woman with many biographical parallels to Brontë and her "troubled refusal," as an American optimist, of Brontë's British world of diminished possibilities. This tension exhibits itself in various ways as Alcott's own writing career progresses, and it parallels her struggle to find her voice as a writer. Eventually, allusions to Brontë become so subtle that Alcott can parallel Brontë's plots and characters in limited ways while creating novels thoroughly steeped in American settings. Only an overt reference to Brontë in her last such book signals the reader that she has not forgotten her literary mentor entirely. This same tension between assent and resistance, which at its best results in a fusion of Alcott's energy and Brontë's "heart" in Alcott's work, also appears when Louisa May Alcott and Charlotte Brontë thematically articulate their respective visions of life.

Part Two

Subtler Ties: Themes

CHAPTER 3

The Inner Life
Self and Spirit

That Louisa May Alcott had Charlotte Brontë's model in mind throughout her writing career is crucial groundwork upon which to build thematic comparisons, for Alcott's dual response to her reading of Brontë's plots and characters manifests itself in the themes of some of the same works in which the connection to Brontë has been established. Alcott's personal connections with Brontë—particularly the tie of gender—resulted in large areas of agreement about which issues were worth writing about; yet, the nature of her responses to these issues, like her plots and characters, demonstrates the tension between personal affinity and cultural distance. Both Alcott and Brontë placed the heroines and heroes they created in circumstances meant to explore the life within, the life between, and the life outside themselves. The extent to which their visions converge and diverge clarifies further the boundaries between personal connections and cultural differences, and enables us to appreciate with more complexity the writer who was Louisa May Alcott.

In exploring the spiritual self through their fictional characters, both Louisa May Alcott and Charlotte Brontë participated in the nineteenth-century Victorians' interest in religious matters. Witness these parallel scenes, in which their heroines confront important issues of their lives in a place neither author frequented: the Catholic confessional. *Villette*'s Lucy Snowe, driven by illness and loneliness, stumbles through rain and wind into a Catholic church and confesses her desperate state to the priest there, even though she is a Protestant. Lucy receives immediate but temporary solace from the priest, whom she eventually discovers is in league with Madame Beck, the villain of the tale. His continuing interest in Lucy stems first from the desire to keep her away from his Catholic benefactor, M. Paul, and failing that to convert her to what Lucy terms his "popish superstition" (*V* 235).

Rosamond Vivian, heroine of Alcott's *A Long Fatal Love Chase*, and also a Protestant, seeks solace in the confessional for the storm of spirit engendered by her continuing love for the husband from whom she has fled after discovering that he is already married. Alcott's Rosamond finds, to her horror, that she has confessed her love to the very man from whom she seeks to conceal it, for Philip Tempest has bribed the priest to allow him to sit in the confessional. However, another priest connected with the same convent helps Rosamond to escape Tempest and his own superior and becomes her dear and trusted friend to the end of the tale.

In these brief passages and in the larger body of their work, it is clear that Alcott and Brontë had in common the general Victorian vision that cast religion increasingly as a concern of women as men strove for money and prosperity, and that both were very much aware of (and in Brontë's case, participated in) anti-Catholic sentiment rampant in both cultures in their time. However, a more comprehensive look at their writing reveals that the tension between agreement and dissent already observed in their work also holds true as each examines spiritual issues. Although some of their experiences of religion were bicultural, Brontë's perspective on these phenomena as a British minister's daughter and Alcott's as the progeny of an American transcendentalist result in different attitudes being manifested in their respective work. As both her negative approach to Catholicism and her portrayals of certain Anglican clerics demonstrate, Brontë seems to mistrust public shows of religious fervor and to consider true religion as essentially a private matter. Alcott, on the other hand, eschews sectarian attitudes and embraces a notion of proper religious behavior that is both more universally encompassing than Brontë's and determinedly public. Further, both writers exhibit an urge to define a distinctly feminine theology. But where Brontë's struggle with this issue begins in hope and retreats to an ever-narrowing despair, Alcott's stories move from despair to a hope whose boundaries expand into an ever wider and more radical view of the spirit.

Some of the important nineteenth-century religious events to which Brontë and Alcott responded—reform movements, missionary movements, and anti-Catholicism—occurred on both sides of the Atlantic. However, the fact that in England the official church was tied closely to the state, whereas in America there was a fundamental belief in the separation of church and state, made every aspect of religious change political in England to a far greater extent than it was in the United States.[1] Anti-Catholic sentiment in England dates at least to the days of Henry VIII, who made himself head of church *and* state in 1534. That the Archbishop of Canterbury and the bishops sat in the House of Lords, and that the monarch—and by 1800, the Parliament— chose the bishops, even further reinforced ties between the English church and state. From the institution of the Test Act in 1673 until its repeal in 1828, no one could hold civil or military rank in England without being a communicant of the Church of England; not until passage of Roman Catholic Emancipation in 1829 could Catholics hold office or vote. Even after Emancipation, however, Catholicism remained suspect in England; laws stayed on the books forbidding Catholic chapels to have steeples and nullifying wills that bequeathed money for "superstitious" practices such as having Masses said for the dead.

Pope Pius IX tested England's limited tolerance for Catholicism in 1850 when he reorganized the Catholic hierarchy of England in ways that suggested to the English that he was attempting to put the Catholic Church on equal footing with the Church of England. The former apostolic vicar of the Central District, for example, was retitled Cardinal Archbishop of Westminster. This seemingly minor event exploded into a major uprising, with Catholic clerics glorying in the return of the true faith to England and Anglicans condemning it as Papal aggression. In fact, Prime Minister John Russell joined the Anglican Bishop of Durham in deeming the act "insolent and insidious" (letter from Russell to Durham, 4 November 1850; rpt. in Helmstadter and Phillips 309–11). A series of highly publicized court cases in the early 1850s involving priests seducing servant girls, improperly gaining funds for the church by deathbed influence, and encouraging wealthy young women to join convents and cede their fortunes to the Church added fuel to the anti-Catholic fires. Parliament in 1853–54 attempted several times to pass laws allowing the inspection of convents "to make sure that no nuns were being entombed alive, exploited for the sake of their money, or otherwise abused" (Paz 17).

Some of these real-life incidents found their way from the courts into art as a whole series of novels of the 1840s and 1850s featured "duplicitous priests, superstitious practices, sinister Jesuits, and the pain of damaged personalities and broken homes" that was traced directly to Catholicism (Paz 59). The penny dreadfuls brought the expression of these themes to new depths, with lurid tales of sex and death in confessionals and behind convent walls (Paz 60–63). The Catholic practice of confession apparently came under regular scrutiny in both life and art, at least in part because of the way confession could replace the control over women's lives exercised by Victorian husbands and fathers with that of the priest. Critics complained that confession "interferes with the confidence which should exist between husband and wife" (Walsh 81).

While this vehement anti-Catholicism was neither universal nor long-lived (things calmed down considerably by 1870), all four of Charlotte Brontë's novels were written between 1846 and 1853, a period which includes the stormiest years of the controversy. Further, she was the daughter of a devoted Anglican cleric whose sympathies were with the Evangelical (Low Church) movement in the Church of England and therefore especially disdainful of the rituals of Catholicism; Fraser writes that while Patrick Brontë's Evangelicalism was "a more cultured and less puritanical breed" than that of some of the later nineteenth-century adherents, "there can be no doubt of the presence in the parsonage of a religion of black and white ferocity and conviction . . . every action informed by consciousness of sin and the imminence of the world to come" (8, 10). Also, unlike her sister Emily, Charlotte apparently did attend her father's church services regularly and enjoyed heated discussions of sectarian issues (Farr 90). That she was acutely aware of the religious events of 1850 is evident from a letter she wrote to William Smith Williams, the reader at Brontë's London publisher, saying, "I have read Lord Russell's letter with very great zeal and relish, and think him a spirited sensible little man for writing it" (Wise and Symington III, 179; 9 November 1850). Thus anti-Catholic sentiment in her work comes as no great surprise; however, while immediately grounded in issues of sectarian politics, Brontë's work extends anti-Catholicism beyond purely political issues to consider its more deeply human implications.

The idea of nuns in convents as a metaphor of containment and repression, for example, seems especially to have captured Brontë's imagination. When Jane Eyre's cousin Eliza Reed becomes a nun after her mother's death, Jane observes that "what [sense] you have, I suppose in another year will be walled up alive in a French convent" (JE 244). Eliza, in fact, becomes the superior of the convent, and as any cynical Anglican would have predicted, endows it with her considerable fortune. *Villette*, published in 1853, conforms to the most lurid anti-Catholic sentiments of the time in its central symbol, the ghost of a nun that appears periodically throughout the novel. According to legend, Madame Beck's girls' school was once a convent, and in the garden behind the school, under an ancient but still-blooming pear tree, lies the tomb of a nun "whom a monkish enclave of the drear middle ages had here buried alive, for some sin against her vow" (V 172). The phantom nun's several appearances in the novel are always connected with feelings of sexual repression. She makes her last appearance when Ginevra Fanshawe elopes with her lover, escaping forever the sexual repressiveness of the pensionnat.

When Charlotte Brontë portrays individual Catholics in her novels, and as her Protestant characters comment upon them, she tends to use them metaphorically to represent the hypocrisy of an outward emotional show of religious thought and feeling that masks either emptiness or active evil within. In Mdlle [sic] Reuter, the directress of the girls' school in *The Professor*, and in her later incarnation as *Villette*'s Madame Beck, Brontë depicts the falseness of these women, who encourage their charges to live lives of pampered luxury and sensuality while they secretly keep these same charges under tight control through constant surveillance—and attributes their hypocrisy largely to their Catholicism. About Mdlle Reuter, the narrator William Crimsworth observes:

> Even if she be truly deficient in sound principle, is it not rather her misfortune than her fault? She has been brought up a Catholic; had she been born an Englishwoman, and reared a Protestant, might she not have added straight integrity to all her other excellences? (87)

Villette's Madame Beck is an even more villainous character than Mdlle Reuter. Madame Beck's machinations to keep M. Paul from Lucy (including drugging her, at one point), not because she loves him but because she wants his money, are a gender reversal of nineteenth-century accusations against priests encouraging vocations (such as Eliza Reed's) and attending deathbeds for the sake of the money that would go to the Church.

Brontë's accusations against Catholicism extend to its deleterious effects upon the schools and students organized under its principles of falsity. *The Professor*'s Frances Henri describes the "Romish school" thus:

> [It is] a building with porous walls, a hollow floor, a false ceiling; every room in this house . . . has eye-holes and ear-holes, and what the house is, the inhabitants are, very treacherous; they all think it lawful to tell lies; they all call it politeness to profess friendship where they feel hatred. (118)

Lucy Snowe perceives that falsity and spying keep the students ignorant of Catholicism's designs on their spirits (and thus under control), even while seeming to indulge their bodies; thus she observes the "Romanism" of Madame Beck's school in *Villette*:

> [L]arge sensual indulgence (so to speak) was permitted by way of counterpoise to jealous spiritual restraint. Each mind was being reared in slavery; but, to prevent reflection from dwelling on this fact, every pretext for physical recreation was seized and made the most of. There, as elsewhere, the CHURCH strove to bring up

her children robust in body, feeble in soul, fat, ruddy, hale, joyous, ignorant, unthinking, unquestioning. (196)

The confessional scene referred to at the beginning of this chapter further demonstrates Brontë's belief in the Roman Church's pervasive secret designs on the human spirit, for even Père Silas's outward compassion toward Lucy has its roots in his impulse to convert her.[2] Although he is by Lucy's own admission "not a bad man, though the advocate of a bad cause" (V 513), she nevertheless casts Silas in the role of Satan as she describes the three temptations to which he subjects her in the name of conversion. When he feeds her an endless supply of tracts espousing Catholicism, she takes solace in the Bible she keeps under her pillow, a book she "was convinced could not be improved on" (V 514). When he regales her with tales of good works, she observes that "For man's good was little done; for God's glory, less." Instead, all the so-called good deeds are tainted by their real motive, to "spread the reign of her tyrant 'Church'" (V 515). Lucy's last temptation, traditionally the most compelling, is that of the Church's elaborate ritual. Conceivably, these ceremonies could be an outlet for Lucy's simmering but always controlled passions. However, she finds that the services have no hold on her imagination: they "struck me as tawdry, not grand; as grossly material, not poetically spiritual" (V 516). In the end, M. Paul, more tolerant than his confessor, accepts Lucy's Protestantism; he in turn becomes virtually the only good Catholic in Lucy's experience. When she learns of his faithful devotion and support to the family of his former love, she muses: "Whatever Romanism might be, there are good Romanists; this man, Emanuel, seemed of the best; touched with superstition, influenced by priestcraft, yet wondrous for fond faith, for pious devotion, for sacrifice of self, for charity unbounded" (488–89). Thus the aptly named Emanuel becomes not just another Catholic, but Lucy's "Christian hero" (491).

As appalling as Charlotte Brontë deemed Catholicism's outward show of devotion with its underlying corruption, she did not limit her criticism of organized religion to the excesses of Papistry. Anglicans, she found, could be as cold as Catholics were demonstrative—and no more Christian. The mission of *Jane Eyre's* Mr. Brocklehurst, who professes that "Consistency . . . is the first of Christian duties" (35), is "to mortify in [the girls at Lowood] the lusts of the flesh" (65); yet, his own wife and daughters accompany him "splendidly attired in velvet, silk, and furs" (65). The Reverend St. John Rivers dedicates his life to his Church, but as he himself admits, he is "a cold, hard, ambitious man" (379). The infamous three curates that grace the opening and closing chapters of *Shirley* engage in an endless round of eating and visiting one another which the narrator assures us is "not friendship . . . not religion . . . piety—never" (7).[3] The narrator contrasts the empty show of religion by these curates with the Christlike actions of Mr. Hall, the gentle, unassuming curate whom the reader first meets at the home of William Farren, where he takes the little children on his lap and offers Farren a loan in his time of desperate need.

Brontë's characterizations of both Catholics and Protestants suggests her belief that public declarations and observations of religion were no sure indication of one's true piety. Thus Lucy Snowe seeks a confessor in a moment of desperation, but ultimately clings to the more private profession of her faith. As she tells M. Paul, "we kept fewer forms between us and God" (*V* 516). The most authentically religious people in Brontë's novels are those, like M. Paul and Reverend Hall, who practice their religion consistently, but not ostentatiously.

In one respect, Brontë's insistence on privacy in religious matters seems contradictory in a society in which a man's very livelihood traditionally was bound to the public practice of religion. Englishmen commonly evaded the Test Act, however, by publicly participating in Anglican rites while privately practicing another religion. Therefore, Brontë was probably especially cognizant that one's outward displays of religious fervor did not necessarily indicate the individual spirit; her work recognizes that dichotomy and privileges the privacy of religious feeling. Conversely, in America, where one's religion was officially a private matter, Louisa May Alcott was just as enthusiastically creating religious people who actively and publicly displayed their beliefs.

Though legally a religiously tolerant country, the United

States was by no means immune to the anti-Catholic sentiment experienced in England in the mid-nineteenth century. Huge numbers of Catholic immigrants, coupled with the Church's interest in sending missionaries to the West, swelled the Catholic population in the United States from 660,000 in 1840 to 3.1 million by 1860. By 1850, Catholics were the largest Christian denomination in America (Nye 284, 308–10). This huge influx awakened the concern of American workers, who were worried about immigration in general causing employment problems, as well as politicians seeking to fuel American fears of possible "Romish" designs on their government. These forces employed the services of such well-known Americans as Lyman Beecher and Samuel F. B. Morse, and even ran Millard Fillmore for president in 1856.

As in England, anti-Catholic feelings surfaced in the popular literature of the time. David Reynolds reports such titles as *Awful Disclosures of . . . the Hotel Dieu Nunnery at Montreal* (1836), a tale in which "priests at a Canadian nunnery [are portrayed] as inexhaustible lechers who had murdered so many illegitimate children they had to dispose of babies' corpses in a lime pit in the basement" (Reynolds 261). Although the "exposé" itself was later exposed as fraudulent, it nevertheless sold over three hundred thousand copies before the Civil War. Reynolds notes that the imagery of "depraved priests and licentious nuns" (85) that permeated popular literature also found its way into the texts of major writers of the day such as Hawthorne and Melville, as it had done in England.

That religious images found their way into Alcott's texts in such different ways than they did in Brontë's can be attributed to several factors. First, in its Constitution, if not in its inception, the U. S. government had officially agreed to stay out of matters of religion.[4] Second, relative to England at least, American religion was much more pluralistic and multi-denominational; as Nye says, "There was . . . no American church but American churches" (284). This pluralism would tend to diminish the impact of any one crusade, anti-Catholicism included. In terms of literature, David Reynolds includes anti-Catholic tracts as part of a much greater body of reform literature and literature exposing the corruptions of "reform," including literature devoted

to temperance, anti-slavery, working conditions, and prison reform. Again, the diffusion would tend to mitigate against the
powerful hold on the imagination of any one reform. But
probably just as important as the overall culture was the fact
that Louisa May Alcott's personal background tended to op-
pose sectarian grievances as strongly as Charlotte Brontë's encouraged them.

Louisa Alcott wrote in a letter in 1884 that "my parents never
bound us to any church but taught us that the love of goodness
was the love of God, the cheerful doing of duty made life happy,
& that the love of one's neighbor in its widest sense was the
best help for oneself" (*Letters* 276). In the same letter, she lists R. W.
Emerson and Theodore Parker, both Transcendentalists and
fallen-away Unitarians (although Parker never formally left the
church), as major influences upon her spiritual life. Her brief
comments sum up succinctly Alcott's ideas of religion: ideally, it
should be non-sectarian, active, and linked inextricably with the
reform movements of the day. As was true of Brontë, Alcott's
depictions of religion and religious figures in her writing articulate her own spiritual sentiments, a philosophy she called "practical Christianity" (*Rose in Bloom* 13).

Despite her personal nonsectarian outlook, Alcott's work
demonstrates that she was certainly aware of non-Catholic
sentiment in American society; most of her references to organized religions are, in fact, to Catholicism. Furthermore, she
could and did present an attitude of religious tolerance toward Catholics in her work while maintaining her own view-
point. For example, she alludes to Catholicism in *Little Women*,
a book which, despite its repeated allusions to God and a
structure based on the Puritan allegory *Pilgrim's Progress*, came
under contemporary criticism for not being quite godly
enough. *The Ladies' Repository*, in its review of the book, demanded that it be banned from Sunday School libraries because "It is not a Christian book. It is religion without spirituality, and salvation without Christ" (472). Her publisher, Thomas
Niles, even asked Alcott to consider removing the Christmas
theatricals from future editions of *Little Women* because Sunday School librarians had complained, but Niles added, "For

my part, I think it is about the best part of the whole book. Why will people be so *very good?*" (26 October 1865; qtd. in Showalter, Introduction to *Little Women* xix)—and Alcott refused to make the change. In fact, even though Mr. March is a minister, no one in the novel ever goes to church, even to be married: Meg's wedding takes place at home, with her father officiating; Amy's occurs in Europe; Jo's is accomplished in a single sentence, with no details about the proceedings.

One of the few allusions to formal religion in Alcott's most famous novel occurs during Amy's stay with Aunt March while Beth battles scarlet fever. Aunt March's maid Esther, a French Catholic who agrees to change her name from Estelle "on condition that she was never asked to change her religion" (192), befriends Amy during her lonely exile from the family. When Amy observes that Esther seems to obtain great comfort from her religious practices, Esther replies, "If Mademoiselle was a Catholic, she would find true comfort; but, *as that is not to be*, it would be well if you went apart each day to meditate, and pray" (193–94; emphasis mine). Esther then helps Amy to set up a small chapel, complete with a picture of the Virgin Mary, for quiet meditation; Amy adds her New Testament and hymn-book to the decor, but draws the line at Esther's gift of a rosary, which she uses as a decoration for her chapel but not as an instrument of prayer. Unlike more vehemently negative depictions of Catholic behavior, Alcott's contains neither pressure for conversion nor criticism of Esther's or Amy's methods of devotion; instead, she projects an attitude of acceptance for whatever method brings the soul to God.

Alcott's portrayals of priests in her sensation stories demonstrate her awareness of the ways they were being caricatured at the time, but her priests are seldom the unprincipled clerics of sensation stories at their most lurid; instead, they tend to be rather fascinating characters. In the confessional scene of *A Long Fatal Love Chase* referred to at the beginning of this chapter, the elderly Father Dominic has succumbed to the temptation of Philip Tempest's bribe and allowed Tempest to take his place in the confessional, thus permitting Tempest to hear Rosamond's admission of her continuing love for him. Certainly, this action fits the stereotype of popular fiction, and parallels Charlotte Brontë's Père Silas, who has no qualms about revealing what Lucy says to him in the confessional. But Alcott's use of the scene is double-edged: on the one hand, Tempest fulfills Victorian ideals by reclaiming the hold on his wife's conscience that the Catholic priest usurps; on the other, Father Dominic is a weak priest, and Tempest's action is, by Alcott's standards, clearly wrong. Further, Alcott counterbalances Father Dominic's weak behavior with that of his young assistant, Father Ignatius, who puts his vow of obedience at risk by helping Rosamond to escape from Tempest and who stands by her to the end of the tale. Though Father Ignatius is consistently ethical in his behavior toward Rosamond, he is clearly in love with her, and some of the scenes between them are among the most passion-charged in all of Alcott's work.

For example, when Ignatius and Rosamond are escaping in a small boat at night, she comments, "You should have been a knight and not a monk"; whereupon, Ignatius tears off his cassock and throws it into the bottom of the boat, exclaiming, "I will be for an hour. Lie there, detested thing!" (141). Later, when they have arrived in England and Rosamond goes to Ignatius's room one evening, she finds that he has fallen asleep reading a biography of Martin Luther; the book lies open to a page

> which seemed to have been much read for several paragraphs were marked and the leaf was worn by frequent turning. It was that point of the story where the great reformer practiced as he preached, and boldly affirming that priests might marry, confirmed his sincerity by wedding his beloved Catherine. (221)

When Ignatius later defends Rosamond from Tempest in a physical fight (and then immediately tends to his wounds), Tempest, clearly understanding the priest's feelings toward Rosamond, demands of the priest, "What will you do [regarding her]?" Ignatius answers:

> I shall love her all my life, shall be to her a faithful friend, and if I cannot remain loyal to both God and her I shall renounce her and never see her face again. You call this folly. To me it is a hard

duty, and the more I love her the worthier I endeavor to become of her by my own integrity of soul. (227)

This chivalric portrayal of the priest, while adhering to traditions of courtly romance, resists many of the stereotypes current in the popular literature: Ignatius has both virility and integrity, and never attempts to convert or to corrupt Rosamond. Further, he is by no means one of Charlotte Brontë's cold clerics; yet there are some of the same hints of the connection between Catholicism and sexual repression here that function as part of Brontë's image of the phantom nun in *Villette*. Alcott, however, applauds the priest's control as evidence of his commitment to an ideal, whereas Brontë treats Catholic sexual repression as hypocrisy.

Alcott again plays at the edges of the popular depiction of priests in her characterization of Augustine Carruth in another sensation piece, "A Nurse's Story." Augustine is the eldest son of a family doomed by hereditary madness; he becomes a priest when he discovers the family secret his parents have kept from their children, "hoping to hide his calamity and expiate his father's sin by endless prayers" (45). The unspoken assumption is that, because of the priest's characteristic melancholic demeanor, no one will notice Augustine's depression, even when it degenerates into madness. However, Alcott avoids the caricature, eventually creating a community of mutual comfort consisting of Augustine, his brother Harry, who becomes a doctor, and their adopted sister, the heroine Kate Snow. While Harry (with the help of Kate, a nurse) tends bodies, Augustine "labor[s] for lost or troubled souls with the devout zeal of a priest of old" (109). The narrator comments that he will never be great, but will be beloved, "for many bless the meek man who so gently comforts sorrow, pities weakness, pardons sins, and so beautifully mingles human charities with divine beliefs" (109). In a comment that prefigures the awareness of Protestant-Catholic conflict but also the ultimately all-embracing Christianity of *Little Women*, the narrator then adds that "Protestants respect his genuine piety, and Catholics will canonize him as a saint" (109).

When this same character appears in the "Companion"

chapter of Alcott's *Work*, he eventually becomes "melancholy mad" (431–32), quietly doing continual penance but separate from the world except for his mother who tends him. While this priestly portrait is less positive than the one in "A Nurse's Story," it still is far from a blanket stereotype of Catholicism. One reason it may be less affirming is that in this novel Alcott reserves the greater praise for the man who most embodies her ideal of practical Christianity: Reverend Thomas Power.

Just as Charlotte Brontë frequently based the clergymen portrayed in her novels (including Brocklehurst and St. John Rivers) upon clerics she had known, Alcott's Reverend Power had his basis in one of the most influential people in her life, Theodore Parker.[5] Parker, a Unitarian minister who became active in the Transcendentalist movement, shared many of Emerson's ideas about the potential godliness of the individual as expressed in the Divinity School Address and was just as controversial among Unitarians for his views, which often questioned the authority of the Unitarian establishment. O. B. Frothingham called him "the greatest [preacher] of his generation" (qtd. in Albrecht 72). He was certainly one of the most popular; his Boston congregation of the 1840s and 1850s had seven thousand names on its register, and he sometimes drew audiences of over three thousand from diverse groups in Boston.

What probably distinguished Parker from Emerson (and from her own father, for that matter) for Alcott was his practical, activist response to religion. He said in a sermon on "The True Idea of a Christian Church": "A church which calls itself Christian . . . must set itself about all this business, and be not merely a church of theology, but of religion, not of faith only but of works; a just church by its faith bringing works into life" (qtd. in Collins 8–9). He then urged Christians to spend more time in "the practical good works of the day" (qtd. in Collins 9). Nor did he merely call others to action. Parker was personally involved in many of the reform movements of the day: abolition, prison reform, education reform, conditions of working people, anti-poverty. To Parker, involvement included giving refuge to fugitive slaves, financial support to John Brown, and personal aid to the many people who came to him needing employment or emergency funds—including Louisa May

Alcott. He held meetings at his home on Sunday evenings to promote conversation and fellowship. Louisa attended one of these in 1856, when she had journeyed to Boston looking for work to help her family out of its desperate straits. She wrote in her journal, "Mr. Parker said, 'God bless you, Louisa, come again,' and the grasp of his hand gave me courage to face another anxious week" (*Journals* 80; November 1856).

As she re-creates Parker in *Work*, Alcott presents him as Reverend Thomas Power, a nonsectarian preacher who works tirelessly in his community, doing charitable works and holding Sunday evening conversations like his real-life counterpart. Although Christie first resists her friend Mrs. Wilkins's suggestion that she attend Power's service, since "she had heard of Thomas Power as a rampant radical and infidel of the deepest dye, and been warned never to visit that den of iniquity called his free church" (200–201), she returns home saying, "I'll never go to church anywhere else" (208). Christie, who had earlier embarked upon an intensive search for God and finally gave up her search for an "all-sustaining power" (147), finds in this particular "Power" exactly what she had sought. Not only does she find that his congregation includes "all classes [and] both sexes" (205), but his sermon strikes deeply into her private soul:

[W]ise counsel, cheering words, and the devout surrender of the soul to its best instincts; its close communion with its Maker, unchilled by fear, untrammelled by the narrowness of sect or superstition, but full and free and natural as the breath of life. . . . For the first time in [Christie's] life religion seemed a visible and vital thing; a power that she could grasp and feel, take into her life and make her daily bread. (213)

Power's influence on Christie, as well as his religion, does supply her with something practical with which to "make her daily bread." He gets her a job as companion to the elderly Mrs. Sterling, where she meets her future husband, David. Mr. Power shows both willingness and ability to reach people at all levels of society. Mrs. Wilkins describes him in homely terms as a "washerwoman" who "starts the dirt and gits the stains out" of souls, even though he doesn't "get half so much credit as them as polishes and crimps" (204). On the other hand, he also tends to the needs of his more "polished" souls through his intellectual gatherings.

Mrs. Wilkins's notion that Reverend Power attends to the needs of all in his flock is seconded on a more abstract level by Elizabeth Keyser, who writes that Power's attitude toward religion "undermines the hierarchical divisions and dualities" (110).[6] This is true on many levels: he appeals to all social classes, to men as well as women, to the spiritual, physical, and intellectual needs of the people for whom he works. His approach is even more inclusive due to its nonsectarian quality. Christie finds displayed in David's study a portrait of a monk flanked on either side by portraits of Mr. Power and Martin Luther, who "stared thoughtfully at one another . . . as if making up their minds to shake hands in spite of time and space" (225).

Alcott's own portrait of Mr. Power is probably her most definitive rendering of "practical Christianity," at least as it connects with any semblance of organized religion. Like Father Ignatius, his human warmth and vitality contrast dramatically with most of Brontë's cold clergymen. He is further unlike them in that, while he is willing to be Christie's friend and advisor as long as she needs him, he never tries to run her life. He tells her about the position with Mrs. Sterling: "If it is not what you want, we will find you something else" (212). When Christie does choose to leave the Sterlings, Power immediately takes her in without question and finds her other work to do; even though he senses that her decision is a troubled one, he allows her to make her own choices. Brontë's St. John Rivers, on the other hand, "acquired a certain influence over me [Jane] that took away my liberty of mind" (JE 402). He orders Jane not only to become a missionary but to become his wife as well, and warns her, "Do not forget that if you reject [my 'offer'], it is not me you deny, but God" (JE 414). While Alcott's presentation of Reverend Power is wholly positive, Brontë is much more ambivalent about Rivers. The fact that she has any sympathy for him at all is evidence that, although his coldness appalls her, she cannot quite condemn his missionary zeal.

Certainly for either Alcott or Brontë to have condemned

missionary zeal would have flown directly in the face of popular opinion, for nineteenth-century society, British and American, honored the missionary spirit. Three separate Anglican missionary societies existed in England by 1815, and another thirteen were founded by century's end. Most of the people involved in the mission movement, according to Latourette (311), tended to be evangelical Christians like Patrick Brontë. The same spirit of evangelism, including the "sense of doom and impending martyrdom" (Welter 91) Brontë captured in St. John Rivers, had caught hold in America, where a popular memoir published in 1829 told the story of Mrs. Ann Hasseltine Judson, one of two wives of a Baptist minister to Burma who died there; Judson's third wife returned to America to great acclaim after his death in 1850, but died shortly thereafter herself (Welter 91, 224n). One difference in American versus British missionary zeal, however, was that in England, foreign missions held the greatest interest; home projects existed in the form of urban missions, but these were mostly token efforts to put forth a facade of interdenominational goodwill. In America, however, there were several kinds of people regarded as "heathens" within the continent, all worthy of "civilizing" as well as evangelizing: immigrants from Europe who migrated West, Indians, and slaves (Nye 292–96). American missions to the West began as early as 1798, and the interdenominational American Home Missionary Society was founded in 1826. Certainly foreign missions were also important, but in somewhat inverse proportion to the home versus foreign interest in England.

The metaphor of good Christians as missionaries permeates many of Alcott's children's books, including the ones in which the Brontëan influence is present. While Brontë's most famous missionary is, of course, St. John Rivers, whose glorious death in India ends *Jane Eyre*, Alcott's missionaries are frequently more secular—and, in the American tradition, more local—in nature. *Jack and Jill*, for instance, abounds with metaphorical images of the children as missionaries. After Mrs. Pecq admonishes the young ladies who have been fantasizing about foreign missions—"We needn't go to Africa to be missionaries; they have 'em nearer home, and need 'em, too. In all the big cities there are a many, and they have their hands full with the poor, the wicked, and the helpless" (JJ 45)—they decide to begin their own version of a home missionary society. In fact, they find tasks very close to home. Merry works on contributing to the comfort of her own family. The motherless Molly decides to take upon herself the "civilizing" of her baby brother, who is largely left alone by the housekeeper, Mrs. Bat, although the difficulty of her task causes her to speculate whether "real missionaries ever killed their pupils in the process of conversion" (JJ 115). Molly's project is consistently rendered in missionary metaphors: Boo's messiness at table leaves him looking "more like a Fiji chief in full war-paint than a Christian boy" (110); Molly's exasperation when he refuses to say his prayers elicits from her the comment, "Then . . . be a real little heathen" (114), causing Boo to relent, "No, no; I wont be a heevin! I don't want to be frowed to the trockindiles. I will say my prayers!" (JJ 114). While the invalid Jill, the third member of the trio of girls, is limited in her activities by her physical condition, she, too, manages to "keep [Mrs. Minot] happy and make the boys gentle and kind" (JJ 226) and realizes, "I've been a sort of missionary without knowing it!" (JJ 227).

Alcott turns to a more traditional, though still nonsectarian, articulation of missionary zeal in *Jo's Boys*, in which Mrs. Jo's beloved but wild Dan goes West to work for the good of the Indians. The end of this novel compares intriguingly with that of *Jane Eyre*. Dan, who is in love with Amy's daughter Bess but in Mrs. Jo's eyes is as unsuitable a match for her as was Jane for St. John Rivers, leaves for the West alone and becomes an Indian agent, a sort of secular missionary, who "lived, bravely and usefully, among his chosen people till he was shot defending them" (365). Though Dan is no clergyman like St. John, Alcott almost immediately follows the report of Dan's martyrdom, and closes the history of Plumfield, with an account of Jo's own son, and Dan's dearest friend, who "eclipsed them all by becoming an eloquent and famous clergyman" (JB 365). Since the young man's name is Teddy, this also may be read as a final tribute to Theodore Parker; however, it is interesting that, while Brontë reacts with some ambivalence toward her clergyman-missionary, Alcott splits the character in two, creating one clergyman and one missionary. The combination allows her to close on a far more hopeful and a far less ambiguous note by reinforcing the idea of practical Christianity with the double actions of Dan and Teddy; Teddy's life balances his friend's martyrdom, ending the novel with joy instead of sorrow. But the lives of both young men are ultimately triumphant, for Alcott celebrated the active, public practice of religion as intensely as Charlotte Brontë honored the private.

But even if the English clergyman's daughter responded to contemporary religious issues with the caution common to conservatives in her culture while the American transcendentalist's daughter embraced them with the expansiveness typical of radicals in hers, neither Brontë nor Alcott was untouched by what Barbara Welter terms the "feminization of religion" in the nineteenth century (83–102).[7] To say that religion became "feminized" is not to imply that women moved into positions of authority in religious groups, for with a few exceptions, this was not true. However, the Victorian concept of separate spheres for men and women assumed that women had a greater "religious instinct" (Heeney 13) than men, and this instinct gradually made them the keepers of religion as the men became more and more involved in the more "corrupting" arenas of politics, business, and industry. Besides instilling religious values in their homes, as in *Little Women* when Marmee involves the girls in giving their Christmas dinner to those more needy than themselves, women became active as Sunday school teachers and in church-related voluntary societies. Women greatly outnumbered men among church members and among church attendees, both in England and America (Paz 273). It behooved ministers, then, to gear their sermons and practices to the needs of the women of their congregations, for even without holding positions of hierarchical power, they made up the majority of the listening audience.

The evidence suggests that ministers did adjust to the needs of their predominantly female congregations, since church doctrine itself became more "feminine" at this time. It emphasized the feminine aspects of God and presented Christ as a self-sacrificing savior (in the same way women were expected to be self-sacrificing). It even contemplated the concept of a female prophet, as does Hester Prynne toward the end of *The Scarlet Letter*. Alcott's favorite preacher, Theodore Parker, insisted that a true godhead must embody feminine as well as masculine characteristics. This was not, however, a universally popular idea. Orestes Brownson, one of the original members of the group that became the Transcendentalist Club, for example, wrote that "The curse of our age is femininity. Its lack, not of barbarism, but of virility" (XIV, 421), and he eventually joined the Roman Catholic Church where the patriarchy was, indeed, safe.

Whether or not the patriarchal structure of Victorian religion was safe from a takeover by women, it is clear from their work that both Charlotte Brontë and Louisa May Alcott struggled with a spirituality that would include the feminine. Robert Bernard Martin says that "*Jane Eyre* is, at bottom . . . largely a religious novel" (81). However, where Martin identifies Jane's religious struggle with an attempt to make religion immediate and relevant to human life rather than something ethereal (which is often symbolized in mythological terms as earth vs. sky, or feminine vs. masculine), Brontë actually expresses the struggle not in dualistic terms, but in efforts to unite the archetypally masculine and feminine properties. In *Jane Eyre*, despite the fact that God remains "He" throughout, the continuing imagery of the moon, which Jane associates with her dead mother's guidance, or at least with some notion of the mystical feminine, permeates the novel. For instance, after Jane discovers the secret of Rochester's marriage, she is warned in a dream to leave Thornfield:

> She [the moon] broke forth as never moon yet burst from cloud; a hand first penetrated the sable folds and waved them away; then, not a moon, but a white human form shone in the azure, inclining a glorious brow earthward. It gazed and gazed on me. It spoke, to my spirit . . .

> 'My daughter, flee temptation!'
> 'Mother, I will.' (JE 324)

In Jane's time of refuge at Moor House, the mercy of Diana and Mary Rivers, whose very names resonate with feminine divinity, serves to mitigate the dominant masculine theology of their brother, St. John Rivers. When Jane returns to Rochester after hearing his voice calling to her (an occurrence Jane calls "the work of nature" [425]), both she and Rochester allude to both the feminine and masculine aspects of God, justice and mercy. Rochester interrupts their reunion to voice a prayer thanking "my Maker, that in the midst of judgment he has remembered mercy" (453). Jane observes ten years later that, when Rochester's sight returned enough to enable him to see his new son, "he again, with a full heart, acknowledged that God had tempered judgment with mercy" (457).

Despite these efforts to assert a more comprehensive understanding of deity, Brontë equivocates at the last moment. The final image of *Jane Eyre* is not that of Jane, Edward, and son in the peaceful "green world" of Ferndean; rather, the narrative of earthly joy suddenly breaks to regard the prospect of St. John Rivers in India, about to receive "his incorruptible crown" (458) of a completely spiritual nature. Jane regards Rivers's death in triumphant terms: he is the "warrior Greatheart . . . in the first rank of those who are redeemed from the earth . . . called, and chosen, and faithful" (457). The ending is puzzling, equivocal; Judith Farr terms it "the defense written by a minister's daughter" (96). Gilbert and Gubar read the passage as "an 'irreligious' definition, almost a parody, of John Bunyan's vision" (370). Rosemarie Bodenheimer claims that the real "mission of salvation" (167) in *Jane Eyre* is Jane's rescue of Rochester, but acknowledges that the novel's end accommodates a "multiplicity" of interpretations and "seems both to credit and to quarrel with them all" (168). Regardless of whether Brontë meant to praise Rivers or to bury him here—or both—the union of God and nature, spiritual and physical, masculine and feminine, that she asserts throughout the novel changes abruptly but undeniably from "and" to "or" in the conclusion. One may have religion of the heart or of the head, but not both.

Brontë also attempts to affirm a more all-embracing spirituality in *Shirley*. Having dismissed the "unholy trinity" represented by the curates of the first chapter, she uses the center of the novel to propose an alternative. As the Whitsuntide (Pentecost) service proceeds inside the church, Shirley and her friend

Caroline Helstone remain on a hill outdoors, in what Ellen Moers describes as a "distinctly feminine landscape" (254), where "undulating pasture-ground" and the insistently red ("rosy," "crimson," "red" [S 319]) tints suggest a decidedly nonphallic environment. In this female haven, Shirley dismisses the Eve Milton created in *Paradise Lost* as "his cook" (320) and creates instead her vision of a "woman-Titan" who "face to face . . . speaks with God" and is "Jehovah's daughter, as Adam was his son" (321). This is the spiritual predecessor Shirley claims as "my mother Eve, in these days called Nature" (321); Shirley declares she will not go into the church, but will remain outside it with her "mother."

Shirley's invocation of the Nature goddess seems successful, for the immediately ensuing "male" image is that of William Farren, who emerges from the church and cares for his children "as tenderly as any woman" (322). Although Joe Scott approaches next, and attempts to re-establish the patriarchy by telling Caroline and Shirley, "ye'd better go into th' house" (326) and by quoting St. Paul to them about women keeping silence, Caroline answers him:

> I dare say, if I could read the original Greek, I would find that many of the words have been wrongly translated, perhaps misapprehended altogether. It would be possible . . . to give the passage quite a contrary turn; to make it say, 'Let the woman speak out whenever she sees fit to make an objection;' — 'it is permitted to a woman to teach and to exercise authority as much as may be. Man, meantime, cannot do better than hold his peace,' and so on. (S 329–30)

As she had done in *Jane Eyre* with Mary and Diana Rivers, Brontë reinforces the feminine images with more mythical feminine images in *Shirley* as well. When Caroline Helstone becomes dangerously ill from what seems at first to be an entirely curable fever, and the male religious structure in the person of Mr. Helstone (who is a minister) can do nothing for her, Caroline and the aptly named Mrs. Pryor enact a kind of Eleusinian ritual between them. Mrs. Pryor realizes that Caroline's real problem is that Robert Moore has abandoned her, and she gives Caroline reason to live by revealing that she is her mother. Caroline and Mrs. Pryor embody the mutuality of renewal that, according to Annis Pratt (172), characterizes the Demeter-Persephone myth: "the child lulled the parent, as the parent had erst lulled the child" (436). As Mrs. Pryor nurses Caroline back to health, Caroline begins to work on her mother's rigid demeanor, using her influence to help her mother become more congenial and less old-fashioned, both in her person and in her dress.

But even after Shirley's creation of her spiritual mother, Eve, and Caroline's discovery of her earthly mother, Mrs. Pryor, the promise of female spirituality is no more fulfilled here than in *Jane Eyre*. Shirley's "woman-Titan" is rewritten in the chapter entitled "The First Blue-Stocking" in volume 3, wherein Louis Moore recalls to Shirley a story she had once written as part of a French lesson. The tale of a mystical union between Genius and Humanity begins as an attempt to define a male muse for the female artist, but is ultimately a "knight in shining armor" story in which Genius "saves" Humanity, and power rests in the hands of the male entity, Genius: "I can take what is mine," he says (*S* 489).

After this encounter, both Shirley and Caroline go back into the church outside of which they formerly sat denigrating Milton's Eve, for they are married there. The exclusively male authority of the marriage ritual is reinforced by the narrator's listing the names of the father, uncle (who is also the officiating minister at Shirley's wedding), bridegrooms, and even the groomsmen involved in the service; the only female names given are those of the brides, who are listed as "daughter of" and "niece of" the male figures. Brontë's model clergyman, the Christlike Reverend Hall, makes a brief appearance to officiate at Caroline's nuptials as though there might be some hope yet for his point of view, but he is overshadowed by the more conventionally phallic forces.

Then, as in *Jane Eyre*, the reader is left with a dichotomy that reinforces the incompatibility between the male and female spirits. The narrator returns to the spot known as the Hollow, "once green, and lone, and wild," to find Robert Moore's mill: "a mighty mill, and a chimney, ambitious as the tower of Babel" (645). The narrator's housekeeper observes that there have been no fairies seen there since the mill was built. "A lonesome spot it was—and a bonnie spot—full of oak trees and nut trees. It is altered now" (646). Once again, Brontë struggles with, but then abandons, the idea that male and female ideas of spirituality could co-exist; unlike the tone in *Jane Eyre*, her attitude here is much less ambivalent. The aura of mourning is palpable.

When Brontë considers the question of religion in *Villette*, she abandons the possibility of uniting the archetypally male and female qualities of spirituality entirely. Lucy's sensible Protestant beliefs are perpetually in conflict with the overly emotional, superstitious practices of the Belgian Catholics. Although Lucy and M. Paul eventually accept each other's sincerity of belief, there is no question of either converting to the other's faith. And, while the larger tragedy inherent in the fact that M. Paul's ship does not quite come in at the end of the novel is that Brontë seems to abandon all hope of equality in relationships between men and women, it means there will be no joyous co-existence of the two spiritualities, either.

Gilbert and Gubar observe that even Brontë's use of *Pilgrim's Progress* is much more conventional in *Villette* than in *Jane Eyre*, for Lucy, unlike Jane, never has any hope of earthly happiness: "Lucy Snowe seems to feel that she will only find true bliss after death, when she hopes to enter the Celestial City" (681n). Thus, although the urge to enhance the standard understanding of religion with feminine considerations erupted frequently in *Jane Eyre*, Brontë seems to have begun the retreat from it almost as soon as she articulated it in *Shirley* and, by the time she wrote *Villette*, was ready to return to the opening words of *Jane Eyre*: "There was no possibility." In her cultural and personal experiences (Paz contends that English women's involvement in religion did not translate into female consciousness raising until about 1870, much later than in America [278–79]), there was little support for such ideas, and though Lucy Snowe allows that we should "leave sunny imaginations hope" (*V* 596), there seems to be no such spirit coming from Lucy's creator.

Christie Devon's creator, on the other hand, leaves the reader with a great deal of hope regarding feminine spirituality. Alcott includes priests on an equal footing with "practical Christian" women in *A Long Fatal Love Chase* and especially in "A Nurse's Story," subtly suggesting the possibility of combining masculine and feminine principles; she addresses this issue much more specifically in *Work*. Critics such as Elizabeth Langland have suggested that *Work* is modeled upon part 2 of *Pilgrim's Progress*, Christiana's story; Christie is a pilgrim who first addresses her own religious crisis, then works to evangelize others.[8]

Christie's deepest moments of religious crisis have much in common with those of Jane Eyre and Lucy Snowe, Brontë's heroines who are referred to in Alcott's *Work*. In her poverty and loneliness during the year following her departure from the sewing shop where she has been working, Christie conducts an intensive search for God, although, unlike the moon and nature imagery in *Jane Eyre*, few hints of feminine spirituality occur before this time. Instead, Christie determinedly examines all the traditional religions: "She went to many churches, studied many creeds" (147). Although she does not seem consciously to realize that she seeks the feminine principle, the terms of her dissatisfaction reveal rather clearly that she does:

> Some were cold and narrow, some seemed theatrical and superficial, some stern and terrible, none simple, sweet, and strong enough for humanity's many needs. There was too much machinery, too many walls, laws, and penalties. . . . Too much fear, too little love. . . . Too little knowledge of the natural religion which has no name but godliness, whose creed is boundless and benignant as the sunshine, whose faith is as the tender trust of little children in their mother's love. (W 147)

The comment about "too much machinery" recalls Lucy Snowe's reflection that Protestants "kept fewer forms between us and God" (V 516); the final line suggests Jane's impulse to seek the feminine principle in Nature.

Like Jane (and like Lucy Snowe as well, for she and Christie both wander in a delirium brought on by fever), Christie's desperation leads her out into the streets in a "long dark night of the soul." As Jane finds comfort in Mother Nature when she flees Rochester ("I thought she loved me, outcast as I was. . . . I was her child: my mother would lodge me without money and without price" [328]), as Lucy finds temporary comfort in Mother Church, Christie also finds comfort in the feminine; her long-absent friend Rachel emerges like a ghost from a mist just in time to keep her from jumping/falling into a river and death. Like both Jane and Lucy, Christie is then delivered into female hands for tending, at which time Rachel disappears back into the mist.[9]

The renewal Christie receives in the home of the washerwoman Cynthy Wilkins is much like Jane Eyre's tenure at Moor House; her willingness to pitch in with the work of the house as soon as she is physically able endears her to Mrs. Wilkins much as Jane's similar impulses impress the Riverses' servant Hannah; the Wilkins children provide additional impetus toward healing, as do Mary and Diana Rivers. Like Jane, who becomes mistress of the village school in Morton, Christie needs more challenging work once she fully recovers her health, and she moves from her refuge to work for Mrs. Sterling.

Unlike St. John Rivers, however, the cleric who enters Christie's life at this time does not stand counter to the feminine principles involved in her recovery; "Mrs. Wilkins' minister,"[10] Thomas Power, reinforces them by accommodating both in his theology. He prays to God as the "dear father and mother of souls" (207). This is the religion Christie feels is "visible and vital," which makes her feel, finally, "Nearer, my God, to thee" (213–14). That the popular hymn which so touches Christie in church was written by a woman[11] further reinforces the feminine aspect of Christie's spirituality.

In fact, as *Work* proceeds, it is the male element that eventually becomes more peripheral, though never absent. Like Shirley on the hillside outside the church, Christie finds "a new heaven and a new earth" (251) in tending a strawberry bed at the Sterlings'. With images of springtime, birth, and Christie's "fingers deeply stained with the blood of many berries" (*W* 249), Alcott makes this landscape as feminine as Shirley's hillside. David and Reverend Power visit her domain, and she welcomes them, but they both leave, while she remains to tend the garden. The "loving league of sisters" (442) Christie forms as the novel closes includes no men; nonetheless, a photograph of David Sterling and a painting of Mr.

Greatheart leading Mercy and Christiana from the City of Destruction, which Christie's former lover Philip Fletcher has just given her, hang on the wall overseeing the women who join hands around the table. Reverend Power, too, is absent from this final scene, but the fact that Christie goes about her own work as "Mr. Power's friend" (427), and that she suggests to her friend Bella Carrol that her own life's work may be along the lines of Mr. Power's "conversations," suggests that she does not mean to eliminate the male principle entirely. Alcott wrote in a letter that "Christ is a great reformer to me not God" (*Letters* 278; 5 February 1884). Both Christie and Mr. Power are Christlike figures in the way they actively pursue reform; that their paths are not mirror images of each other does not necessarily mean either is unimportant—the point is that, to Alcott, both men and women were worthy of the Christlike role of "great reformer."[12]

Although Alcott's fiction does not equivocate about or deny the possibility of the role of the feminine principle in religion in the way Charlotte Brontë's does, neither does it go nearly as far in embracing religious beliefs outside mainstream American Protestantism as Alcott herself did. In an early journal entry, the thirteen-year-old Louisa had recorded "an early run in the woods before the dew was off the grass" that "seemed like going through a dark life or grave into heaven beyond" and "as if I *felt* God as I never did before" (*Journals* 57; 1845); at a much later date (1885), Alcott added to this entry that "I most sincerely think the little girl 'got religion' that day in the wood when dear mother Nature led her to God" (*Journals* 57). In a series of letters to her longtime correspondent Maggie Lukens in 1884, Alcott expressed her admiration for Emerson, who

> is called a Pantheist or believer in Nature instead of God. He was truly *Christian* and saw God *in* Nature, finding strength & comfort in the sane, sweet influences of the great Mother as well as the Father of all. I, too, believe this, & when tired, sad, or tempted find my best comfort in the woods, the sky, the healing solitude that lets my poor, weary soul find the rest, the fresh hope, or the patience which only God can give us. (*Letters* 277; 5 February 1884)

THE INNER LIFE

This spirit is certainly present in Alcott's fiction; in *Jo's Boys*, for example, Mrs. Jo seeks to preserve her beloved Dan from destruction by urging him thus: "Nature is your God now; she has done much for you; let her do more, and lead you to know and love a wiser and more tender teacher, friend, and comforter than she can ever be" (*JB* 129). But in that same letter to Lukens, Alcott went on to assert that "The simple Buddha religion is very attractive to me, & I believe in it" (*Letters* 278) and even to attest to a belief in transmigration of the soul: "I think immortality is the passing of a soul thro many lives or experiences, & such as are *truly* lived, used & learned help on to the next. . . . I seem to remember former states before this" (*Letters* 279). These thoughts are not particularly shocking in view of the influence of Oriental philosophy on two of Alcott's mentors, Emerson and Thoreau, but they suggest that Power's "free church" and Amy March's experiments with Catholicism only begin to express the radicalism that Alcott herself felt in regard to spiritual matters. She never backed off from or recanted these ideas in her fiction as did Charlotte Brontë, but clearly she held ideas that would have shocked *The Ladies' Repository* even more than what she explicitly expressed as "practical Christianity."

Louisa Alcott and Charlotte Brontë's portrayals of religious issues in their fiction, even in similar scenes such as the ones with which this chapter begins, demonstrate an awareness of and involvement with spirituality that Victorian society expected of its women. Although they responded to sectarian concerns largely in ways typical of their cultural and personal backgrounds but antithetical to each other, their responses also suggest important areas of mutual concern. The public nature of religion in England clearly suggested to Brontë that *true* religion was a private matter just as official religious privacy in America led Alcott to conclude that *true* religion must be public; yet, their characters who are the most positive models of Christian behavior, such as Mr. Hall, M. Paul Emanuel, Mr. Power, and Christie, are in all cases those whose public behavior matches their private belief. Further, though culture divided them, gender united them in the search for a feminine principle of spirituality. While Alcott pursued this with transcendental American optimism and Brontë with British Protestant caution, the art of each expresses the yearning for a theology that would embrace male and female aspects of God, head as well as heart. It is this yearning, at least in part, that sends female artistic creations of both writers into Catholic confessionals in search of internal peace. However, the way in which Brontë's characters are answered with equivocation or outright refusal to validate their premises, whereas Alcott's generally succeed in their spiritual quests, embodies what American writers generally termed "failure of nerve" on the part of the British (but what Brontë herself would probably have termed simply realistic) and verifies the American character of Alcott as a writer and as a transcendentalist, although one more practical than many of the thinkers around her. Thus, even in this important consideration of the inmost workings of the human spirit, Alcott draws upon but ultimately "translates" the influence of Charlotte Brontë.

CHAPTER 4

The Consociate Life
Self and Others

Just as both Charlotte Brontë's and Louisa May Alcott's work affirms that spirituality must link public and private, head and heart, both also assert the need for links between the self and other people. Solitude, more than poverty or hard work, drives the heroines of each writer to the point of despair. *Work*'s Christie Devon is so utterly alone after quitting her job in a lace factory that "[t]he world looked very dark to her, life seemed an utter failure, God a delusion, and the long, lonely years before her too hard to be endured," and the narrator comments, "It is not always want, insanity, or sin that drives women to desperate deaths; often it is a dreadful loneliness of heart, a hunger for home and friends, worse than starvation" (150). In *Villette*, Lucy Snowe's lowest moments come when she is alone during the pensionnat's two-month summer holiday with a servant and a "deformed and imbecile pupil" (227) whose guardian will not allow her to return home. At this point, Lucy admits, "A sorrowful indifference to existence often pressed on me—a despairing resignation to reach betimes the end of all things earthly. Alas! When I had full leisure to look on life as life must be looked on by such as me, I found it but a hopeless desert" (228).

As each writer explored alternatives to the problem of solitude, the Victorian "cult of womanhood" loomed over her consciousness; the ideal role for any woman was to be the "angel in the house" making life pleasant for her husband and family. Charlotte Brontë cannot accept the utter passivity and loss of self inherent in this definition of womanhood. Witness, for example, Jane Eyre's thoughts on the subject:

> [W]omen feel just as men feel; they need exercise for their faculties, and a field for their efforts as much as their brothers do . . . and it is narrow-minded in their more privileged fellow-creatures to say that they ought to confine themselves to making puddings and knitting stockings, to playing on the piano and embroidering bags. (JE 110–11)

Nevertheless, Brontë seeks marriage as the preferred narrative outcome for her heroines; however, within the marriages she creates, she strives to adjust the "angel" ideal in order to put man and woman on equal footing within the home. Like her impulse to develop a more complete spirituality, the impulse toward a more complete marriage also begins in a hope that eventually dissipates. In her writing, Brontë also explores alternatives to married life. But in view of the fact that neither her personal nor her cultural experiences validated the possibility of permanent relationships between women, it is not surprising that her literary attempts to evade solitude eventually collapse, like Lucy's hopes, into the "despairing resignation" of a woman alone. Alcott, on the other hand, begins from a more positive stance on the position of a woman alone, but also accepts her society's notion of family as the basis of female power. She builds outward from this basis of family in an effort to create relationships in which self-reliance can co-exist with communal values. Furthermore, she proposes these optimistic, inclusive constructs in many of the works that manifest the influence of the more skeptical art of Charlotte Brontë.

While Brontë's Jane Eyre resists Rochester's attempt to characterize her as an angel, saying, "I am not an angel . . . and I will not be one till I die" (262), Jane's creator found it increasingly difficult to construct a narrative alternative to the image of the woman on a pedestal, adored (and largely ignored) by her man. Although she repeatedly attempts to propose equality in relationships, Brontë's suspicion that equity in relationships between the sexes is ultimately impossible becomes a belief more clearly stated in each of her successive novels.

Certainly nineteenth-century culture did nothing to reassure her that gender equality was possible or even desirable, but perhaps some of her difficulties in fully imagining her ideal state also stem from a personal impulse where love is concerned. Brontë herself once turned down a proposal of marriage because "I had not . . . that intense attachment which would make me willing to die for him, and, if I ever marry, it must be in that light of adoration that I will regard my husband" (Letter to Ellen Nussey, 12 March, 1839; Wise and Symington I: 173). Although in *Jane Eyre* she seems to regard this attitude as a sign of immature love ("I could not, *in those days*, see God for his creature: of whom I had made an idol" [277; emphasis mine]), her own words indicate a personal impulse to circumvent the Victorian ideal by finding a man whom she could put on a pedestal. In her novels, she consistently creates just such unequal power relationships between her lovers: in *The Professor* and in *Villette*, the teachers Frances and Lucy fall in love with men who are older, more experienced teachers. In *Shirley*, the title character is an independent heiress who marries her tutor despite his difference in class; and of course *Jane Eyre*'s Rochester is her employer and nearly twenty years older than herself. Although her project seems to be to discover a fundamental, internal equality between men and women despite external differences, she consistently sets up situations in which there is much to overcome in order to get to that point. She and her heroines succeed in this quest, at least to some degree, in her first two novels, but by the time she writes *Villette* she despairs of ever achieving the desired balance.

In Brontë's first novel, *The Professor*, she at least insists on freeing the "angel" from total involvement with the house, for Frances Henri continues to work after she marries Crimsworth. However, he notes that she treats him as "the master in all things" and acts the part of a "submissive and supplicating mortal woman" (209–10). While Jane Eyre asserts and Rochester assents to her equality of spirit with him in *Jane Eyre*'s center, critics have noted (see Gilbert and Gubar, chapter 10) that Brontë still finds it necessary to raise Jane through her inheritance, and to cripple Rochester, in order to make their positions more equal before uniting them at novel's end. Even at this, they are only able to maintain this delicate balance by remaining apart from society at Ferndean.

As Gilbert and Gubar note, "Qualified and isolated as [Jane's] way may be, it is at least an emblem of hope. Charlotte Brontë was never again to indulge in such an optimistic imagining" (371). Certainly the endings of *Shirley* and *Villette* do nothing to contradict this assertion. It was noted in chapter 2 that Brontë employs a whole series of passive verbs in describing Shirley's preparation for her marriage. Shirley's independence, and virtually her existence, seem to end when she accepts Louis Moore's proposal of marriage. She is quite literally silenced: the proposal scene is reported in Louis's words as an entry in his journal, and Shirley never speaks another word in the novel except for the narrator's report that Shirley *said* that "Louis ... would never have learned to rule, if she had not ceased to govern" (638).

Like the rest of Brontë's heroines, *Villette*'s Lucy Snowe continues to refer to her lover as "master" even after declarations of love and equality. In *Villette*, Brontë despairs of even the imperfect unions she has previously proposed. M. Paul Emanuel sets up Lucy in a school of her own before leaving on his ocean voyage, but is shipwrecked and never returns to consummate the relationship. Brontë has, by this time, abandoned even her modest hope for the happy ending expressed in *Jane Eyre*; she no longer believed that her world—or fate—would permit a woman without money and beauty to have both Jane's "exercise of faculties" and love as well.

But Brontë's eventual despair regarding heterosexual relationships does not result in her proposing either the life of a woman alone or in relationships with other women as a joyous alternative to marriage, although both situations appear in her novels. Her interest in the life of unmarried women reflects not only her personal situation (she remained single to age thirty-eight), but many attitudes common in nineteenth-century England. At the same time that the "angel in the house" was held up as the societal ideal, demographics worked against this role as a possibility for many women. The 1851 census for England and Wales (rpt. in Black 46–69) shows that women over twenty years of age outnumbered men by nearly

400,000 in a population of about 10 million. The same census report lists only about 2.7 million, or about 54 percent of England's female population, over twenty years of age as wives and mothers (Black 46). Even taking into account that a portion of these women may eventually have married, this leaves a large number of women in the single state, a difficult and sometimes desperate position since there were few opportunities for female employment. The fate of the unmarried woman, also referred to as "superabundant," "redundant," or even "excess," became a subject of great interest in newspapers and magazines of the period.[1] Some writers, such as Dinah Mulock Craik, posited a kind of power intrinsic to female solitude; however, her description of this life reveals that its main feature is stoicism, not joy:

> A finished life . . . though most likely it will be strangers only who come about the dying bed, close the eyes that no husband ever kissed, and draw the shroud kindly over the poor withered breast where no child's head has ever lain; still such a life is not to be pitied, for it is a completed life. (308; qtd. in Auerbach 20)

Despite this less-than-rousing affirmation of the woman alone, solitary spinsterhood was the least objectionable alternative to marriage, according to public opinion. Though sometimes characterized as mutually beneficial, female friendships were generally suspect because women themselves were suspect. In her (in)famous *Girl of the Period* essays published in the *Saturday Review* beginning in 1868, Eliza Lynn Linton characterized friendships between women as filled with jealousy, rivalry, and contempt for one another's intellects (I, 184). At their best, sustaining friendships between women were cast as "rehearsals" for the "real" relationship: marriage. The "heterosexual" nature of such friendships was frequently noted:

> In these undying, clinging attachments, it may sometimes be noted that one of the women is masculine in her very womanhood, dominating in intellect or will, or possessed of some subtle force of which we know nothing, and the other is 'a woman indeed'—defenceless, tender, instinctively craving after that

'shadow of a substance' for which she was made to long. (Ireland v; qtd. in Nestor 16)

The best that could be said for this particular kind of relationship was that it provided the partner who was the "woman indeed" with some practice for the life of "substance"—that is, marriage—if she was ever lucky enough to achieve it. But for the most part, female friendships were a consolation prize for "losers in the demographic lottery" (Nestor 15).

The only thing more frequently suspect than a pair of women was a community of women; writers such as Craik and Frances Cobbe held that putting groups of women together would only exacerbate all their weak qualities. While this attitude might in part be attributed to a mistrust of nunneries and therefore a part of the general anti-Catholic bias in England, the abundance of unwed women had led to the establishment of Anglican as well as Catholic sisterhoods, so it cannot wholly be a result of sectarian prejudice. Craik warns that "there would necessarily ensue . . . frivolity, idleness, and sick disordered fantasies" (*About Money* 160) in communities of women. To carry this one step further, the ultimate evil seems to have been communities of women *governed* by a woman. As Frances Cobbe noted,

> The possession of unnatural authority [by Mother Superiors] has continually proved too strong a temptation; and the woman who in her natural domestic sphere might have been the gentlest of guides, has become . . . the cruellest of petty despots. (786)

While such publications as the *English Woman's Journal*, established in 1858, and *Victoria Magazine*, in 1863, and literary works such as Elizabeth Gaskell's *Cranford* (1851–53) protested vehemently against such damning portrayals of unmarried women, Mrs. Linton's famous characterization of those who would celebrate women banding together as a "shrieking sisterhood" seems to have held sway with public opinion.

Pauline Nestor (5) cites Gaskell's *Life of Charlotte Brontë* as one of the works that stood in adamant opposition to Mrs. Linton's concept of the "shrieking sisterhood." Some of this may be due to Gaskell's shaping of Brontë's life according to her own positive ideas regarding female community, but the facts of Charlotte Brontë's life were certainly there to be shaped in such a manner. She celebrated her relationships with other women, including those with her sisters Anne and Emily, and with two school friends, Ellen Nussey and Mary Taylor, with whom she corresponded all her life. In opposition to contemporary attitudes that female friendships formed among schoolgirls were transitory, she once wrote to Ellen, "I think, dearest Ellen, our friendship is destined to form an exception to the general rule regarding school friendships" (5 September 1832; Wise and Symington I: 104–5). She was also able to celebrate the unmarried life; in a letter to her former schoolmistress about the schoolmistress's single life, she wrote:

> I always feel a peculiar satisfaction when I hear of your enjoying yourself. . . . [I]t seems that even 'a lone woman' can be happy, as well as cherished wives and proud mothers. I am glad of that. I speculate much on the existence of unmarried and never-to-be-married women nowadays, and I have already got to the point of considering that there is no more respectable character on this earth than an unmarried woman. (30 January 1846; Gaskell 201)

While this letter begins with Brontë's joy at her former teacher's ability to travel and enjoy herself in the company of a woman friend, her use of the word "respectable," not happy, in describing the unmarried state suggests a certain ambivalence on her part about such a life. Certainly her attitudes respecting marriage betray ambivalence where she herself was concerned. She once wrote to Ellen Nussey that her unhappiness in her position was "not that I am a *single* woman and likely to remain a *single* woman but because I am a *lonely* woman and likely to be *lonely*" (qtd. in Peters 384). Another time she had written to Ellen, refuting gossip that she was returning to Belgium to a lover:

> Not that it is a crime to marry, or a crime to wish to be married; but it is an imbecility, which I reject with contempt, for women, who have neither fortune nor beauty, to make marriage the principal object of their wishes and hopes, and the aim of all their

actions; not to be able to convince themselves that they are un-attractive, and that they had better be quiet, and think of other things than wedlock. (April 1843; rpt. in Gaskell 173)

Whether Brontë's personal respect for the single life ulti-mately represents confidence in female self-reliance or stoic acquiescence to fate, the female characters she creates never find permanent joy either in female friendships or in com-munities of women. Of course, she found little in her own life to affirm that such joy, even if encountered, would be per-manent. Her experiences at the Cowan Ridge school, and later at the Pensionnat Heger in Belgium, were filled with misery; her friendships with Mary and Ellen, though lifelong, were honored more by the post than by their physical presence; within her family, she lost her mother when she was five years old and also all of her sisters, the women with whom her female bonds were strongest. In her fiction, we see some cel-ebrations of female relationships, but the relationships are severed by death or marriage. Other times, women come to-gether without achieving real community. This finally leaves her with the image of woman alone, a prospect that, as both Dinah Craik and Mrs. Linton averred, was a position of power if not happiness. But alone in her isolation at Haworth, the power of the lone female must have had little resonance for Charlotte Brontë. Instead, what she explores in *Villette* is the psychological damage visited upon a woman of intelligence and imagination by a life devoid of human contact.

Brontë's most positive characterization of the male/female relationship is in *Jane Eyre*; she presents some of her most positive relationships between women here as well. Jane has several sustaining relationships with women, despite her in-auspicious beginnings with her Aunt Reed and cousins. The servant woman Bessie functions as a surrogate mother, Miss Temple at Lowood school as a mentor, and Helen Burns as a sister. At Moor-House, with the mythically named Mary and Diana Rivers as her associates, Jane's female relationships become more intensely spiritual. All these encounters are crucial to Jane's successful development; however, they all drop to sec-ondary significance as her union with Rochester approaches.

Except for Helen, who dies, all these friendships are indeed mere "rehearsals" for marriage, both Jane's and those of the other women involved. Although Jane owes Miss Temple "the best part of my acquirements; her friendship and society had been my continual solace; she had stood me in the stead of mother, governess, and latterly, companion" (JE 84), Miss Temple drops out of Jane's life entirely when she (Miss Temple) marries. Bessie is never mentioned after Aunt Reed's death. Though Jane once found "a reviving pleasure . . . of a kind now tasted by me for the first time—the pleasure arising from perfect congeniality of tastes, sentiments, and principles" (JE 354) in her relationship with Diana and Mary Rivers, they are relegated to the status of once-a-year visitors after all the women marry.

Some of Brontë's female friendships also exhibit the surrogate heterosexuality noted in the popular press, more subtly in *Jane Eyre* but emphatically in *Shirley*. Jane calls Diana Rivers the "superior" and "leader" of the trio at Moor-House; she is "handsome" and "vigorous"; Jane likes "to sit on a stool at Diana's feet, to rest my head on her knee, and listen" (JE 355). Both she and Mary defer to Diana's greater vigor, both physical and intellectual. In *Shirley*, the title character herself comments upon the masculinity of her name; she is truly the "male" half of the Shirley–Caroline friendship which dominates much of the novel. Shirley is independent and strong, a landowner and heiress; Caroline is weak and dependent. Although Caroline vows that "I am supported and soothed when you—that is, *you only*—are near, Shirley" (264), Shirley herself senses that Caroline's affections are beginning to lie elsewhere, and pleads with her friend not to let Robert Moore, whom she deems "The Troubler," come between them—that is, not to let their friendship be merely a "rehearsal" for marriage.

Which, of course, it eventually is. Both women complete the marriage plot; because they marry brothers, they ostensibly can remain friends. However, Brontë gives us no assurances that this will happen, for their double marriage takes place only a few paragraphs before the end of the book. In any case, Caroline seems to have "replaced" Shirley with Robert as of the moment of their engagement, even siding against her as Shirley reluctantly acquiesces to setting a wedding date—a date Caroline herself eagerly anticipates.[2]

If one-on-one female relationships in Brontë's work are susceptible to the breaches of death and marriage, communities of women are even more problematic. While the Lowood school brings Jane Eyre her first taste of positive female contact, even its female atmosphere is not unequivocally positive. Miss Temple dominates Lowood in Mr. Brocklehurst's absence, but the vicious Miss Scratcherd abides there, too. About the teacher with whom she shares a room for the two years she herself works at Lowood, Jane can only say, "How I wished sleep would silence her!" (86) because she wants space for her own thoughts. The only girl Jane seems to have any relationship with in eight years at the school is Helen, who dies early in Jane's experience there. Lowood accomplishes Brontë's purposes in Jane's development—education and her first tastes of love and friendship—but leaves her with no permanent female bonds.

The groups of women together depicted in the girls' schools in The Professor and Villette,[3] on the other hand, reflect the most negative of popular English opinions on such groups. The young ladies are lazy in their studies and generally seem to bring out the worst in themselves as they spy on one another at the behest of the directress. Both Mdlle Reuter and Madame Beck represent the worst of all possible scenarios: the woman in charge of a group of women. In their manipulations and machinations, they embody Frances Cobbe's "petty despots," not only in relationship to the protagonists whose love relationships they try to sabotage, but also respecting the young women whose minds they are supposedly forming. In fact, controlling the girls' bodies turns out to be even more important than enriching their minds. As noted previously, much of this attitude can be attributed to Brontë's anti-Catholic sentiment; both schools are foreign, not English, and Catholic. It is as though Brontë is using the characteristics of the anti-female sentiment in the popular press to emphasize the anti-Catholic notions here, making Madame Beck the embodiment of the worst traits of Catholics and females at once.

Brontë depicts the individual friendships Lucy develops with Ginevra and Paulina in *Villette* more positively than the power relationship that obtains between Madame Beck and the students and teachers of her school on the whole, but even these relationships betray stereotypical attitudes toward female friendships. Lucy functions as the "male" part of both relationships, the tough, wise advisor to both ultra-feminine women—Ginevra even calls her "Diogenes"—as opposed to a supportive peer. Further, the relationships serve as "rehearsals for marriage" for Paulina and Ginevra. Lucy's awareness of what happens to both women after their marriages indicates that they continue to communicate with her, but neither figures in Lucy's story again after she reports their marriages.

Brontë tentatively proposes the validity of the single life in *Shirley*, in which many episodes revolve around two unmarried women, Miss Mann and Miss Ainley, and the widowed Mrs. Pryor's relationship with Caroline, the young woman she reveals to be her daughter. Some critics feel that these characters and their relationships were part of Brontë's original preparation for a plot structure in which Caroline Helstone coped successfully with single life, a plan she altered when her sister Anne (in many respects, the model for Caroline) died when the novel was half-completed (J. M. S. Tompkins 25–28). Yet, despite the continuing attention given to unmarried women, and the early assertion (by Robert Moore, who should know) that "Men, in general, are a sort of scum" (85), the best that unattached women like Miss Ainley are eventually allowed to hope for is a nunlike existence, "without a bright hope or near friend in the world," an existence that fixes its hopes on "the bliss of the world to come," and which Caroline compares to "the Hindoo votary stretched on his couch of iron spikes" in the way that it "violate[s] nature" (390). Although Mrs. Pryor values the single life and encourages Caroline to share it with her, Robert Moore eventually rescues Caroline from this fate through marriage; Mrs. Pryor is relegated to the status of an honored boarder in Caroline and Robert's home, an outcome that assures her financial and emotional security, though it also displaces her dream of a female community with her daughter.

In *Shirley*, regardless of its problematical ending, both heroines are allowed to complete the marriage plot because one is rich and one is beautiful. In Brontë's last novel, *Villette*, despairing of traditional marriage at least for poor, plain women like Lucy Snowe[4] (and possibly for herself, then a single woman in her mid-thirties responsible for the care of her increasingly infirm father), she finds no permanently sustaining relationships between women, and turns instead to exploring the psyche of the woman alone.

Villette's Lucy Snowe is neither rescued from the single life nor blessed with communal happiness within it. Lucy is not destined to find community with the pupils of the school she has founded. Although her school prospers and eventually becomes a boarding school after its humble beginnings as a day school, the school represents financial, not emotional, security. As Nina Auerbach points out, Lucy's original move into the classroom is pointedly characterized as abandonment of the nursery, where she has been governess to Madame Beck's children. The novel itself is "a study in the power of the female world that has left the family behind" (Auerbach 97), a statement even more true at the end than when Lucy first enters the classroom. Nestor correctly characterizes its ending as "fundamentally antipathetic to mutuality and communality alike" (140). Auerbach somewhat more positively reads the ending as "a triumph of decent and orderly deviousness" in which Lucy, "Having learned to rule . . . receives her little nation" (112) and joins the ranks of the most powerful people in the novel: Madame Beck, Madame Walravens, and Père Silas. However, this interpretation seems overly optimistic and somewhat cynical in light of what Lucy acknowledges as the source of her happiness during this time: M. Paul's love.

The penultimate chapter of the novel promises Lucy interdependence and the love and work for which she has longed; this combination brings her the most joy she ever experiences as she works and carries on a long-distance relationship with M. Paul for the next three years. In Lucy's words,

> The secret of my success did not lie so much in myself . . . as in a new state of circumstances, a wonderfully changed life, a relieved heart. The spring which moved my energies lay far away beyond

seas, in an Indian isle. . . . [H]is letters were real food that nourished, living water that refreshed. (594)

This situation, in which Lucy has both love *and* fulfilling work, is the closest Brontë ever comes to achieving in fiction what seems to be her ideal situation. Yet her personal and cultural circumstances were also telling her imagination that it was an impossible dream. So Brontë lets her heroine live her dream for three years, but when it is time for Lucy and Paul's ship to come in, it sinks in a storm off the coast of England.

What will she do *without* her "real food" and "living water"? True, Lucy has power, like the three characters she mentions as the novel closes, but she had early characterized these three as "a basilisk with three heads" (559), almost an unholy trinity in their mutual Catholicism. Therefore, the cry of the Banshee immediately preceding Lucy's final nod to the novel's three most powerful worldly forces calls for a reading of the ending which is mixed at best. Lucy's "Farewell" at the end of *Villette*, despite her financial success, has overtones of Craik's "completed life," and of Brontë's own assertions that women with "neither fortune nor beauty" should "be quiet, and think of other things than wedlock." This is not to suggest that Brontë even remotely approves of the conditions that dictate such a fate for a woman of Lucy's intellectual and imaginative potential; rather, in depicting Lucy Snowe's increasing psychological instability through this novel, a situation due to her continued isolation from human love, Brontë rages against a situation she sees no prospect of changing. As with her proposals regarding spirituality, her writing regarding relationships initially proposes great possibilities, but what limited hope she ever has of turning the possibilities into realities collapses by the end of *Villette*; like Lucy herself, her creator leaves hope to those with "sunny imaginations" (V 596).

One such "sunny imagination," that of Louisa May Alcott, was just beginning to show forth its light on the printed page as Charlotte Brontë's death ended her brief but brilliant literary career. Although Lucy's comment is her disparaging reference to naive, unrealistic souls who do not understand life's hard realities—as du Plessis writes, "the unprecedented utopian hope of marriage and vocation for the female hero is castigated as reader banality" (12)—Alcott's hope stems not from naiveté but from a very American brand of optimism that, as Faulkner was to say a century later, expected humankind not only to endure but to prevail. As Brontë's personal and cultural circumstances provided fertile ground for the growth of her pessimism, optimism was nurtured in Alcott through her personal ties to American transcendentalism; she was the daughter of Amos Bronson Alcott and the devoted student of both Emerson and Thoreau. However, the dire economic circumstances of her early life and her mother's influence also developed in her a devotion to practicality. Her own responses to the ideal of the Victorian "angel of the house" begin from a premise of female self-reliance and expand outward from it to propose communities based upon but reaching beyond the powerful Victorian family unit.

Alcott needed Emersonian self-reliance as a starting point, for the permanently single life was less likely for American than for British women and therefore more an aberration from the norm. The extent to which women outnumbered men in Charlotte Brontë's England meant that even if every eligible male married one of the eligible females (discounting class differences entirely), around 10 percent of the women would have remained unmarried; census data show 46 percent of the women, in fact, unmarried in 1851 (Census Table rpt. in Black 46). American women at this same time married at a rate of 93 percent (Census Table rpt. in Daniel Smith 121). In fact, one of the remedies to the crisis of "excess women" suggested by the British popular press was to encourage women to emigrate to "the colonies," where there was actually a shortage of eligible females.[5] Far from resigning themselves to the distinct possibility of permanent singlehood, Sarah Elbert writes, "Marriage was still the most important event of a woman's life in America" (113). While the Civil War was to change these circumstances considerably by creating newly single widows and reducing the number of marriageable men (for women born between 1860 and 1880, the proportion of single women increased to a high of 11 percent), it was still much less common for a woman to remain single in Alcott's America than in Brontë's England.

The single life, then, represents to Alcott much more of an

overt choice than the doomed fate it represents to Brontë. Unmarried herself, Alcott consistently created characters for whom this life was a joyful and conscious choice, even in those works in which Brontë's presence is markedly felt.[6] *Work*'s Christie Devon even uses Brontë's own marks of marital ineligibility—"I have no beauty, no accomplishments, no fortune" (82)—while she is *turning down* a marriage proposal and choosing to remain single. Although Christie does eventually marry in the novel, she is soon widowed and the novel closes with her at age forty, seemingly enjoying her life as a single mother and feeling no impetus to change it. Some of *Work*'s other single women include the widowed Mrs. Sterling, David's sister Rachel/Letty, who, as a "fallen woman," would have been forever ineligible for marriage by Victorian standards, the former slave Hepsey, and the beautiful Bella Carrol, who remains unmarried rather than taking the chance of passing down the family madness to another generation. While these women all have reasons for their single state, none of them shows any signs of regretting it.

In some of her other Brontë-influenced works, Alcott depicts the single life even more clearly as a conscious choice. Faith Dane, Sylvia's unmarried cousin who is the wisest person in *Moods*, is described as "past thirty, shapely and tall . . . singularly attractive . . . possessed of a well-balanced mind, a self-reliant soul, and that fine gift which is so rare, the power of acting as a touchstone for all who approached" (144). When Sylvia asks her why she has never married, Faith says simply, "I never met the man who could satisfy me" (271). Although the three March sisters who survive to adulthood in *Little Women* all eventually marry, Marmee advises them early on that it would be "better [to] be happy old maids than unhappy wives" (98), and the first volume of the book closes with Jo still determined to remain unmarried. Alcott's comments about her "perverse" publishers who insisted she marry off all her characters in the second volume indicates that she would have preferred to leave at least this one March sister to her single life (*Letters* 121–22; 22 January 1869). In the last book of the March trilogy, *Jo's Boys*, Alcott creates a new Jo in Nan, who dedicates herself to medicine and spinsterhood in the first chapter and maintains it to the last, despite young Tom's attempts to persuade her otherwise. Although Meg's son John alludes to the demographic fact of the 1880s that the population of New England has an excess of women[7] — "which accounts for the high state of culture we are in, perhaps" (22) — Alcott's women who remain single usually do so by choice and happily, not by default and stoically. Mrs. Jo even wonders, "I sometimes feel as if I'd missed my vocation and ought to have remained single" (JB 23).

Alcott's own busy spinsterhood probably provided some of the background for this positive perspective, but another reason Alcott's single women seem to remain happy is that for them, unlike for Brontë and her heroine Lucy Snowe, the single life in America does not have to mean desperate loneliness; it is a life shared with friends. Although two of Alcott's important mentors, Emerson and Thoreau, both wrote essays on the subject of friendship, Thoreau's influence seems closer to Alcott's concept of the term. Emerson's idea of friendship, like many of his ideas, is to use the human relationship to transcend the human and approach the spiritual. As Christopher Newfield comments, Emerson's "Friendship" essay specifically concerns itself with male friendship; further, even among men, Emerson never "imagines male friendship leading to the equality of a band of brothers" (187), but always depicts a teacher/pupil (or, as Newfield puts it, "master/slave" [187]) relationship in which the more spiritual member of the relationship lifts the lesser one to a higher plane. This Platonic approach to relationships is consistent with the goal of the male/female relationship as he presents it in "Love."

Thoreau, as he so often does, honors the Emersonian ideal but links it much more clearly to the real world. In his own essay entitled "Friendship," Thoreau describes friendship as a linking of spirits, and even suggests it results in the "apotheosis" (181) of the friend; however, he also reaches out to embrace a more worldly, encompassing view of the possibilities of friendship:

> [W]e cannot have too many friends; the virtue which we appreciate [in a friend] we to some extent appropriate, so that thus we are made at last more fit for every relation of life. A base Friendship is a narrowing and exclusive tendency, but a noble one is not exclusive; its very superfluity and dispersed love is

the humanity which sweetens society, and sympathizes with foreign nations, for though its foundations are private, it is in effect, a public affair and a public advantage. (188)

In addition to the philosophical ideas Louisa Alcott may have absorbed from these two transcendental influences, she had ample support for female friendships in the world immediately around her. American culture provided much more support than did English culture for the premise that women's coming together could be a joyous and mutually beneficial enterprise. Carroll Smith-Rosenberg argues that sexual segregation due to the concept of home as woman's separate sphere created emotional distance between women and men but also encouraged the development of what she calls intense "homosocial" bonds between women, who did not exist as "isolated dyads, but were normally part of highly integrated networks" (60–61) of women. Unlike the systematic undercutting which the British press (fairly or not) accused English women of perpetrating against one another, Smith-Rosenberg says that "hostility and criticism of other women was discouraged" (64) in these networks.

Young American girls were initiated early into the idea of female communities, for almost all children in New England attended school for a year or more (Cott [101] reports virtually universal literacy in New England by 1840; in contrast, 45–49 percent of the women of England were illiterate at this time [Stock]), "while middle-class girls routinely spent at least a year in boarding school" (Smith-Rosenberg 66). Both Smith-Rosenberg and Cott note that, again unlike the situation in England, the friendships formed in these early years continued across lifetimes, even after marriage (Smith-Rosenberg 62–63; Cott chapter 5, esp. 176–78). These same bonds would often form among young women working in newly burgeoning factories and mills, again continuing long beyond the time when they would leave the working world (Cott 55–57).

Alcott features successful all-female networks in the town, the working world, and the boarding school in her novels *Work* and *Jo's Boys*, both of which make direct references to Charlotte Brontë and her works. In *Work*, the friendship Christie develops with Rachel in the lace factory where both are briefly employed endures for the rest of their lives; Christie stands up for Rachel when the supervisor fires her after learning of her past, and it is Rachel who saves Christie when she is on the verge of suicide. The scene with which *Work* closes is one of Alcott's most famous tributes to female community. Pledging to "know and help, love and educate one another" in a "loving league of sisters" (442), Christie, her daughter, her mother-in-law, Rachel, the washerwoman Cynthy Wilkins, the former slave Hepsey Johnson, and the wealthy heiress Bella Carrol join hands around Christie's table and pledge themselves to a continuing solidarity that transcends boundaries of age, class, and race. This is, indeed, as Thoreau said, the "humanity which sweetens society." Thus, in a novel in which Alcott early on argues directly against Jane Eyre for marrying "that man," her closing scene also argues against the exclusionary nature of the British class system and against the practice of abandoning one's friends after moving on to further adventures, two ideas that Brontë's art generally upholds.

Ironically, it is in the scene from *Jo's Boys* where Alcott directly expresses her admiration for Charlotte Brontë that she most directly opposes Brontë's vision of the female educational community in *Villette*. In the chapter entitled "Among the Maids," Jo and Meg bring together the young female scholars for an evening of sewing and conversation, in form much like the *lecture pieuse* which M. Paul occasionally invades to bring a bit of the literature of the day, along with his commentary on it, to the young women of the pensionnat. Though Meg institutes the evenings at Plumfield ostensibly because she is afraid the young ladies are neglecting their domestic educations in favor of their Latin (a charge frequently made in the early days of women's education, when utilitarian principles still held sway), Jo turns them into a forum for discussing issues of the day. On the evening in question, there ensues a lively conversation on the subject of "old maids," in which Jo observes that many of the current population of unmarried women are actually widows; one of her charges adds, "Old maids are n't sneered at half as much as they used to be, since some of them have grown famous and proved that woman is n't a half but a whole human being, and can stand alone" (285). It is when the succeeding discussion turns to literature that Jo makes her comment that Charlotte Brontë's books "thrill me" more than those of George Eliot because in Eliot "the heart is left out" (290). Clearly Alcott found much to admire in Brontë, even if her own cultural situation contradicted the air of dark despair, or, at best, resignation, with which Brontë regarded the life of the single woman.

Alcott's fiction is not anti-marriage, however; despite her own singlehood and her support for unmarried women, she creates happy marriages for characters, including two of the characters most like herself, Jo March and Christie Devon. Nevertheless, the approach to marriage in her fiction reveals that she had grave doubts about this particular human relationship unless, as Charles Strickland argues, it produced "a genuine partnership of privilege and responsibility" (113). Strickland's comment leads to two of the reasons that Alcott was wary of matrimony from the female point of view: it threatened women's equality and it threatened their independence. In fact, as the discussions throughout this study indicate, many of the places in her work where Alcott alludes to but resists Charlotte Brontë are places wherein Alcott senses that "unmated pairs" are being joined together, a situation she considers responsible for "half the misery in the world" (*Letters* 108; 18 February 1865). This is especially true in regard to the marriage between Jane and Rochester in *Jane Eyre*, against which Christie Devon argues passionately because she "cannot think it a fair bargain" (*W* 81). In replacing the Jane–Rochester relationship with that of Christie and David in *Work*, Alcott substitutes well-matched people whom she considers to be true equals for the power relationship that she senses in Brontë.

Several critics have noted (see Strickland, Elbert) that Alcott's wariness regarding marriage has more to do with a woman's loss of independence than with any other issue. Emerson had commented in "Self-Reliance" that "Society is a joint-stock company, in which the members agree, for the better securing of the bread to each shareholder, to surrender the liberty and culture of the eater" (32). Although Emerson's complaint chiefly concerns the liberty of ideas lost when an individual conforms to society, the economic metaphor is especially appropriate to Alcott, whose most memorable heroines marry for love and demand intellectual and spiritual mutuality from their mates, but always realize the importance of financial independence as well. Strickland writes that, to Alcott, "Marriage meant subservience . . . without the compensation of financial security" (49). Elbert contends that Alcott believed "Wage earning for women . . . made escape possible from the tyranny of patriarchal families" and that "women needed wages to command respect from others in the nineteenth century" (74). Alcott herself wrote in her journal (on Valentine's Day, no less!), having just received a one-hundred-dollar retainer to write an advice column, that "liberty is a better husband than love to many of us" (*Journals* 165; 14 February 1868).[8] Christie Devon's first words in *Work* are "Aunt Betsey, there's going to be a new declaration of independence" (1), by which she means she is going to support herself. Alcott's concern that marriage would mean the end of whatever financial independence a woman might have were well-founded, for even by 1890 only 2.5 percent of the married women in America worked outside their homes (Smith 122). Women in the public sphere, married or single, were highly suspect in Victorian society, British and American. A famous American indication of the intensity of this attitude was the situation that came about at the first Women's Rights Convention at Seneca Falls in 1848. This meeting of some of the most radical feminists in America was chaired by Lucretia Mott's husband, James, because no woman dared risk the impropriety of speaking publicly before a mixed audience.

What the women's rights movement quickly came to recognize, however, was that social equality for women was dependent upon economic equality. In the marriages Alcott creates that most refer to those in Brontë's works, Alcott underscores, in a recognizably American way, the importance of economic self-reliance. Given the English class structure, the only way Brontë can assure Jane Eyre's continued economic independence after her marriage is through the inherited income her uncle's will provides; that she does so is a sign that she and Alcott both recognized the importance of continued independence as well as the link between personal and economic equality. With her first novel heroine, Edith Adelon of *The Inheritance*, Alcott echoed Brontë's concerns regarding social and economic dependency in British terms: Edith's precarious social position has come about because her father (Lord Hamilton) had married beneath himself in rank, and so kept the marriage a secret. Further, Edith herself declares the folly of persons of different social and economic classes marrying, deterring Lord Percy from proposing until after she has been revealed to be a noblewoman (and heiress) after all.

Alcott's more mature, and more fully American, heroines, however, do have other options, and for women like *Work*'s Christie Devon, retired domesticity like Jane Eyre's is not enough to ensure happiness even if one is financially stable.[9] Strickland writes that

> *Work* is an eloquent plea for women like Christie (and Alcott) who wish, no less than men, to hold on to their integrity and independence, and who deserve men who will both love and respect them as human beings. It is, then, a feminist work, but it is not a tract against marriage and family life. (113)

In *Work*, Christie and David marry dressed in their respective uniforms, he in his soldier's dress and she in her nurse's attire. Far from retiring from public life into the domestic "sphere" after their marriage, Christie leaves for the Civil War a week after her husband does and works as a nurse until David is killed. At the end of the novel, Christie begins a very public career as a liaison between working women and the "ladies" who are trying to improve their conditions without understanding much about them.

In the *Little Women* series, Alcott creates her version of a "genuine partnership" in the marriage between Jo and Friedrich Bhaer by keeping her heroine financially independent. In an allusion to societal expectations, as she accepts Friedrich's proposal Jo says, "No one can say I'm out of my sphere now," but then adds, "I'm to carry my share, Friedrich, and help to earn the home. Make up your mind to that, or I'll never go" (*LW* 480). Although her future husband's reply is a noncommittal "We shall see," this is in fact what happens. Jo becomes the headmistress of Plumfield, which she founds with her inheritance from Aunt March, and in *Jo's Boys* returns to her writing and becomes a famous author. The partnership she creates includes both love and work so that the heroine can maintain her selfhood after the marriage. What Brontë had asserted as an only temporarily attainable ideal in Lucy's situation while M. Paul was away, Alcott's optimism enables her to propose as a permanent narrative outcome—with the not inconsequential bonus of having her partner actually with her to enjoy it!

Alcott's work most assuredly supports the life of single women in community with other women; it supports married life as well through her creation of marriages-as-partnerships (even Faith Dane, the consummate spinster of *Moods*, calls marriage "the great event of a woman's life" [179]). However, some of Alcott's most interesting relationships are those in which she blends notions of traditional Victorian family life with the theory (if not necessarily the practice) of transcendental communities such as the one she herself experienced at Fruitlands, in an attempt to mitigate the solitude required by self-reliance with the benefits of community, and to mitigate the impractical idealism of transcendentalism with the practicality of the traditional family. In *Work*, *Little Women*, *Jo's Boys*, *Jack and Jill*, and in the sensation tales *A Long Fatal Love Chase* and "A Nurse's Story," Alcott proposes communities whose core is always some vision of family, but at the same time, reaches outward toward sometimes ingenious permutations of the traditional family.[10]

In her study of mid-nineteenth-century American novels by and about women, Nina Baym notes that women *writers* of that period conceived of the idea of woman's role in society in terms very different from the enforced domesticity and separatism the idea of "women's sphere" connotes. The Victorians were quick to acknowledge that women could be a good influence on men (Welter 25–26) and that "women are less prone than men to the more blatant vices [and therefore] men and women can provide a healthy corrective for each other" (Strickland 110); they even used this idea as an argument for co-education (Butcher 33). However, women writers took these ideas a step further. While recognizing that home and work were different, Baym contends, women writers recognized that men's values penetrated into and controlled the life of the home, and they began to propose in their work a new system whereby

> the direction of influence could be reversed so that home values dominated the world. . . . When accepting, as one's basic relation to another, obligation rather than exploitation, doing another good rather than doing him in; when books and conversation and simple comfort seem superior to ostentation and feverish pleasure—then . . . a true social revolution will have taken place, American life will have transformed. . . . Some of the writers liked to use Pascal's circle, whose center was everywhere and circumference nowhere, as the image of woman's "sphere." (48–49)

One can certainly imagine Charlotte Brontë embracing the relation between men and women expressed here in terms of an immediate, private family like her own. Good families in Brontë's work do, indeed, revolve around mutuality and take care of one another. For example, *Jane Eyre*'s Mrs. Fairfax lives at Thornfield because she is a distant relative to Rochester; Jane values her newfound cousins Diana, Mary, and St. John Rivers and shares her inheritance with them because they are family; Caroline Helstone takes her mother into her home in *Shirley*.

Alcott, on the other hand, frequently proposes more expansive visions of community in the very works in which the influence of Brontë is present. The core of women Alcott envisions at the end of *Work* is the only one in this discussion that remains all female. Nevertheless, it has its basis in family, for its center is Christie, her daughter, her mother-in-law, and her sister-in-law. In *Jack and Jill*, Mrs. Minot and her sons form the family core, which expands to include Janey (because she is Jack's friend and he was involved in the accident that disabled her) and eventually most of the town's young people, who are all Jack and Janey's (Jill's) friends. In *Little Women*, what begins as a matriarchy presided over by Marmee expands to include Mr. Laurence and Laurie (who, rescued from his wanton ways by Amy, marries her), Meg's husband and children,

Jo's family, and Mr. March when he returns from the war. Although the community embraces men, women's values take precedence; the family gathers around Mrs. March at the end of the novel.

Even in Alcott's sensation fiction that alludes to Brontë, she sets up mutually supportive communities based on family that include men and women. In *A Long Fatal Love Chase*, which frequently parallels and even quotes *Jane Eyre*, the heroine flees from her demonic husband and takes refuge with a group of people that includes her husband's first wife and son, along with the priest who has helped her to escape. In "A Nurse's Story," Kate Snow moves from her original position as companion to Elinor Carruth to her place as a de facto "daughter of the house" (108) after both Elinor and her sister Amy die. Mrs. Carruth exacts a promise from Kate on her deathbed "to be a sister to my sons" (108), after which Kate and the sons live together "always cheerful, always busy . . . and no brothers could be more devoted than they, no sister prouder than I of the two earnest, useful, noble men, whose lives are passing side by side with mine" (109). When, toward the end of the story, the three come upon their lost half-brother, Robert Steele, he, too, comes to live with them until his death.

Alcott's communities seem designed to strike a balance between the traditional Victorian family, which though supportive could also be confining and isolating, with the ideals of nineteenth-century Utopian communities, which reached beyond family ties to bind people together, but often lacked the structural support to keep them together for long periods of time. The Fruitlands community in which Alcott herself was involved, for example, lasted only about six months. Critics who discuss Louisa May Alcott's experiences at Fruitlands have sometimes used her satirical piece "Transcendental Wild Oats" to demonstrate Louisa's unalterable opposition to transcendentalist communities (see Showalter, "Introduction," and Auerbach); however, since Louisa Alcott repeatedly turns to positive visions of unorthodox communities in her fiction, one must grant that the concept had at least some attractions for her. Alcott's communities wrestle with two basic problems important in the demise of Fruitlands: their impracticality and their notion of the "consociate family" (the phrase Alcott and Lane used for their enterprise in their letter to the *Herald of Freedom*), a group of people living together and held together by like-mindedness rather than biological ties.

Inattention to the practical matters of life was the way of life at Fruitlands. Among other things, the community came together in June, too late for planting, sowed a variety of seeds in the same field, and eschewed the use of fertilizer—despite their stated goal to support themselves through farming. Even more reprehensible, in Louisa Alcott's eyes, was their peculiar idea of the division of labor: the men engaged themselves in "being," while the women and children did most of the "doing." Mrs. Alcott was heard to answer a question about whether they employed beasts of burden at Fruitlands by replying, "Yes, one woman" (Shepard 307).[11] One consistency in all of Alcott's fictional communities is that all the people involved contribute in practical ways to the whole. In *Work*, for example, Christie plans to pursue a public career in order to bring the working and moneyed classes of women together, Bella is to hold "Conversations" (very likely modeled upon Margaret Fuller's "Conversations") for the improvement of upper-class women, and several of the others will work among the needy in their community—each "ready to do her part to hasten the coming of the happy end" (442), the advancement of all women. One can see this principle of universal but divided labor even in "A Nurse's Story," when "Harry [a doctor] tried to save the shattered body, Augustine [a priest] to uplift the sad soul, and I [Kate Snow, the narrator] to warm and cheer the desolate heart" (114) of Robert Steele after the trio brings him from an asylum to live with them. For Alcott, the exclusive pursuit of the cerebral life of the philosopher does not contribute to a workable community; even her more spiritual characters, like Augustine, have tangible work to do.

An even more delicate, and difficult, problem at Fruitlands was the question of family units. As Richard Francis's examination of Fruitlands shows, Charles Lane's and Bronson Alcott's differences over what they meant by a "Consociate Family" was the philosophical death-knell for Fruitlands as surely as impracticality was the physical one. Francis uses

Bronson Alcott's journal entries regarding family to argue that "he believes that one must concentrate one's efforts on the paradigm [of family] that lies to hand; if it can be perfected, society as a whole will be redeemed" (234). Crucial to this idea of family, for Alcott, was sexuality, for he strove for the union of body and spirit. Lane, on the other hand, while praising the family profusely in a two-part article he wrote for the *Dial* in 1843, characterized it as something eventually to be transcended. He took as his model the celibate Shakers, who dissolved individual family groups in favor of the larger community. Lane, according to Francis, envisioned family as "nothing more than a group of like-minded individuals" that would gradually attract more adherents "until eventually the 'family' is coextensive with society as a whole" (222). The question of whether Bronson Alcott would abandon his conjugal family in favor of a sexually segregated, celibate style of life apparently drove him to the brink of an emotional collapse. Louisa Alcott's stance on the issue seems clear, for in "Transcendental Wild Oats" she specifically says it is "my faithful wife, my little girls . . . mine by ties that none can break" (378) that bring Abel Lamb back to sanity. To her, family is the core of a successful community, and most of her successful fictional communities are so based.

Nevertheless, despite her bitter portrayal of Charles Lane as Timon Lion in "Transcendental Wild Oats," Alcott seems fundamentally to have realized with him that sexuality complicates the problems of community, and of relationships in general. In Alcott's early novel *Moods*, Faith Dane comments that "unhappy marriages are the tragedies of the world, and will be till men and women are taught to make principle not pleasure, love not passion" (271) the bases from which they choose their mates. In the communities in the previously mentioned sensation pieces (whose configurations certainly rival all the oddness that Fruitlands had to offer), the male figures of Father Ignatius and Robert Steele have relationships with the heroines that are among the most passion-charged in all of Alcott's work. In bringing these men and women together in community, she defuses the problem in the first case by making her virile man a priest with unshakable integrity, and in the second by turning a possible lover into a brother, then making him a physical and emotional cripple.[12] The other brothers in "A Nurse's Story" also live celibate lives due to the family's heritage of madness, and again Alcott describes their determination as "principle oppos[ing] passion" (109). Surely Alcott's own singlehood, the problematical nature of her own parents' relationships, and even the notions of her hero Emerson, whose essay called "Love" glorifies a particularly Platonic, spiritual ideal, made it difficult for Alcott, as for Brontë, to conceive of passionate relationships that were also practically workable. However, her overt insistence that love and passion are different, and the way she values the former, suggests that her characterizations are deliberate rather than by default. Perhaps Alcott sensed that passion led to the loss of emotional and artistic independence just as surely as social constraints led to the loss of financial independence for the nineteenth-century woman.

Alcott's diverse efforts to create the ideal community culminate in her last full-length novel, *Jo's Boys*, but reach back to *Moods* for their basis. Adam Warwick, the Thoreauvian hero of *Moods*, puts forth this view during a discussion on divorce: "I would begin at the beginning, and teach young people that marriage is not the only aim and end of life" (146). In *Jo's Boys*, Alcott does begin at the beginning, with a school community of boys and girls, then frames this entity within a larger community of adults and children. The resultant group values individualism and at the same time has family at its core.

The co-educational community of young people in the novel, made up of students at the Plumfield school and Laurence College, reflects Alcott's support of an American trend that began with the establishment of the nation's first co-ed college, Oberlin, in 1837. It gathered momentum after the Civil War as arguments that women were a good influence on men began to supersede the utilitarian argument that it was most efficient for men and women to be educated separately, since their roles in life were different. By 1890, about 43 percent of American colleges admitted women (Butcher 33). The transatlantic cultural differences in this area are striking; Queen's College in London, the first higher educational institution for women in England, was not established until 1852, and the first English university to open its degrees to women, London University, did not do so until 1878 (Crow 152–53, 296).

At Alcott's Plumfield, the founders "believed so heartily in the right of all sexes, colors, creeds, and ranks to education, that there was room for every one who knocked" (282) and the "young women . . . were among the best students in the college" (39). George and Dolly, two former Plumfield boys who have gone on to Harvard (notorious in publications such as the *Women's Journal* for its resistance to co-education), represent opposing, Old World notions of co-education in the novel. Early on, while attending a party at the Laurences' home, Dolly declares that he "Never saw girls eat such a lot. It proves that they ought not to study so much. Never liked co-ed" (104). Later in the novel, during another visit to Plumfield, Dolly reconsiders: "But if we've got to turn the grindstone, it would be mighty nice to have some of the little dears to lend a hand," and his friend replies, "I'd like three this minute, —one to fan me, one to kiss me, and one to give me some iced lemonade!" (272). Mrs. Jo overhears the conversation and tries to set her two former pupils straight:

> I was glad to hear you say you would like to have girls at your college; but I hope you will learn to speak more respectfully of them before they come; for that will be the first lesson they will teach you. . . . Frivolous girls may like to be called 'little dears' and things of that sort; but the girls who love study wish to be treated like reasonable beings, not dolls to flirt with. (273)

At the end of the novel, the young men return to Plumfield for Class Day; after watching many of the young women carry off honors, George surrenders: "You know, I'm quite converted to co-education and almost wish I'd remained here. It gives a grace to study, a sort of relish even, to see charming girls at it" (319).

Neither males' edification nor their salvation seems to be at the root of Alcott's support for co-education, however, as much as the way that learning to accept one another as human beings helps to defuse the "passion or principle" dilemma and to create self-reliant human beings—people who have real choices in life. Alcott echoes her father's ideas when she has Jo's nephew John assert that "grandpa is right in saying we must each be what God and nature make us. We can't change it much,—only help to develop the good and control the bad in us" (191). She reinforces this idea with the proliferation of careers she grants her characters, male and female: artists, doctors, teachers, an actress, a tailor, an alderman, a clergyman, and even a lay "missionary" to the Indians. Some characters, male *and* female, remain single, while others marry.

Regardless of the students' eventual life choices, however, they all remain part of the essential community of Plumfield and Laurence College because they are not considered just students, but family. The school founded by Jo and her husband is built around family. Jo and Friedrich and their sons, Meg and her children, Laurie and Amy and their Bess, and Mr. March all live on the grounds. Jo's boys—and girls—continue to be family, and Plumfield their home, long after they finish school. Although the timing of the novel is such that the second generation of students is at Plumfield as the first is either scattered or finishing at Laurence, even the scattered ones continue to return to Plumfield and to figure throughout the novel. All the men and women involved with the schools take a personal interest in the students, offering them advice on fashion and health, financial support, help with their homework, and motherly tending when they are ill. By basing the school on the concept of family, Alcott ensures a community that will endure even as its "children" grow.

Alcott's other principles of community are also in evidence in *Jo's Boys*. She defuses the problem of passion in her community by making Laurie Jo's brother through his marriage to her sister Amy. Laurie remains the one who, in some respects, knows Jo best—he attempts to lift her spirits by suggesting that they write and produce a play, for example—but the marital relationship Jo has with Friedrich emphasizes a concept of love that broadens beyond physical passion.[13] Toward the end of the novel, Jo heads off what she believes would be a disaster, Dan's interest in Amy's daughter Bess. She sees Dan's volatile nature as one capable of worshiping but not properly loving the artistic young woman, she sees the danger of Bess abandoning her artistic gifts, and she discourages the relationship.

Also crucial to Alcott's community are the contributions of each of the adults in ways that are real and practical, yet also recognize their individuality. Friedrich is the college president, Mr. March the chaplain and teacher of philosophy, Laurie a financial contributor, and the March women "divided the care of the young people among them, each taking the part that suited her best" (9). Even though each of the families has a home on the grounds and separate familial relationships, their common life's work is to reach out to the larger community of the scholars in their care, and eventually to reach out to the world, the even larger community that Jo's boys—and girls—will affect. As Nina Auerbach puts it, this community is one "[b]eyond sisterhood, [in which] Mother Bhaer presides over a Utopian community of cooperation among and between the sexes . . . whose influence spreads into the capitals and the wasteplaces of the world" (71). While one might argue against the feasibility of such an endeavor, Alcott's depiction of it demonstrates the things she most values in relationships: family-based communal work combined with self-reliance, the values of Fruitlands and Emerson.

Alcott's most encompassing response to the problem of solitude, then, neither denigrates marriage nor requires it as a condition of human happiness. In this respect, she and Charlotte Brontë agree with each other and disagree with many of their cultural contemporaries. On a deeper level, both Alcott and Brontë suspected that Victorian culture's admiration of woman as long as she stayed in her "sphere" did not create for woman a role that was separate but equal, but separate and powerless. Thus both, in fact, treated in their fiction the problem of forging relationships in which the price a woman paid was not the loss of self. Brontë begins with optimistic relationships in *The Professor* and in *Jane Eyre*, then abandons her hope of reconciling self-reliance and love and resigns herself to a mutually exclusive dichotomy; the characters in *Shirley* get love and *Villette*'s Lucy Snowe maintains her independence. But while Brontë's explorations of relationships collapse inward to Lucy's disturbed and disturbing resignation, Alcott works outward from a core of self-reliant individuals that recognizes the power of the family community.

Her most successful characters do, in fact, achieve both independence and union with others as well. However, this is partly because Alcott accepts a much broader notion of successful human relationships than those provided by the marital relationship; women together and communities that include women and men who are not spouses also function successfully in her work, many times in the same fiction in which she draws on Charlotte Brontë's own characters. The way Alcott "translates" this influence, then, reveals once again the tie of Brontë's British influence being loosened by Alcott's fundamentally American approach to the issues being considered. But despite their progressions in nearly opposite directions from a fundamental agreement on a woman's need for and right to both self-reliance and love, Alcott was to find her most solid connection to Charlotte Brontë in the one thing she supposed kept the "heart" she found in Brontë's art alive, whether in solitude or in community: work.

CHAPTER 5

The Professional Life
Self and Work

Perhaps no other theme connects the fiction of Louisa May Alcott and Charlotte Brontë so powerfully as their mutual insistence on the value and necessity of meaningful and fulfilling work for women. Alcott's and Brontë's concerns with this theme reflect their personal involvement with the issue as women whose families came to depend upon them for financial support as well as their conflict with societies that limited women's opportunities: the need for meaningful work is thus a psychological issue as well as a practical one. All of Brontë's heroines assert this need explicitly; even her most self-abnegating character, Caroline Helstone of *Shirley*, urges her country's fathers to "seek for [your daughters] an interest and an occupation which shall raise them above the flirt, the manoeuvrer, the mischief-making tale-bearer . . . give them scope and work" (*S* 393), while her most independent, *Villette*'s Lucy Snowe, insists that the years when her lover M. Paul is away are "the three happiest years of my life" because "I worked—I worked hard" (*V* 593). Louisa Alcott voices her enthusiastic assent from the other side of the Atlantic in the words of *Work*'s Christie Devon: "I have been and mean to be a working-woman all my life" (*W* 428). The heroines of both writers are happiest when working and miserable, almost to the point of insanity or suicide, when they have nothing to do. This chapter explores the way each writer deals with the issue of women's work in her own fiction, from the pressing need for work they both feel to the ways each deems it acceptable to meet those needs. While Brontë and her society define acceptable work in much more narrow terms than do Alcott and hers, some of Alcott's considerations, though grounded in American cultural standards, seem to be a response to her reading of Brontë. Finally, each writer eventually explores the ramifications of the work she has chosen for herself: that of the woman writer.

Both Brontë and Alcott had personal reasons to concern themselves with issues of women's work, for both were thrust into the position of supporting themselves and their families. Branwell Brontë's increasing dissipation and Anne and Emily's inability to cope with working away from home drove Charlotte Brontë and her sisters' efforts to found a school they could operate from Haworth. The sisters' understanding that they needed more education themselves in order to support this undertaking was the impetus for Charlotte and Emily's studies at the Heger "finishing school" in Belgium, an experience that furnishes much of the background for *Villette*. The declining health of her father and siblings, and the death of the latter, made Charlotte's need to support herself even more pressing, for her father's death would end the support of even his modest income as a cleric. Across the Atlantic, Bronson Alcott's innate impracticality and his radical educational ideas made him an unreliable source of income, thrusting the burden of support upon his wife, who started what was essentially an employment agency in Boston, and, increasingly, upon his daughter Louisa.

As Celine Carrigan notes, however, Charlotte Brontë's heroines, unlike their creator, are generally "free from the burden of imposed responsibility" (214). They work to support themselves, but do not have others dependent upon them; rather, they assert her belief that work in itself is respectable and healthy for women. The heroine of Brontë's first novel, Frances Henri, even insists on working after she marries, a position Anne

Smith terms "revolutionary in 1846" (xv). Her other heroines, though less revolutionary in this regard, all work until they marry: Jane Eyre is a teacher and governess; Lucy Snowe is a teacher, governess, and companion; Shirley Keeldar is an eminently competent businesswoman, at least until she turns over all her affairs to her husband-to-be.

What is more remarkable than the fact that these women work is their contention that work is an essential part of their being. William Crimsworth, the narrator of *The Professor*, comments about his wife, Frances:

> I knew she was not one who could live quiescent and inactive, or even comparatively inactive. Duties she must have to fulfill, and important duties; work to do—and exciting, absorbing, profitable work; strong faculties stirred in her frame, and they demanded full nourishment, free exercise. (P 206)

In subsequent novels, Brontë ceases to hide behind a male narrative voice (even though she continues to publish her work as "Currer Bell") to assert the value of work. Jane Eyre insists on work as requisite to mental health. She terms her life at Lowood "uniform; but not unhappy, because it was not inactive" (JE 84). In words reminiscent of Crimsworth's, Jane entertains the thought that employment has a worth far beyond economic security when she finds herself restless at Thornfield, despite her secure position and her success in tutoring Adele:

> It is vain to say human beings ought to be satisfied with tranquility: they must have action; and they will make it if they cannot find it. . . . It is thoughtless to condemn [women], if they seek to do more or learn more than custom has pronounced necessary for their sex. (JE 110–111)

In *Shirley*, female characters in all walks of life demonstrate their support for nontraditional employment for women at a time when a woman's "natural" profession was considered to be that of wife and mother. In addition to Caroline Helstone, whose comments begin this chapter, Shirley herself—who as her father's heir manages her estate—is a potent example of women's capabilities beyond homemaking. Even twelve-year-old Rose Yorke utters a vehement tirade, supported by Scripture, against women being forced to funnel all their energies into traditional household work:

> [I]f my Master has given me ten talents, my duty is to trade with them, and make them ten talents more. Not in the dust of household drawers shall the coin be interred. I will *not* deposit it in a broken-spouted tea-pot. . . . I will *not* commit it to your worktable. . . . I will *not* prison it in the linen-press . . . and least of all . . . will I hide it in a tureen of cold potatoes, to be ranged with bread, butter, pasty, and ham on the shelves of the larder. (*S* 400)

Brontë's last completed novel, *Villette*, demonstrates both the positive value of work and the dangers of its absence. Lucy Snowe's worst period of depression occurs during the school vacation, when she has little company and virtually nothing with which to occupy herself. Conversely, she says the years when M. Paul is away and she runs her school are her happiest times because they are filled with difficult but fulfilling work. Brontë died too soon to see the range of respectable professions for English women extend beyond those of teacher and governess as it did later in the century.[1] Nevertheless, she insisted throughout her fiction that meaningful work was necessary to a woman's well-being.

Jane Eyre and Lucy Snowe both work to achieve independence and to support themselves, but not, as did Brontë, to support others who depended upon them. This is true of many of Alcott's heroines as well. Even though Alcott herself worked to help support her family until she died,[2] her heroines seem to have a different project in mind, something more akin to what Susan Harris calls "willing [the] self into power and existence" (54) by setting out to work. In the early chapters of *Work*, a novel that refers openly to Brontë, Christie Devon actively seeks work even though she has a home with her aunt and uncle. From her initial pronouncement that "There's going to be a new Declaration of Independence" (*W* 1) to her almost immediate admission that "I'm sick of this dull town"

(*W* 2), Christie's attitude combines personal restlessness and the Protestant work ethic. It exudes confidence in the possibility of fulfilling the rags-to-riches dream according to the Franklinian model: "There is plenty of work in the world, and I'm not afraid of it; so you'll soon hear good news of me" (*W* 5). Even Alcott's sensation heroine Rosamond Vivian seeks outside work as an antidote for her restlessness and her dreary life as an unappreciated nurse and companion to her elderly grandfather; but as she expresses her need for activity to Phillip Tempest, she also rehearses with him the narrowness of opportunities for young women in her position:

> "Turn governess and drudge your youth away as most indigent gentlewomen do.". . .
>
> "I don't know enough and am too young, I think."
>
> "Be an actress, that's a fine life enough."
>
> "I've no talent and no money to start with if I had."
>
> "You can stitch your health and spirits into 'bands and gussets and seams' as a needlewoman. How does that suit?"
>
> "Not at all; I hate sewing."
>
> "Then marry some rich old man who will let you have your own way in everything and die by the time you are tired of it."
>
> "A rich man wouldn't care for a poor girl like me and I should not like money without love."
>
> "Bewitch a young man and let him make an idol of you for a time.". . .
>
> "I don't know any." (*Love Chase* 28)

Both of these Alcott heroines lose their sense of purpose in life when they have no work to do. Christie Devon nearly throws herself into a river before being rescued by her friend Rachel; Rosamond becomes despondent when her husband has her locked up in an asylum where "books were denied her, also pen or needle and she was left to brood over her unhappy fate. Tempest proved his wit in leaving her no employment" (*Love Chase* 176). She, too, nearly goes mad with nothing to occupy her time or her thoughts.

Regardless of these authorial affirmations of women's need for employment and warnings of the consequences of its absence, Victorian culture on both sides of the Atlantic made it difficult for women to support themselves and to maintain respectability at the same time. As the Industrial Revolution transformed the main location of labor from within the home to outside it, society increasingly recognized the potential for corruption in the working world—its "meanness and wicked-ness and misery" ("The Intellect of Women" 417), as a *Saturday Review* article put it—and increasingly insisted that only men should brave this potential damage. Women, on the other hand, should maintain their purity and essential goodness by stay-ing at home in their more "natural" role of "angel in the house," creating an oasis of incorruptibility where their husbands could find a respite and where their children could be raised with-out harm. This was the "logic" that produced the nineteenth century's version of the notion of separate spheres for men and women and a corresponding "cult of true womanhood" (Welter 21–41; also see Weiner 31–36 and Strickland 8–10). While the notion in general had efficacy both in England and in America, it took slightly different forms in each culture.

In England, there was little question that *some* women would work; the 1861 census, for example, terms 29.5 percent of the women "employed," up slightly from 28.9 percent in 1851 (Crow 158). However, English society drew clear distinc-tions along class lines; more than three-quarters of these women worked as domestic servants or in textile and dress-manufacturing factories (Crow 318). Thus, work for pay was largely the prerogative only of lower-class women, and car-ried with it a commensurate suspicion that the working woman's morals had been corrupted through her experience in the marketplace. British society seemed determined to pro-tect only its "respectable" women from such corruption; middle-class women working for pay cast doubt both upon their own morality and the earning power of the men upon whom they supposedly depended—despite the fact that in-creasing numbers of women had neither husbands nor chil-dren for them to hover over as "angels" and that manufactur-ing left less and less for them to do at home. As Florence Nightingale writes in *Cassandra* (1852), "Widowhood, ill-health, or want of bread, these three explanations or excuses, are supposed to justify a woman in taking up an occupation" (33).

In fact, while the scene quoted above from Alcott's *A Long Fatal Love Chase* takes place on an island off the coast of England, even the few employment opportunities Rosamond delineates characterize American, not British, society. For the British woman, approved work was even more limited than in Rosamond's litany. Even if extreme need justified a gentlewoman taking up an occupation, British society still attempted to maintain her in her "proper sphere"—that is, in the home, caring for children. Thus most middle-class women, untrained in household work (which would have been beneath them in any case) were qualified for only two occupations: governess or prostitute, according to the *Saturday Review* ("Wanted A Governess," 3 September 1859; qtd. in Crow 68).

While the *Review* article expresses a preference for the former occupation over the latter, the extent to which British society considered working for hire fundamentally immoral often made governesses, like their lower-class sisters, morally suspect as well. The occupation of governess was a subject of much consternation in early British Victorian society. Even though in terms of numbers, the plight of women working as domestic servants might have been a more visible issue than that of governesses (about 750,000, as compared with about 25,000 governesses, in 1851), the governess problem engendered so much discussion in journals, books, and *Punch* caricatures that by 1859 Harriet Martineau complained that readers must be "wearied . . . with the incessant repetition of the dreary story of spirit-broken governesses" ("Female Industry" 294). While the intense focus on the problems of governesses with little attention paid to those of the more numerous lower-class working women is most assuredly a reflection of the British class system, no doubt governesses posed an especially difficult problem. As Mary Poovey suggests, middle-class families sought to use governesses as a "boundary" between themselves and lower-class society, yet found that what they represented threatened that very boundary. On the one hand, governesses were supposed to be gentlewomen,[3] but the lower classes, not gentlewomen, were supposed to need to work, so governesses shared at least this one trait with the lower classes. Were they also repositories of sensuality, as society suspected working-class women of being, or were they fair angels beyond it, as befitted their class? Another complicated issue was that governesses tended children, but that was supposed to be the function of the middle-class mother; in other words, they were paid for what was assumed to be a profession that was "above" the marketplace, usurping another woman's role as they did so. The conjunction of class concerns and moral concerns, then, complicated middle-class attitudes toward governesses (Poovey 127); families had a vested interest in employing as governesses women who were beyond reproach morally (that is, who were gentlewomen) but, since women who worked for wages were necessarily tainted, families attempted to resolve some of the many contradictions a governess's very existence raised by keeping them apart from themselves socially. This resulted in what Jeanne Peterson calls "status incongruence" (15): governesses were women whom no one knew how to treat because they existed in some nebulous place above the level of servant but below the level of family. Small wonder if this confusion led to ambivalence and even resentment in both directions.

Brontë both illuminates and criticizes the British prejudice against governesses in *Jane Eyre*. Although Jane's first interview at Thornfield, with Mrs. Fairfax, had left her pleasantly surprised— "this is not what I have heard of the treatment of governesses" (*JE* 97)—she soon learns that Mrs. Fairfax treats her as an equal because their positions, in fact, are closely related: "this affable and kind widow was no great dame, but a dependent like myself. . . . The equality between her and me was real" (*JE* 101). Rochester himself proposes to judge Jane on her merits; he allows that "Not three in three thousand raw school-girl-governesses would have answered me as you have just done," but adds, "I go too fast in my conclusions: for what I yet know, you may be no better than the rest; you may have intolerable defects to counterbalance your few good points" (*JE* 136). But when Blanche Ingram and companions arrive at Thornfield in volume 2, they have no such impulse toward fairness. In Jane's very presence, they disparage governesses as detestable, ridiculous, incompetent, capricious, insolent, immoral, distracting nuisances (*JE* 178–80). While

Brontë's resentment toward this attitude is clear in her portrait of Blanche as a shallow hypocrite interested more in Rochester's money than in his charms, the story as she unfolds it makes clear her commensurate investment in British social standards. Jane marries Rochester, but not before her uncle's legacy ensures that she need no longer labor for wages; further, the couple do not take their place in English society at the end of the novel, but withdraw from it at Ferndean. In *Jane Eyre*, Brontë creates a way out of Jane's employment as a governess that suits her but is also at least marginally acceptable to her society.

Marrying or going abroad, in fact, were virtually the only positive exits from life as an English governess, once one entered it. Jane Eyre notwithstanding, marriage was unlikely, for a governess's position depended on her repressing her sexuality as much as possible so as not to be considered low-class or threatening to her employer's wife. Treatises on the plight of governesses in the 1840s, in fact, frequently noted that former governesses made up the largest numbers of women in lunatic asylums, often linking this fact with their sexual repression—another issue that may have been too close for the comfort of the average Victorian gentlewoman (Poovey 129–30).

Going abroad was a happier alternative for the restless governess in that a woman performing a governess's tasks would be apt to be considered a teacher without as many resultant social restrictions as in England. However, this also entailed the loss of one's place in English society (Peterson 20). Brontë opts for this solution to Lucy Snowe's dilemma in *Villette*. Although Lucy works both as a companion to Miss Marchmont and governess to Madame Beck's children before becoming a teacher, she makes it clear that resuming either life would be a symbolic failure to her because she would necessarily be dependent upon the whims of a family. After Lucy's reunion with the Brettons in Villette has made it abundantly clear to her that she may be a welcome guest in middle-class homes, but only as a poor relative and never an equal, Lucy refuses Mr. Home's offer to be Paulina's companion:

> [T]o be either a private governess or companion was unnatural to
> me. Rather than fill the former post in any great house, I would

deliberately have taken a housemaid's place, bought a strong pair of gloves, swept bedrooms and staircases, and cleaned stoves and locks, in peace and independence. . . . I would have made shirts, and starved. (*V* 382)

Unwilling to live her life as a dependent, belonging no-where, Lucy clings to the choice that offers her financial inde-pendence, clarity in who and what she is, and, not inciden-tally, the possibility of passion, even though that choice carries with it an acknowledgment of giving up whatever small claim she has to a position in British society.

While Alcott's adaptations of Jane Eyre and Lucy Snowe in her own work demonstrate that she admired their drive for autonomy, and while she makes use of occupations such as teacher, companion, and even governess in her own work, her characters also sweep bedrooms and make shirts without suf-fering permanent damage to their psyches or reputations. She seems to applaud Brontë's interest in the problems of work, but responds in typically American fashion. American Victorianism employed its own "cult of domesticity" as far as acceptable occupations for women were concerned, but the parameters of respectability tended to be much broader be-cause Victorian culture in America took shape differently than it did in England. Daniel Walker Howe contends that, insofar as Victorian culture involved the rise of the middle class,

> Victorianism in Britain and America developed within different contexts. . . . In England such people [middle class] lived at the periphery of polite society and political power; in America they dominated economic, social, and political institutions. Aristocratic culture patterns, against which middle-class Victorian standards had to contend in Britain, were weak in the United States. For this reason one could argue that Victorian culture was experienced more intensely in the United States than in Victoria's homeland. (508)

Duncan Crow affirms this assessment of continuing class conflict within British Victorianism when he discusses the "wild hopes," soon dashed, to which the Reform Act of 1832 gave rise. As Crow puts it, "The lower classes soon discovered that their hopes [for a more egalitarian society] had been totally without foundation" (32); a whole series of reforms, led by the Chartists, continued to press the issue through the 1830s and 1840s. Even with this continued agitation, however, and even as middle-class people acquired wealth, they did not also acquire social status. "To cross the gulf [between middle class and aristocracy] and be received in Society was an exercise that many attempted but few succeeded in" (Crow 33).

In America, on the other hand, the less-defined class structure enabled early Victorian culture to emphasize more universal opportunities to employ the Protestant work ethic and thus to achieve success; while more conservative elements of society were always uneasy with the idea of women working, many of the restraints associated with Victorian culture seemed to become more entrenched only after the Civil War (see Weiner 31–46; Baym, *Woman's Fiction* 48–50; Welter 40–41). Further, especially in the early part of the century, women could move in and out of the labor force with no particular societal sanctions (typically, young women might work until they married), a mobility that class divisions in England would not have allowed. Thus, many occupations that even in America would have been deemed unacceptable for women as long-term careers were more palatable as temporary employment. In addition, a variety of professions opened up to American women far earlier than they did in England.

For instance, on Harriet Martineau's visit to America in 1836, she reported that women there worked at teaching, doing needlework, taking in boarders, working in mills, doing shoe binding, typesetting, bookbinding, and as domestic servants (Weiner 31). According to Russell Nye, the rapid expansion of the public school system created a demand for teachers that women quickly filled; also, the first woman to graduate from Harvard Medical School set up practice as early as 1835 (552). Nancy Cott notes that "New England textile factories from the start employed a vastly greater proportion of women than men"; statistics on cotton mills between 1818 and 1833 indicate that the *average* proportion of female workers was 87 percent (37). As with the question of social and economic equality, Alcott's early novel *The Inheritance* exhibits a more

British—adopted, rather than adapted—response to the problem of women's work. Edith's position as governess allows the haughty Ida (herself a dependent, but nevertheless "legitimate" because highborn) free rein to despise her, and when Lady Hamilton's bank notes are missing, it is easy for the family to believe the supposedly lower-class Edith to be guilty of the crime. However, Alcott's considerations of women's work in her later Brontë-influenced stories reflect a more openly American attitude, not only when she features the work of governesses and teachers, but also in the ways she expands her characters' horizons beyond these occupations.

When, for example, Alcott casts her characters as governesses, as she does in some of her best children's stories, sensation stories, and a novel of the 1860s, she joins Brontë in deploring the conventional British attitude toward the occupation. However, while Brontë's commentary is that of an insider, herself a victim and a member of the system she describes, Alcott couches her protest in a distinctly American and democratic point of view. In the "Camp Laurence" chapter of *Little Women*, Laurie's English friends are unpleasantly surprised to discover that Meg March works as a governess; they respond to this news with condescension and patronizing platitudes. As Miss Kate walks away, commenting, "I didn't come to chaperone a governess," Meg is left to observe to John Brooke, "I forgot that English people rather turn up their noses at governesses, and don't treat them as we do," to which Brooke replies, "Tutors, also, have rather a hard time of it there, as I know to my sorrow. There's no place like America for us workers, Miss Margaret" (LW 134).

In her direct assault on the British status quo as it appears in *Jane Eyre*, Alcott creates in "Behind a Mask" a governess-heroine who meets with success even though, unlike Jane, she is most assuredly not a gentlewoman. In fact, part of the joke that Jean, a divorced actress, plays on the Coventrys is in leading Lord Coventry to believe that she is of noble lineage; since, as Alcott rather pointedly demonstrates, nothing about Jean enables him to prove otherwise, he believes she is of his class and eventually marries her, though, as Jean realizes, he never would have considered that option while he believed her a commoner. What Jean is, despite her working-class origins, is charming, talented, intelligent, and eventually a good wife, as the narrator assures us. Further, Alcott points out that Jean is able to get along with and positively influence both the upper-class family and the servants in the Coventry household: no "status incongruence" for her.

In *Work*, Christie Devon labors for a time as a governess, constantly overhearing the class-conscious remarks made about governesses by the social climbers in Mrs. Saltonstall's set: "[S]he's a dowdy thing, always trailing round with a book and those horrid children. No danger in [Philip Fletcher's] marrying *her*" (*W* 78). Once again, the final joke is not on the governess, but on the gossipy society women who model themselves upon their idea of contemporary European fashion; Christie has some sympathy for Fletcher himself, but ultimately enjoys letting Mrs. Saltonstall know that her brother has proposed to her, his sister's governess. That Christie is reading *Jane Eyre* when Philip approaches her to propose and that she disparages Jane's choice in marrying Rochester and then refuses Philip suggests that by this time Alcott is consciously rewriting Brontë's tale from her American point of view.

Alcott's most memorable heroine, Jo March, shares with both Jane Eyre and Lucy Snowe the profession of teacher when she works as a teacher and governess to Mrs. Kirke's children in New York; Jo, like Jane, moves on from this occupation, eventually becoming, like Lucy, directress of her own school, although Jo more often appears either as a nurturer or an administrator than as a classroom teacher. For both writers, running a school ensures their heroines' independence, but Brontë's ending to Lucy's story suggests her lack of optimism that Lucy can have both independence and love, whereas Alcott's asserts her belief that both are possible. Indeed, it is the extended-family structure of Plumfield that makes it so successful.

Although her most famous heroine, like Brontë's Lucy, pursues a teaching career, Alcott's American perspective allows her to consider a much wider range of employments for other heroines: both Rosamond Vivian of the sensation tale *A Long*

Fatal Love Chase and Christie Devon of *Work* make their way through the world as nurse, seamstress, companion, and servant, in addition to Christie's turns as factory worker and actress. Some of Rosamond's activities are calculated to keep her hidden from the husband from whom she is fleeing in the sensation tale, but in *Work* Christie pursues a variety of careers with little fanfare or attention to the class status connected with each.[4] By the time she wrote *Jo's Boys*, Alcott was actively urging her young female readers to consider occupations for themselves; Jo's *girls* become artists, doctors, and actresses, some marrying, some remaining single. While this novel appears much later (1886) than either Brontë's works or even Alcott's own stories of Rosamond and Christie, its radical premise becomes more evident when one observes that, even by 1870, only 15 percent of all American women were listed as being in the labor force, a number which rose only to 19 percent by 1890 (Weiner 4)—still much smaller percentages than that of their British sisters. A further indication of Alcott's radicalism is that Christie's marriage and motherhood do not end her career; she marches off to the Civil War as a nurse almost immediately after her wedding, and the end of the novel finds her on the threshold of yet another career as a liaison between the working women and middle-class women in her community. How far Alcott's art goes beyond life as she knew it is evident in the fact that married women in the American labor force numbered only about 2.5 percent by 1890 (Weiner 6); working mothers do not even show up in large enough numbers to be included in American labor statistics until 1940.

While Alcott joined Brontë in championing the plight of the governess but proposed a much wider range of possibilities for female employment in general, some of the most interesting parallels and contrasts between the two writers occur when they consider two careers for women which seem to have fascinated them both: actresses and writers.

Overall, middle-class opinion of theater and performers in the mid-nineteenth century seems equally disparaging in England and America. Jonas Barish, in fact, traces the basic mistrust of acting as far back as the time of Plato, who associated acting with loss of self on the grounds that "imitation is formative—those who imitate tend to become what they imitate" (Barish 21). Not even a thinker as influential as Plato could ever put an end to theater, however, and in England women have been playwrights, actors, and even theater managers since the Restoration. Social mores from the mid-eighteenth century on mitigated against women being in public view with men other than their fathers or husbands (Gardner 7), however, adding sexual sanctions to long-standing suspicions of theater in general on the grounds that it nurtured an unhealthy and immoral human penchant for public display (Barish 326). Indeed, insofar as immorality was concerned, the London stage from 1660 through the eighteenth century had a reputation for being a platform from which an actress could become the mistress of a wealthy man (Johnson, *Actress* 30).

Charlotte Brontë, whose performance in family theatricals as a child has already been noted, frequently presents acting in her adult writing either as falseness or as loss of control. In *Jane Eyre*, for example, Rochester's Parisian lover who betrays him and leaves him to raise Adele is an opera dancer named Celine Varens. Brontë reinforces the idea of the falseness associated with acting in the "Charades" game in which Rochester and Blanche Ingram enact a wedding scene, and also when Rochester tries to pass himself off as a gypsy fortune teller. Although Rochester is proud of his masquerade, Jane tells him, "I shall try to forgive you: but it was not right" (204).

In *Villette*, acting becomes synonymous with lack of control. In Lucy Snowe's performance at Madame Beck's *fete*, after characterizing her performance with words like "power" and "possessed" (*V* 210), she "put[s] by" her "keen relish for dramatic expression" because "it would not do for a mere onlooker at life" (211). The most stunning theatrical performance in the novel, of course, is the performance by Vashti[5] that Lucy attends with Graham Bretton. Like Lucy's own performance earlier, the night at the theater is marked by a stunning display of power, yet Lucy finds the power disturbing. She comments on the actress's spellbinding performance:

I found upon her something neither of woman nor of man: in
each of her eyes sat a devil. These evil forces bore her through
the tragedy. . . . It was a marvellous sight: a mighty revelation.
It was a spectacle low, horrible, immoral. (*V* 339)

Like the seasickness that punctuated Lucy's previous flir-
tation with hope on her voyage from England, her hopes for a
relationship with Graham are dealt their death knell when
Vashti's performance is punctuated by disaster: a fire breaks
out in the theater, and in it Graham rescues a young woman
who captures his affections as Lucy never could. Lucy—and
Brontë—clearly recognize the power of theater but associate
this power with an inevitable loss of self.

Certainly the very concept of theater was also inherently evil
to many in post-Puritan America. Albert Palmer, writing in 1895,
estimated that at mid-century 70 percent of the American people
regarded even *going* to the theater as sinful (165). Claudia Johnson
quotes mid-century clergymen's sermons against the theater,
including one who declared that Lincoln's assassination was a
warning from God about the dangers of the theater ("Third Tier"
582). Moreover, there is evidence that public opinion equated
actresses with prostitutes from the time women first appeared
on the stage (see Auster, especially chapter 2).

But some specific aspects of nineteenth-century American theater may have encouraged Louisa May Alcott to take a
more positive view of it than did the general public. First, as
both Auster (18, 25–27) and Johnson ("Drama" 332) observe,
the theater was one place in America where an independent
woman could have a career that had pay equity with men at
a time when other women who did the same work as men
(in sales, factories, and teaching, for example) made about
one-third to one-half their salary (Johnson, *Actress* 56–57). Further, the salary an actress could command for the amount of
time and effort required would have made it especially attractive. The lowest-paid extras made as much as the high-
est-paid mill girls, who typically worked fourteen hours a day,
six days a week. Although actresses' salaries were lower than
those of teachers, the shorter hours and less stressful working conditions often enabled actresses to train for other jobs

while supporting themselves in the theater (Johnson, *Actress* 51–55). This is evident in Alcott's *Work*, for although Christie initially takes a job as a servant because she "found her want of accomplishments a barrier to success" (W 16) in finding a job as a governess, she gets precisely that job after quitting the theater: "since her last effort in that line she had increased her knowledge of music, and learned French" (W 59).

Another reason Alcott may have found the theater especially interesting is that the 1840s and 1850s, formative years for her, "were probably the most theatrically significant decades of the century" (Johnson, "Drama" 330). These years were marked by a proliferation of female playwrights and stars. One who was both was Anna Mowatt, whose upper-class background helped to add respectability to the stage when she not only wrote one of the century's most successful American plays (*Fashion; or, Life in New York*; 1845), but acted as well. Also among them was Charlotte Cushman, America's first internationally renowned actress, who so impressed Alcott (she reports having a "stagestruck fit" after seeing Cushman perform in Boston [*Journals* 90; June 1858]) that she wrote her into *Jo's Boys* as Miss Cameron, an actress who takes an interest in Josie's theatrical aspirations. What Miss Cameron teaches Josie seems to reflect the contemporary view of Cushman (see Auster 16–17) as a moral, influential woman who took time to encourage other actresses: Josie learns from the actress "to see how sacred good gifts are, how powerful, and how faithfully they should be used for high ends, each in its own place helping to educate, refine, and refresh" (JB 167). A similar character appears much earlier in Alcott's *A Long Fatal Love Chase* as Madame Honorine, a respected actress who uses her power and independence to help the beleaguered Rosamond escape the villainous Phillip Tempest.

Even conservative New England was, in fact, beginning to see how the stage could be used for "high ends" during this time. While plays had traditionally been regarded by detractors as "sacrilegious, immoral, and false" (Johnson, *Actress* 18), a relationship between the American reform movements and theater was forged when *The Drunkard* was performed at the Boston Museum in 1843, bringing members of the Temperance Society into the audience. Reform-minded groups favoring abolition and other causes soon found that they could raise money and preach at the same time through properly selected plays (Johnson, "Drama" 331), often staged by community theater groups made up of the reformers themselves. Alcott herself indulged her love of theater by performing in such productions from the late 1850s through the 1860s (see Stern, "Trouper"). Her contemporary Louise Chandler Moulton recalled her "taking part in a play for the benefit of some charity she would not otherwise have been able to assist," and added, "One does not half know Miss Alcott who has not seen her—as Mrs. Jarley—display her 'wax-works.' I think it is quite the best bit of broad comedy I can remember" (41).

Finally, the stage was one of the battlegrounds where the struggle for recognition of American art and culture as separate from the British culture was being fought, sometimes quite literally. One famous incident in the conflict was the Astor Place riot, which ensued in 1849 when the most successful British actor of the time, William Macready, and his American rival Edwin Forrest appeared in New York as Macbeth at the same time; thirty-one people died and forty-eight more were injured in the struggle (Auster 14–15; Hornblow 38–42).

Even though at mid-century theater was being used by some as a point of divisiveness between British and American society, a fascination with actresses and acting was one of the imaginative links between Charlotte Brontë and Louisa May Alcott. Alcott, like Brontë, performed in family theatricals as a child; when Alcott uses theater and acting motifs in her writing, however, she separates her attitude toward acting as a profession, which she respects, from her attitude toward falseness in personal relationships, which she, like Brontë, disdains.[6]

In *A Long Fatal Love Chase*, for example, Rosamond reacts to Philip's "masquerade" much as Jane does to Rochester's. Philip bribes a priest and takes his place in the confessional in order to hear Rosamond admit her continuing love for him, just as Rochester tries to draw Jane out in the gypsy fortune-telling scene. Alcott consciously refers to *Jane Eyre* in this episode, even titling the chapter "Flee Temptation," and her character reacts to Tempest's falseness with the same reserve with which Jane responds to Rochester's. Although Tempest, like Rochester, wishes to treat his falseness as a practical joke, Rosamond, like Jane, "shrink[s] instinctively from one who possessed so little of either virtue [truth or fidelity]" (*Love Chase* 133).

Vashti, the actress who fascinates but disturbs Brontë's Lucy Snowe, appears in one Alcott sensation story almost as a code word for "actress." In "Behind a Mask," Jean Muir refers to Lucia, the Coventry's resident cousin who is informally engaged to Gerald Coventry as the tale begins, as "Vashti" in the letters she writes to her friend Hortense. Although the name originally comes from a Biblical queen, the link with the character named Lucia, whom Jean disdains for her hypocrisy (she acts like an "icicle" while burning with uncontrollable jealousy toward Jean [197]) makes it more likely that the reference is to Brontë than to the Book of Esther. Further, Alcott does not condemn professional acting here, but rather Lucia's real-life hypocrisy.

When Alcott includes professional acting in her fiction, she seems as fascinated as Brontë by the power of theater but more positive in her outlook. Elizabeth Keyser, in her discussion of *Work*, notes that Christie's acting "expresses rather than conceals emotion" (114)—unlike the deceptive charades in *Jane Eyre*—and that Alcott avoids "The danger of women's acting, that of losing themselves" (120)—unlike Lucy and Vashti in *Villette*.[7] Christie abandons professional acting because she feels it is making her too narcissistic, but when she "performs" again for her friends on her birthday, her acting reveals to them some of her finer qualities of which they were not aware. After Christie performs Shakespearean scenes as Juliet, Lady Macbeth, and Portia, her future husband, David Sterling, observes to their friend Reverend Power, "I'd no idea she had it in her" (*W* 273) and says to Christie herself, "I feel as if I never had [seen you before]" (275).

In general, although Alcott disagrees with Brontë's negative attitude toward the power of theater, she often alludes specifically to Brontë when creating her own version of the profession. The parallels between Lucy Snowe's acting in *Villette* and the "Actress" chapter of *Work* were discussed in chapter 2; although both women leave acting behind, Lucy avoids it because the loss of self terrifies her, but Christie worries that it will make her too self-centered. In Alcott's sensation stories, where powerful women often have free rein, actresses bearing Brontëan names often appear in more sympathetic form than in Brontë's own works. Two of them, for example, echo the name of Rochester's dancer-lover Celine Varens. Although Rochester's account of Celine contains nothing but scorn and disgust for the woman who was unfaithful to him and abandoned her child to run off with an Italian lover, Alcott's adaptations enable the reader to understand, if not always sympathize with, the woman's point of view.

Virginie Varens, the heroine of "V. V.," is initially a sympathetic character, a seventeen-year-old actress under the power of a Machiavellian cousin who hopes to marry her and who has carved his initials, V. V., in her wrist, covering the scars with an iron bracelet. The image recalls the scene in *Jane Eyre*, when Rochester and Jane have returned from a tense shopping expedition, marked by her resistance to every luxury he tries to force upon her. Rochester finally says to her, "it is your time now, little tyrant, but it will be mine presently; and when once I have fairly seized you, to have and to hold, I'll just—figuratively speaking—attach you to a chain like this (touching his watch guard)" (273). Although in the end Rochester reverses this image by giving Jane his watch and watchguard, saying "Fasten it into your girdle, Janet, and keep it henceforward: I have no use for it" (451), Alcott's heroine meets with no such good fortune.[8] When Virginie marries, Victor murders her husband and threatens to frame her for the murder. Virginie becomes a much less sympathetic character after this, when, with the guidance of Victor, she plots to win the heart of the wealthy Earl Douglas and drives his intended fiancée to suicide. Douglas uncovers her guilt and threatens to send her to "a gray old tower" he owns in Scotland, "with no life near it but the sound of the wind, the scream of the gulls," where "you shall live cut off from all the world, but not from God" (128). She escapes this fate through poison imbedded in another piece of iron jewelry, an opal ring. Although Virginie is by no stretch of the imagination an admirable heroine, it is significant that she eludes her fate rather than submits to it and that her guilt is somewhat mitigated by the fact that the male characters, especially Victor, are more evil and manipulative than she. Most important, the acting that comes under

Alcott's censure is the falseness that takes place *outside* the theater, not the artistic endeavor of acting itself.

Another intriguing variation on Brontë occurs in "A Double Tragedy," in which a much more sympathetic actress, Clotilde Varian, is thwarted by a vicious male character Alcott names St. John. This St. John is no clergyman, like the one Brontë creates in *Jane Eyre,* but has some of his icy, domineering character nonetheless. "Pride and passion, courage and indomitable will met and mingled in his face." He looks at Clotilde with "the lordly admiration and pride which a master bestows upon a handsome slave" (134). As it happens, Clotilde is St. John's wife. His version of their relationship is that he married the beautiful young Spanish woman, but their bliss soon dissipated in "domestic tempests," after which he was forced to leave his "fiery angel" in a chateau (better than an attic!) and to disappear. Two years later, hearing that St. John has died, Clotilde returns to her prior stage career and is about to marry a fellow actor, when St. John reappears to reclaim what he clearly considers to be his property. St. John orders Clotilde to "submit" (140) to him, and threatens her lover's life, but she arranges for some stage machinery to fall on St. John and kill him, whereupon she commits suicide. Here Alcott adapts Brontë's St. John so that even the long-suffering Rosamond Oliver would be glad she didn't marry him; but for her actress she has sympathy and pity. Brontë suspects acting, offstage or on, but while Alcott joins her in abhorring falseness in human relationships, she enjoys rather than mistrusts the possibilities of power and revelation that stage acting symbolizes for her.

It seems fitting to close these observations on women and the working world by reconsidering, this time from the standpoint of art rather than biography, the writers' characterizations of the profession each chose for herself: writing. The most memorable characters Alcott and Brontë ever created are themselves writers. Neither Jane Eyre nor Lucy Snowe ever writes for pay, yet Brontë casts both their stories in the first person, allowing them, though subtly, to author their own lives. *Jane Eyre* is even subtitled "An Autobiography"; in the convention of early novels, it takes notice of its readers repeatedly, including one of the most famous addresses in literature: "Reader, I married him."

While Jane as narrator tries to explain every action that she thinks readers might find objectionable, Lucy Snowe as *Villette*'s narrator is not nearly as interested in staying in the reader's good graces. She keeps the secret of Dr. John's identity from the reader for nearly one hundred pages of text, commenting haughtily that "I preferred to keep the matter to myself" (248). She avers that she is writing "a heretic narrative" (235).

Brontë uses Lucy's story to lash out, in a larger context, against cultural conditions that dictated, as had Southey, that "Literature cannot be the business of a woman's life." In one scene, which Nancy Miller calls "a parable—which is not to say a recommendation—of the conditions of production for female authorship" (113), Lucy is virtually dragged from her work by two professors (appropriately named Boissec and Rochemorte) who refuse to believe she has written a piece that M. Paul has submitted to them as evidence of his students' work. Lucy's terror of their scrutiny renders her unable to respond to them either verbally or in writing, until she gets angry at them and produces a stunning though viciously satiric model of "Human Justice" (*Villette*, chapter 35). Anger toward her readers erupts again on the last page of the novel when Lucy rather perversely throws out a hopeful lifeline to those "sunny imaginations" (596) who need happy endings, then ends her story with an account of the success of the three most repulsive characters in her tale and no account of the rest of her own story, only a last "Farewell."

The artist/writer who is Charlotte Brontë remains hidden behind her writer/characters Lucy and Jane and additionally behind the pseudonym Currer Bell when she puts her art before the public. Given Southey's early warning to her and her interest in being considered a writer, not a "woman writer," one can well deem her use of these shields, as well as Lucy's repressed rage, to be manifestations of her "anxiety of authorship" (Gilbert and Gubar, chapter 2). Ironically, Brontë seems to have thrived, as a writer at least, on just such anxiety. Neither *The Professor*, with its first-person male narrative voice, nor *Shirley*, narrated mostly in the third person, succeeds as literature nearly as well as do Brontë's two novels in which her women writers author their own lives while under continuing duress.

Across the ocean, the American popular market (aside from

certain male writers unhappy with their lack of success in it) welcomed women writers (Nye 52), and Louisa Alcott seems to have found this atmosphere quite as much an impetus to developing her talents as England's conservatism was to Charlotte Brontë's. With her customary optimism and ability to enjoy her life's experiences, Alcott invites the public to witness much of the progress of her own writing career in the person of her most famous character, Jo March, acknowledging frequently and publicly in her lifetime that Jo's career as a writer was essentially her own. Jo's writing "vortex," the mixed reviews given her first novel, the difficulties of writing after her sister's death, and her experiments in sensation fiction—all recorded in *Little Women*—essentially reflect her own experiences as a writer. She even pokes a bit of pointed fun at celebrity-seekers who hound successful writers in the "Jo's Last Scrape" chapter of *Jo's Boys*.

Given the American cultural climate and the existence of authors, even female authors such as Charlotte Brontë, as precursors, Alcott did not seem to labor under the burden of "anxiety of authorship." Nor does Bloom's "anxiety of influence" seem an appropriate description of her attitude, since Alcott seems perfectly comfortable with drawing, sometimes verbatim, from her models as she adopts and adapts, without any particular need to depose them. Alcott may sometimes join in with Brontë's defense of woman in the nineteenth century and at other times propose quite different approaches to addressing the problems she faced, but she never disparages Brontë as a writer. In fact, she seems to appreciate the groundwork Brontë has laid and to honor her as a "foremother." What anxiety Louisa May Alcott encountered as a writer, and another reason she would not have considered Brontë her "competition," was her own struggle with notions of talent vs. genius—notions, as Brodhead shows, that were exacerbated as much by the literary climate in America as Brontë's anxieties reflected that of England. Simply put, by not claiming genius for herself, she didn't have to deal with her relationship to an acknowledged genius.

Certainly this attitude was not without its complexities in her life, as discussed earlier, but also in the writers she creates. The very fact that Alcott deflects the talent/genius argument away from her alter ego Jo and onto Laurie and Amy in *Little Women* may suggest, in an "absence as presence" way, that it remained a troubling issue for her in the most accomplished period of her career. That a tale as late in Alcott's career as *A Modern Mephistopheles* was published anonymously and that its hero, Felix Canaris, is nearly crippled by the "fear of the world and the loss of fame before [his] eyes" (*AMM* 25) as he attempts to follow up his first, phenomenally successful, book with another suggests that this was no moot point for her even in 1877. However, the fact remains that Alcott hid behind the cloak of anonymity for *Mephistopheles* as part of a "Guess who wrote this?" game, not under threat of censure. Whatever demons may have tortured her from time to time, she seems to have been able to live with them by focusing her energies in the practical determination to make the best use she could of her gift, whether it be talent or genius, in order to take fullest advantage of the American literary market as she assessed it.

Admittedly, while that attitude may have made her a more productive and financially successful writer and even protected her from disappointment, it may also have kept her from daring to be as accomplished a writer as she might have otherwise become—daring, that is, to be an artist. For although Jo's (and Alcott's) writing "vortex" resembles Charlotte Brontë's "influence ... which becomes ... master" (qtd. in Gaskell 236), Brontë's attitude toward the art of writing stands in marked contrast to Alcott's attitude toward the professional work of writing. In considering the occupation of authorship, more than any others, Alcott ultimately distances herself from Brontë by creating writers with little if any hint of the influence of Charlotte Brontë, writers who are successful but not geniuses. It should be noted that, though their lives are not without complications, they are also people who take joy in the work of writing. Thus, the two writers absolutely agree on the need and value of work for women—including themselves—and they both resist the boundaries within which their respective societies seek to contain "women's work." But Alcott, as an American writer, finds those boundaries, at least in practical terms, much less confining than does her lifelong literary heroine, Charlotte Brontë.

Whether presented overtly, as in a Jo March, or covertly, as in a Jane or Lucy, the concept of authorship has often been expressed in literature by means of the metaphor of parenting, a metaphor that has special implications when the author is female (see Gilbert and Gubar, chapter 2), and which suggests one final contrast linking the life and art of Alcott and Brontë. Beginning from the Lacanian premise that "the literal is associated with the feminine, [while] the more highly valued figurative is associated with the masculine" (Homans 5), Margaret Homans reads nineteenth-century British women writers' characterizations of motherhood as a literal translation of creativity, that is, as an act that often pushes the artist from the symbolic order back into the literal world where she becomes object rather than subject, and is therefore no longer capable of creativity. Specifically, she reads in Jane Eyre's dreams of children the "terror [which] originates in the heroine's confinement to the world of objects" (87). In considering Jane as the writer of her own story, we might carry this reading a step further to note that when Jane does actually come to the point in her story where she has a child, her art—her narrative—stops. In Alcott's work, however, both Christie in *Work* and Jo March Bhaer work after motherhood. While Christie for a time "forgot there was a world outside" (*W* 413) after her daughter's birth, she embarks on a new and challenging career—her life as a creative work—at the end of the novel. Jo's writing career is also interrupted, but not ended, by her marriage and subsequent motherhood. In fact, in *Jo's Boys* she is a successful writer who is perpetually hounded by celebrity-seekers. Thus Brontë's characters affirm the either/or notion of creativity, while Alcott's propose the conjunction "and" to link other creative activities with motherhood.

The irony of these characterizations is the uncanny way in which, for both writers, their earlier art predicted the courses of their later lives. For Charlotte Brontë, motherhood did mean death; she died of complications from her pregnancy, leaving what would have been her fifth novel, *Emma*—whose fragments "show a less egocentric, more objective, and socially . . . subtler Charlotte Brontë than we have hitherto encountered" (Anne Smith xvii)—unfinished. Louisa May Alcott became a single parent like Christie Devon when her sister May died shortly after childbirth and asked that Louisa raise her infant daughter, which she did for the last eight years of her life—and she never stopped writing. Though only an accident of fate, this final parallel signals the essential difference between Louisa May Alcott and Charlotte Brontë; despite the many ties that personal and cultural similarities engendered, Alcott's life, unlike Brontë's, ultimately supported her belief that she inhabited a world of promise and possibility.

Conclusions and Considerations

"But Is She Any Good?"

The particular approach to the literary legacy of Louisa May Alcott employed here—exploring whether and to what extent Alcott's lifelong interest in Charlotte Brontë translated into artistic influence as she established herself as a writer—has as its larger goal gauging with more accuracy Alcott's place in nineteenth-century American literature. Demonstrating the continuing, though changing, influence of Brontë on Alcott does not diminish Alcott's talents, or suggest that she lacked the imagination to create her own stories, for regardless of inherent talent—or genius—the stories we know and care about become a part of us that we employ whenever we tell our own stories. Rather, establishing Alcott's interest in this British writer, then exploring the ways in which she seemed to resist and finally to write beyond Brontë's influence, enables us to see Alcott herself more clearly, to add more dimension to our understanding of Alcott as a reader of literature and also as a particularly American writer. Tracing the boundaries of Brontë's influence in Alcott's writing brings two particular aspects of Alcott's artistry into sharper focus.

In terms of artistic technique, pointing out the various ways Alcott uses Brontë throughout her novels, children's stories, and sensation fiction is a way of tracing Alcott's development as a writer. In her early work, Alcott seems entranced by Brontë's accomplished character development, particularly in her creation of Jane Eyre, Rochester, and Lucy Snowe. However, Alcott seems to realize almost immediately that she cannot directly adopt British forms or characters into her American work; they do not "translate" well into an American milieu. As Alcott develops artistic control, her work becomes more cohesive and more consistently American; she overtly argues with Brontë's characters in her own work, even parodying situations, especially from *Jane Eyre,* and rewriting them. In her revisions of Brontë, Alcott typically gives more power of action to her heroines than does her English counterpart, even while retaining language and plot situations that specifically echo Brontë.

In her most mature work, Alcott moves from adoption of Brontë, through revision, to what I have termed adaptation: she successfully fuses the depth of character and sometimes even elements of plot that she finds in Brontë with an inclination toward a more active form of heroism than Brontë's female characters exhibit; in so doing, she creates some of her most successful works. The deftness with which she eventually could adapt her sources is evident in one of her last novels, *Jo's Boys,* in which Alcott refers to Brontë overtly and admiringly in the text, while the actual scenes in which Brontë's "influence" are felt are subtly transformed into Alcott's new terms.

Examining the technical aspects of Brontë's presence in Alcott's writing reveals tension between Alcott's admiration for Brontë's characters and the inclination to employ her own artistic style as she endows her own characters with as much power but more efficacy than Brontë's; examining some of the major themes that both Alcott and Brontë treated in the works in which Brontë's influence has been established reveals a related, but subtler, tension. What Robert Weisbuch characterizes as a fundamental connection between the (male) American and British writers in his transatlantic study—the common heritage of Shakespeare, Chaucer, and Milton—is enhanced in the Alcott–Brontë connection by the powerful commonality of gender. As nineteenth-century women, both writers show great interest in issues of spirituality, interpersonal relationships, and opportunities for self-fulfillment as these issues are shaped by their positions as women. But Alcott's response to these issues is also shaped by her personal and cultural ties to Victorian America rather than England. Her responses to her reading of Brontë repeatedly rewrite British reserve and repression in terms of American optimism and progressivism. She, like Brontë, is aware of the special problems gender entails, but like her American literary influences, such as Thoreau, Emerson, and Hawthorne, her awareness of the difficulty of action is tempered by the belief that one must act nevertheless. Not for her was the "failure of nerve" that American writers associated with their British counterparts. So Alcott is indeed what Elaine Showalter (*Sister's Choice* 20) terms a "hybrid" writer; she responds both as a woman and as an American in creating her own texts. She rethinks Brontë's powerful but repressed women characters but also rethinks the philosophies of American transcendentalism and American Victorianism, developing a "Newness" of her own. Thus she presents characters—Kate Snow of "A Nurse's Story" for instance— who observe life with the intensity of Lucy Snowe, banter like Jane Eyre with powerful men, and exert influence from within a family, while at the same time the self-reliance and openness to new situations she exhibits seem to extend and redefine the family as a community.

Thus, in some respects, my examination of Alcott's work reaffirms Weisbuch's thesis that American writers were powerfully influenced by their British counterparts even as they sought to define themselves in a separate American context. Whether because the tie of gender is more powerful than the male attitude of rebellion or because Alcott considered herself a "talent" rather than a "genius" and never felt the sense of British-American competition with Brontë that seemed to characterize the writers Weisbuch considers, Alcott seems content good-naturedly to parody or rewrite Brontë in her own work, and ultimately merely to appropriate what is useful and blend it with her own inclinations, rather than to react to it with outright hostility. Even when Alcott's creations are most in opposition to Brontë's, as in the unrestrained co-educational atmosphere of *Jo's Boys*, she is ready to acknowledge her admiration for the "heart" she finds in Brontë's writing, the quality that united them despite the oceans—physical, personal, and cultural—that separated them. One might extend these considerations even further by examining other transatlantic connections of Alcott's, for instance her love of Dickens and Goethe, perhaps even balancing them with Elizabeth Keyser's suggestions in *Whispers in the Dark* regarding the American influence of Hawthorne in her writing. The end result would be a more complete assessment of Alcott as a reader and a writer, augmenting current criticism that more often assesses her in feminist or in cultural contexts than in literary ones.

If one is to argue for Alcott's place as an American writer, the question that must be answered in regard to her work is one that both Jane Tompkins and Susan Harris recently have asked in regard to nineteenth-century women writers in general—and one that Alcott's musings about "talent" and "genius" suggest she asked herself: "But is it any good?" (see Harris's article and chapter VII of *Sensational Designs*). To the extent that Alcott writes what Nina Baym calls "woman's fiction," Ann Douglas in *The Feminization of American Culture* would certainly answer "No," for Douglas treats the whole genre as a negative phenomenon:

> "Feminization" inevitably guaranteed, not simply the loss of the finest values contained in Calvinism, but the continuation of male hegemony. . . . The triumph of the "feminizing," sentimental forces that would generate mass culture redefined and perhaps limited the possibilities for change in American society. (13)

Douglas considers only Margaret Fuller and Harriet Beecher Stowe in her early work (which, however, degenerated into a career that she calls "profoundly disappointing" [253]) as women writers who escaped the anti-intellectual feminization that ultimately upholds the status quo and so distresses her. Jane Tompkins, however, argues in direct opposition to Douglas:

> [T]he popular domestic novel of the nineteenth century represents a monumental effort to reorganize culture from the woman's point of view; . . . this body of work is remarkable for its intellectual complexity, ambition, and resourcefulness; . . . in certain cases, it offers a critique of American society far more

devastating than any delivered by better-known critics such as Hawthorne and Melville. (124)

Susan Harris, who at least entertains the idea that some nineteenth-century women's fiction *could* be valuable, suggests looking at these texts "as both reactive and creative rather than asking them to self-consciously embody 'timeless truths.'" She argues for examining them in the light of historical, rhetorical, *and* ideological parameters in order to determine their overall worth (45). Applying her parameters to Alcott's work reaffirms Alcott's importance as an American writer, although I would go even further and remove the quotation marks from the idea of "timeless truths," for Alcott's work stands that test as well, continuing to speak powerfully to readers more than a century after her death.

Alcott utilizes her best technical attributes—powerful characterizations developed through dialogue and plot, use of vernacular, and control of several plot threads at once—in the standard literary forms available to her as she explores ideas that often argue directly against the status quo. In her domestic fiction, and in her children's fiction as well, she defies convention by creating realistic rather than perfect characters and by repeatedly asserting her belief in female self-sustenance. She argues for a more comprehensive view of spirituality, of community, and of women's lives than was supported by her society as a whole.

Alcott's work, even her best work, is by no means flawless, often because incongruities arise from her efforts to work within genres while consciously realizing that her ideas defy literary as well as societal conventions. However, even these disruptions may prove instructive to the critic seeking a fuller understanding of the concept of genre. For example, after Beth dies in *Little Women*, the narrator comments, "Now, if [Jo] had been the heroine of a moral storybook, she ought at this period of her life to have become quite saintly, renounced the world, and gone about doing good in a mortified bonnet, with tracts in her pocket. But you see Jo wasn't a heroine" (*LW* 435). Alcott then creates an alternative response for Jo by turning her attention to writing. Christie's struggles toward success in

Work often seem to be Alcott's struggles to write a novel that conforms to the Tompkins definition of the novel of sentiment—it is by, for, and about women—while disrupting some elements of the status quo as her heroine seeks to achieve independence. When Christie Devon thinks David is more interested in his old friend Kitty than in her, the narrator breaks in to observe:

> If she had been a regular novel heroine at this crisis, she would have grown gray in a single night, had a dangerous illness, gone mad, or at least taken to pervading the house at unseasonable hours with her back hair down and much wringing of the hands. Being a commonplace woman she did nothing so romantic. (W 310)

Alcott does not wish to write a "moral storybook" for children or a "regular novel" for adults, for some of her ideas were too revolutionary to be contained in the forms she had chosen. On the other hand, she writes in these genres partly because she does not wish to eschew the forms, or the conventions they represent, entirely. She believes wholeheartedly in what Victorian society only gave lip-service to—the power of womanhood and of family—and seeks to put that power into action in her writing. Thus her use of conventional forms while proposing radical social ideas may be read as an attempt to stretch literary genres beyond conventional uses as well.

Sometimes the tension shows, as in the somewhat aimless romantic chapters of *Work* and its eventual ponderous utopian ending after the liveliness and realistic nature of the beginning—life and realism which derive in no small way from Alcott's comic rewriting of *Jane Eyre*. In her most successful works, there is less tension between form and content than elsewhere; in "Behind a Mask" and "A Nurse's Story," for example, the form of sensation fiction enables Alcott to write her female characters in as strong terms as she wishes. Here, the power of Brontë's female characters provide important groundwork for the ones Alcott creates. In *Little Women*, both generic tension and Brontëan influence dissipate as she creates her most American of characters in Jo March.

Another technical aspect of Alcott's work that characterizes some of her finest writing is the humor, even satire, she uses in rewriting other literature, such as the *Jane Eyre* take-offs in *Work* and in "Behind a Mask," and in rewriting her family history as she does in "Transcendental Wild Oats." Again, the specific reliance on Brontë seems to diminish as Alcott comes into her own as an American writer, though the thematic concerns for the position of woman in the nineteenth century remain.

In addition to both the reactive and creative aspects of Alcott's work—the skill with which she presents a picture of nineteenth-century American life and challenges the reader to imagine a world beyond its boundaries—the hold Alcott's work maintains on the modern reader suggests that it may also embody some of those nebulous "timeless truths." Well over a hundred years after its initial appearance, *Little Women* has never been out of print. Writers as diverse as Gertrude Stein, Simone de Beauvoir, and Adrienne Rich have testified to this book's importance in shaping their own careers. Continued popular and critical interest in Alcott's work has spurred recent republication of her sensation tales and adult novels, and first-time publication of two manuscripts, one of which (*A Long Fatal Love Chase*) catapulted her onto the *New York Times*'s Bestseller List in 1995. A new film version of *Little Women* opened in theaters in December 1994, generating articles in popular magazines (see Carey, Mahoney, Rohrer, Walton) that affirm the continuing relevance of the issues Alcott raised, as well as the power with which she raised them, over a century ago.

Readers still are concerned with what came to be one of Alcott's—and America's—most important themes: reconciling the need for individual fulfillment with the need for community. This certainly has been a concern of American life and literature at least since Emerson proposed "Self-Reliance" as a counterpoint to the Mayflower Compact in 1841, and provides even more impetus for the study of Alcott's work. As Susan Harris puts it, unlike the way that "[c]anonical male novels value the individual over his society" (54), novels by women feature "protagonists willing themselves into existence in an effort to *create* their own society," and in doing so, "women's novels anticipate the *real* problem of the twentieth century: how to nurture and protect a self . . . that is trying to work out the parameters of its obligations to others" (55). This makes Alcott's work important in terms of illuminating nineteenth-century literature and in illuminating the present as well. Alcott may have drawn much support from Charlotte Brontë as a foremother in that she created powerful females who did, indeed, will themselves into existence, but essentially she found no validation there for the concurrent notion of creating a new society; for that, she needed to rely on her Americanness. Ultimately, Louisa May Alcott could not be a Charlotte Brontë because she was not Charlotte Brontë; though personal background, gender, and a passion for writing linked them in important ways, her specific talents, cultural background, and temperament were different. She learned a great deal from her transatlantic mentor but needed to move in new directions as she willed herself into existence as a writer. As a result, examining the ways in which Alcott drew upon her reading of Charlotte Brontë in creating her own works is a step toward appreciating Alcott's unique talents more fully and toward placing her firmly among those nineteenth-century American writers eminently worthy of readers' continued attention.

NOTES

Chapter 1. Transatlantic Ties

1. Modern biographers continue to grapple with the problem of the accuracy of Gaskell's portrait of Patrick Brontë and of the children's early life at Haworth. Juliet Barker in *The Brontës* (1994), for example, contends that he was neither "the half-mad and violent eccentric described by Mrs. Gaskell" nor "a weird recluse" (108), that Gaskell's accounts of his dietary restrictions are contradicted by the recollections of Brontë servants, and that he was "clearly not only concerned for, but interested in, his children" (109). She also challenges Gaskell's view of the Brontës' extreme isolation at Haworth (90–99). On the other hand, Lyndall Gordon's *Charlotte Bronte: A Passionate Life* (1994) seems generally to accept Gaskell's view. What is most relevant here, however, is that Louisa May Alcott read Gaskell's version, in which the portraits of the father and of the sibling relationships did contain many parallels to her own situation.

2. In addition to Louisa Alcott's own comments on her father in her *Selected Letters* and *Journals,* major sources for information on Amos Bronson Alcott's life are Odell Shepard's *Pedlar's Progress* and Madelon Bedell's *The Alcotts.*

Chapter 2. Adoption and Adaptation

1. Nina Baym defines woman's fiction as works that are "written by women, are addressed to women, and tell one particular story about women. They chronicle the 'trials and triumph' . . . of a heroine who, beset with hardships, finds within herself the qualities of intelligence, will, resourcefulness, and courage sufficient to over-

come them," beginning with Catherine Sedgwick's *New-England Tale* in 1822 and remaining popular until after 1870 (*Woman's Fiction* 22). Although Alcott's original *Moods* clearly falls within the parameters of her study, Baym's only mention of Alcott is to equate the publication of *Little Women* with "the decline of woman's fiction" because it represented "the transformation of woman's fiction into girls' fiction" (296). She does admit, however, that Alcott "stands out above all the rest [of the women writers in her study] for creating not one, but several authentically human women characters" (299).

2. Many critics call reading pessimism into the opening words of *Jane Eyre* a misreading, since Jane hates walks and is in fact glad that the weather is miserable and so there is "no possibility of taking a walk" (7). However, Brontë's work at its most cheerful contains only constrained optimism, and this passage is at best equivocal; how is it possible to consider "There was no possibility" as the beginning of an optimistic tale?

3. Joel Myerson and Daniel Shealy discovered the manuscript of *The Inheritance* among the Alcott papers at Harvard's Houghton Library in 1988 when they were preparing a volume of Alcott's then-unpublished letters. A note attached to the manuscript in Alcott's hand indicated, "My first novel written at seventeen." There is no indication that Alcott ever tried to have it published in her lifetime. Editors Myerson and Shealy brought it to publication in 1997 in concert with a television movie *loosely* based on Alcott's story. The film version transplants the characters from England to America, and expands the horse-taming incident so extensively as to make the resulting tale resemble *National Velvet* as much as it does Alcott's text!

   In addition to the parallels with *Jane Eyre*, the novel may pay tribute to another of Alcott's lifelong favorite writers, Goethe. According to her journals, Emerson gave her *Wilhelm Meister* as a gift when she was fifteen, and "from that day Goethe has been my chief idol" (60; addendum to 1847 entry, dated 1885). The angelic Edith, picked up on Lord Hamilton's trip to Italy, resembles the lyrical child Mignon (also an orphan picked up in Italy) who so entrances Wilhelm; particularly, she entrances the family and their guest, Lord Percy, with songs she learned from her mother in Italy. Mignon, with her poignant song "Kennst du das Land?" ("Do You Know the Land?"), was one of the most well-known aspects of Goethe's novel. Even Beethoven once set it to music.

4. In fact, Elbert's comment is true in only the most general sense. Geoffrey Moor is no St. John Rivers; he is not a proper mate for

Sylvia because he doesn't understand her and because she doesn't love him, but he does love her and tries to make her happy. Brontë portrays Rivers as a cold clergyman who only wishes to make Jane his wife so she can "respectably" accompany him on a missionary expedition to India. When Jane refuses him, he informs her that "It is not me you deny, but God" (JE 414) and predicts for her a place "'in the lake which burneth with fire and brimstone'" (JE 422). On the other hand, when Sylvia finally reveals her true feelings about Warwick to Moor, now her husband, he rages but then grieves, asks her forgiveness for not knowing better that she was not ready to marry, and offers to go abroad until and unless she sends for him. Further, as suggested earlier, Alcott veers almost immediately from Adam as a Rochester figure; moreover, as Sylvia's wise friend and confidante Faith Dane helps her to understand, Warwick, unlike Rochester to Brontë, is not a suitable match, either.

5. I have come upon only three other possible references to Brontë's *Shirley* in Alcott's work, and these rather tenuous. A "Dr. Shirley" appears amid several other Brontëan references in the "Companion" chapter of *Work* and in "A Nurse's Story," which is in many respects the same tale. The third reference is in the title of another thriller first printed in *Frank Leslie's Illustrated Newspaper,* "Taming a Tartar." Although this story involves the conflict between an English woman and a "wild Russian," and most overtly alludes to Shakespeare's *The Taming of the Shrew,* the fact that the long confrontational scene in *Shirley* in which Louis Moore persuades Shirley to marry him repeatedly alludes to Shirley's dog, Tartar, with Moore attempting to prove that he should replace Tartar as Shirley's "dear companion" (S 620), suggests Brontë as a possible inspiration. *Shirley* is by no means Brontë's best work, but it does seem odd that it touched Alcott so little, considering its concern with female friendships and with spinsters.

6. Alcott's stories seldom end with marriage; even when a marriage takes place close to the end, "marriage" clearly means what comes *after* the ceremony. In *Little Women,* for example, Meg's marriage takes place in the opening chapters of volume 2, and several later chapters are devoted to the problems of adjusting to marriage and changing family dynamics when children are born. Jo's marriage takes place in a single line—"Jo found herself married and settled in at Plumfield" (484)—and the novel immediately turns its attentions to the school she and Friedrich found together. Alcott even teases about this in one story. "Psyche's Art" ends with the following paragraph:

Now, in order that every one may be suited, we will stop here, and leave our readers to finish the story as they like. Those who prefer the good old fashion may believe that the hero and heroine fell in love, were married and lived happily ever afterward. But those who can conceive of a world outside of a wedding-ring may believe that the friends remained faithful friends all their lives, while Paul won fame and fortune, and Psyche grew beautiful with the beauty of a serene and sunny nature, happy in duties which became pleasures, rich in the art which made life lovely to herself and others. (226)

This calls to mind Brontë's last novel, *Villette*, in which, after describing in great detail a storm that rages for seven days just as M. Paul's ship is about to come in, and would not quit until "The destroying angel of tempest had achieved his perfect work," she suddenly stops and continues:

> Here pause: pause at once. There is enough said. Trouble no quiet, kind heart; leave sunny imaginations hope. Let it be theirs to conceive the delight of joy born again fresh out of great terror, the rapture of rescue from peril, the wondrous reprieve, from dread the fruition of return. Let them picture union and a happy succeeding life. (596)

As so often happens when these two writers suggest similar plot lines, Alcott's is full of hope, but Brontë's leaves hope as the final refuge of the hopelessly naive.

7.   Elizabeth Keyser's superb *Whispers in the Dark* contains the first scholarly examination of allusions to Charlotte Brontë in Alcott's writing. In her study of Alcott's career, she notes references (from *Jane Eyre* only) in "Whispers in the Dark," "Behind a Mask," and *Work*. Keyser's thesis, in a thorough and informed analysis of Alcott's entire writing career, is that Alcott does not, as many critics have suggested, abandon or attempt to stifle her progressive social views beginning with the writing of *Little Women*, but shapes the radicalism in her texts in increasingly subversive ways so that the discerning reader can still detect a critique of traditional values within them. Alcott's allusions to Brontë, Margaret Fuller, and especially to Nathaniel Hawthorne are, to Keyser, evidence of her continuing adherence to unconventional ideas.

In *Work*, Keyser notes connections to *Jane Eyre* in the "hereditary madness" plot of the "Companion" chapter (see note 10 below), in

Christie's impulse to cast David as a Byronic hero, and in the proposal scene between Christie and Philip Fletcher, where she rightly
comments in a note that Christie rejects Philip in an "impassioned
speech similar to the one in which Jane declares her equality with
Rochester" (204, note 7). However, I differ with Keyser's discussion at
several points. First, she says twice that Christie is "under the influence
of *Jane Eyre*" when she is "tempted to marry Philip Fletcher" (101), with
the contextual implication that she wishes to follow in Jane's foot-
steps because she is still in an immature, romantic state. Christie's
own comments reveal resistance to, rather than influence by, the
Jane/Rochester match. Christie "makes up her mind to accept, if this
promotion was offered her" (79) after she has overheard the gossips
at the seashore commenting negatively upon Fletcher's noticeable
interest in his sister's governess: after several derogatory remarks
on Christie's lack of style, they say, "No danger of his marrying *her*"
(78). This attack on her vanity, and the thought of an end to her
financial struggles, convinces her to hear Philip out, although she
recognizes it would mean "to marry without love" (79). Further, even
when "her reply was all ready," he asks and "she found it was not, and
sat silent" (82), even *before* Fletcher makes his condescending remarks.
Christie may be under the influence of poverty, vanity, and loneliness, but here, and in this whole first section of the book, Alcott
works strongly *against* the influence of *Jane Eyre*. As Elaine Showalter
puts it more accurately, Christie "*revises* the romantic fantasies of *Jane
Eyre*" (Introduction, *Alternative Alcott* xxxii; emphasis mine) in this scene.

Second, in describing Christie's depression and near suicide,
Keyser contends that she "tries to find salvation in living for others
but only succeeds in bringing herself to the verge of suicide" (102),
an allusion to the fact that Christie continues to give away part of
her earnings to those less fortunate than her, even after she loses
her factory job. Alcott clearly indicates that it is life *without* others
that brings Christie to this point: she specifically writes that it is *not*
"want, insanity, or sin," but "a dreadful loneliness of heart, a hunger
for home and friends, worse than starvation" (150) that is Christie's
overwhelming problem. This is an important distinction because it
is a fallacy in too much modern scholarship about Alcott. She—
and her heroines—value both independence *and* community.

Finally, Keyser describes *Work* as a three-phase novel, consisting of "youthful ambition and adventure, disillusionment and
despair, and recovery facilitated by courtship and marriage" (101).
Although her pursuant discussion of the novel demonstrates that
Keyser knows this summary to be incomplete, this is still troubling

because Alcott so strongly resists the notion that life ends with marriage (see note 6, above). In fact, in *Work*, there is both more adventure and more despair *after* the marriage. Life, she knew, does not go in a straight line according to the male *bildungsroman*, but in cycles.

8. For *Pilgrim's Progress* as a model for *Work*, see the essays by Elizabeth Langland and Paula Kot; Langland argues that *Work* parallels Christian's journey, while Kot suggests the true parallel is with Christiana's.

9. The fact that Alcott's employment as companion to the invalid Anna Weld took place during 1865–66, and that she published a thriller called "A Nurse's Story" with the same plot during this time (December 1865–January 1866) suggests to me that this chapter was not part of the original story of "Success," but was added sometime after she first worked on the project in 1863–64. Further, the tone of this chapter is markedly more serious than Christie's adventures thus far in the novel, and the more accomplished writing alludes to Brontë in the oblique and subtle ways characteristic of her later work.

10. Elizabeth Keyser rightly notes that Alcott seems deliberately to put the hereditary madness in the father's line rather than the mother's. However, I am not convinced that this necessarily means that "Alcott directly associates madness with patriarchy" (107) in any other than a strictly biological sense.

11. Sarah Elbert's newly edited version of *Moods* reprints the entire 1865 edition, then adds the portions new to the 1882 edition in an appendix entitled "Selections from *Moods*, 1882," pp. 225–80 in this volume. All quotes from the 1882 version of *Moods* refer to these pages. Elbert writes that "The revised *Moods* is a tidier, more formulaic work, but it is the first version . . . that moves readers deeply" (xv). For the reasons discussed in this chapter, I find that the later version represents an Alcott more mature both as a writer and as a thinker than the earlier one. Also, I am much more moved by the Sylvia who comes into sharper focus as a character due to Alcott's revisions and who lives and tries to put her life back together after making a terrible mistake, than the one who conveniently dies and therefore doesn't have to deal with the consequences of her error.

12. Ironically, the only time Emerson ever seems to comment directly on Charlotte Brontë is in a reference to the novel Alcott virtually ignores: *Shirley*. In a journal entry dated April 6, 1850, he writes, "I think a novel like *Shirley* must cultivate its readers. It is very useful to each in his kind" (Emerson, *Journals* 109).

13. In no way do I mean to imply that Charlotte Brontë was a sensation

novelist. Although she makes use of coincidence, gothic occurrences, exposition of social problems, and strong central female characters as did the sensation writers, her fiction is clearly at a different level of art than that of the story papers for which Alcott was writing. The possibility that she could employ certain elements of Brontë's fiction as she participated in this genre, however, was clearly not lost on Louisa Alcott.

14. Thanks to Greg Eiselein of Kansas State University for the initial suggestion that "Behind a Mask" might have some plot connections with *Vanity Fair.* Indeed, Jean's actions and character have much in common with those of Becky Sharp, who also tries to marry her way to fortune and is often motivated by a desire for revenge upon characters who belittle her for reasons of social class. Becky, however, settles too soon for the younger son, Rawdon Crawley, and so is unable to marry Sir Pitt when he finally proposes to her. Even the name "Coventry" may be taken from this novel; Rawdon eventually takes a military post at Coventry Island to get away from Becky, where he dies of yellow fever.

15. Rosamond's name may allude to the "Fair Rosamond" of English legend, who was a mistress of Henry II. Henry built a virtually inaccessible house for her, called Labyrinthus, but Queen Elinor found her way to it and poisoned Rosamond. Sir Walter Scott alludes to her story in two of his novels, *The Talisman* (1825) and *Woodstock* (1826). Alcott seems to have in mind the inaccessibility of Rosamond's island home, and possibly the disaster that ensues when one person (Tempest) makes his way to her. Another possible source is the eponymous heroine of Maria Edgeworth's *Rosamond* (1801), a collection of stories for children which Abba Alcott read aloud to her daughters on Louisa's eleventh birthday, according to her 1843 journal (*Journals* 47; 29 November 1843).

    In a chapter on American women writers' fascination with the character of Shakespeare's Miranda, Elaine Showalter says the character's name in Alcott's story is Miranda (*Sister's Choice* 35). While Philip Tempest *calls* her his Miranda once, while alluding to her loneliness and isolation, Rosamond is her name throughout the story. Showalter also says the story was written in 1867. However, Alcott had already received a refusal from publisher James Elliott, who, after commissioning it from Alcott, returned it to her saying it was "too long and too sensational" (*Journals* 153), in September 1866.

16. Alcott was not alone in her troubled attitude regarding Rochester. The *North American Review* complained that "the profanity, brutality, and

slang of the misanthropic profligate give their torpedo shocks to the nervous system" ("Novels of the Season" 357). Lydia Maria Child, after writing to her friend that she "sat up all night" to finish reading *Jane Eyre,* and that "I could have loved him [Rochester] with my whole heart," had to admit that "I wanted conscience to come in and check him. . . . I wish he had said, 'Jane, I *cannot* deceive you.' . . . [I]t would have saved the nobleness of Rochester's love for Jane, which has only this one blot of deception" (Meltzer and Holland 239). She must have forgotten about the gypsy scene and about Rochester's perverse proposal, in which he first suggests she take a job in Ireland as governess to "the five daughters of Mrs. Dionysius O'Gall of Butternutt Lodge" (*JE* 253).

17. In *Hospital Sketches* and in "My Contraband," two early works based heavily upon Alcott's experiences as a Civil War nurse, Alcott easily adopts the first-person narrative voices of nurses Tribulation Periwinkle and Faith Dane, respectively. In two sensation stories, "A Skeleton in the Closet" and "A Double Tragedy," she takes on the male persona of the heroine's lover, with less success (as had Brontë in *The Professor*).

18. Sarah Elbert notes (*Hunger* 195–96) that the term also is used repeatedly by another of Alcott's favorite writers, Charles Dickens, in reference to Esther in *Bleak House* (1854), and suggests Dickens as the source of the title of Alcott's novel. The editors of Alcott's *Selected Letters* claim that publisher Thomas Niles himself suggested the title in a letter dated 16 June 1868 (*Letters* 119, note 1).

19. At a forum organized by the Harriet Beecher Stowe Foundation in Hartford on March 16, 1995, participants were encouraged to respond to the book and movie versions of *Little Women.* Two responses were especially interesting in view of this discussion of Professor Bhaer as a mate for Jo. One woman said that the marriage never really bothered her because "Jo was always doing something unusual, so this was just another one of her unusual behaviors." Another woman, whose parents were Irish immigrants, said she and her mother found the marriage offensive to the idea of the American dream because Jo married "a foreigner."

20. Brontë's attitude toward the spying in *Villette,* especially as Madame Beck and her cohorts use it, sounds like Michel Foucault's description of the principle of surveillance in *Discipline and Punish.* Although Foucault's book is ostensibly a history of prison systems, the use of constant surveillance in order to control people's actions is a philosophical principle that Madame Beck uses most effectively in her pensionnat.

Chapter 3. The Inner Life

1. Details of English religious history here are mostly drawn from D. G. Paz, *Popular Anti-Catholicism in Mid-Victorian England*, and Kenneth Scott Latourette, *The Nineteenth Century in Europe* (Volume II of *Christianity in a Revolutionary Age*). On the American side, Russell Blaine Nye's *Society and Culture in America, 1830–1860*, and Ira Mandelker's *Religion, Society, and Utopia in Nineteenth-Century America* were most helpful.

2. Given the extent to which Brontë drew upon her experiences at the Pensionnat Heger in creating *Villette*, it is tempting to assume that Brontë's anti-Catholicism may have been formed there. However, Aïda Hudson contends that "Charlotte's anti-Catholicism was fully developed before she ever went to Brussels" (75). Hudson cites as convincing evidence an early Brontë poem entitled "Apostasy." In the poem, a priest badgers a dying woman who has converted to Protestantism to reconvert. The woman refuses; the poem ends with the lines, "Not Death shall shake, nor Priestcraft break/My rock-like constancy."

3. Brontë seems to have mistrusted public displays of religion of any kind. As Peters asserts, "Religion for Charlotte, Emily, and Anne was always to remain a private affair, a communication between God and individual" (60).

4. At the time of the American Revolution, nine of the thirteen American colonies had established churches that citizens were required by law to support and attend. However, disestablishment followed revolt, beginning with New York in 1777 and ending with Massachusetts in 1833 (Douglas 23). The claims of both religious freedom and lower levels of anti-Catholic sentiment in America expressed here should be understood as *relative to* the situation in England. One need only consider the fact that the United States did not elect a Catholic president until 1960; even then, there was enough mistrust of Catholicism in the country that the Republican campaign claimed that if John Kennedy were elected, his first allegiance would necessarily be to the pope, not to the American people. In turn, Catholic joy at Kennedy's election suggests their hope that American Catholics, if not the Vatican, would occupy an important part of Kennedy's attentions.

5. Useful references on the life and philosophy of Theodore Parker are Henry Steele Commager, *Theodore Parker*, R. C. Albrecht, *Theodore Parker*, and Robert E. Collins, *Theodore Parker: American Transcendentalist*.

6. Estes and Lant claim that "the force Mr. Power represents is the hierarchical, patriarchal power that Christie previously shunned" (244), that "he is a Satanic figure" (245) because he tempts Christie

back into the heterosexual world and out of her all-female "Paradise," and that because Alcott occasionally records criticism of her father and Emerson, "It would not be surprising, then, if her feelings toward Parker were also characterized by this ambivalence" (244). Their negative reading of Power's character ignores Alcott's uniformly positive references to Parker in her letters and journals and also the text of *Work*, where Mr. Power's character is never anything but good. The anti-male bias that informs this essay is unfortunate, for the overall idea of Christie as a female redeemer is an interesting one in light of Alcott's comment that "Women need a religion of thier [sic] own" (*Letters* 277; 5 February 1884).

7. In addition to the works cited here, both Ann Douglas and Amanda Porterfield substantiate the powerful influence of American women in reshaping church doctrine in the nineteenth century. Douglas, however, considers it to be a largely deleterious phenomenon.

8. Anne Phillips contends that Alcott's interest shifts from "self-actualizing" to "self-negating" images—from "pilgrims" to "missionaries" (213)—as she moves her characters from childhood into adolescence through the 1870s, using *Little Women* and *Jack and Jill* as her respective examples. This same pattern, though in much more positive form, characterizes her treatment of Christie's developing spirituality in *Work*, published in 1873. Christie's shift shows a relatively fully actualized forty-year-old self moving outward to make a difference in the larger world, rather than an adolescent giving up the struggle for selfhood and retreating into conformity.

9. In *Jo's Boys*, Dan's recovery from despair in prison begins with Mason, a suffering fellow prisoner he befriends and cares for, progresses when Mason sends the prison chaplain to him with a deathbed message, and culminates with a sermon given by a woman who comes to talk at the prison on the Sunday before Thanksgiving. The situation is almost a perfect gender reversal of Christie's recovery in *Work* through the efforts of Rachel, Mrs. Wilkins, and Reverend Power.

10. This appellation, linking Power with the feminine, serves as a chapter title in *Work*.

11. The hymn was written in 1841 by Sarah Adams (Welter 89).

12. Alcott's characterization of Christ puts Estes and Lant's reading of Christie as a "Female Christ" on rather shaky ground, for throughout the essay, they insist on reading *supernatural* interpretations of Christie's actions into Alcott's text, such as her working of miracles and her death, resurrection, and ascension. Alcott's letters to Maggie Lukens detailing her religious beliefs (*Letters* 275–80; 14 January 1884, 5 February 1884, 14 February 1884) make clear her more human understand-

ing of Christ. They also refer to the influence of Theodore Parker, who preached against belief in miracles. Thus it seems unlikely that *Work* was meant as a "parable" (226) whose hidden meaning has to do with the coming of Christie as the kind of female savior envisioned by Hester Prynne. Christie, however, *is* a Christ figure in Alcott's terms—a great reformer—and so is Reverend Power.

Chapter 4. The Consociate Life

1. Extensive work on how nineteenth-century periodicals present the problem of the "superabundant" woman has been done by Nina Auerbach (American and British) and Pauline Nestor (British), whose introductions pointed the way to valuable resources for this study. Duncan Crow's *The Victorian Woman* also makes much use of periodicals in its examination of varied aspects of the Victorian woman's life, principally though not exclusively in England.

2. Nestor states that at the end of *Shirley*, "Brontë suggests the completeness of the bond where feminine and masculine are integrated rather than opposed and she does so through a narrative voice not identified as belonging to either gender" (124). While the question of *Shirley*'s narrator is an interesting one, this seems an overly optimistic reading of the end of this novel. The truly "integrated" relationship, the friendship between Shirley and Caroline, has been usurped by the male-dominant marriages, and the novel ends with the observation that manufacturing has driven all the magic out of the land. This is domination, not integration.

3. An essay in the *Imperial Review* entitled "True Colleges for Women" highlights one of the most troubling aspects of girls' schools in its statement that

> the congregating of young girls at a certain age, either in boarding-schools, true college, or any other gregarious establishment . . . is a downright forcing of minds which ought, for the moment, to be kept as dormant as possible. By minds we do not mean intellects; we mean what everybody who is acquainted with human nature will understand. It is on this account, and on this alone, that female boarding-schools are so unspeakably pernicious. (1867; qtd. in Crow 199)

Clearly, the threat to the girls' "dormant" sexuality is the true issue. Brontë incorporates this attitude into her portrait of Madame Beck, obsessed with her students' private lives even as she minimizes her attention to their intellectual pursuits.

4. Both Paulina and Ginevra are beautiful and rich, and both get the traditional marriages that, according to Brontë, such as they can expect. Lucy's final comment on the former is that "Graham and Paulina were blessed, like that of Jacob's favoured son. . . . It was so, for God saw that it was good" (533). Ginevra, an immensely likable character despite her many shortcomings, "got on—fighting the battle of life by proxy, and, on the whole, suffering as little as any human being I have ever known" (577). Their marriages and resulting happiness make it clear that Brontë's resignation refers specifically to the many women like Lucy (and, like Brontë's image of herself) who, without the advantages of wealth or beauty, could not really expect to marry.

5. U. S. Census data for 1850 report 11.8 million men and 11.3 million women, almost the reverse of the situation in England, with double the population (U.S. Dept. of Commerce Chart A 91–104; 14).

6. While many other examples of the principles of relationships discussed in the rest of this chapter—marriages, the single life, and community life—can be found in other works by Alcott than the ones discussed here, I am limiting the discussion to those works in which specific connections with Brontë have already been demonstrated. For a selection of Alcott's works and excerpts of works that especially emphasize her celebrations of single women and communities of women, see *Alternative Alcott*.

7. The 1880 U.S. Census reported an even larger gender gap than in 1850, 25.5 million men to 24.6 million women. However, the figures for New England do show the discrepancy noted by Jo's nephew: 7.1 million men and 7.3 million women (U.S. Dept. of Commerce charts A 91–104 and A 172–94; 14, 22).

8. Alcott, desperate to pay bills and send some money home, declared that "If he [Mr. Bonner, who commissioned her to write the advice column] had asked me for a Greek oration I would have said 'Yes'" (*Journals* 164).

9. Nina Baym's intriguing comment on the relationship in *Jane Eyre* is that "Jane's goal in the novel is dominance while the goal of all the American heroines [in her study] is independence" (*Woman's Fiction* 30). While most critics focus on the *equality* of Jane and Rochester, or whether or not Jane is truly an equal at the end of the novel, it is certainly true that Jane thrives on Rochester's physical and emotional dependence upon her, which gives her power over him, and that most relationships in Brontë focus on issues of power. Issues of dominance vs. independence would seem to mark the American-British literary (in addition to the political) struggle in general, and also to reflect a difference between a society built

upon social classes in contrast to a society constructed upon democratic principles. It would be worth exploring whether, as America's rich and poor have moved further apart into increasingly well-defined social classes, contemporary literature has increasingly concerned itself with power issues.

10. I am tempted to use Sandra Zagarell's phrase "narratives of community" to describe these works. However, except for the children's novels, the plot does not revolve around the community in Alcott's works in the same sense as it does, for instance, in Elizabeth Gaskell's *Cranford*, where the community itself is the hero, which is how Zagarell defines the genre. In Alcott's adult works, community is more of a proposed narrative outcome, an alternative denouement to death or marriage—or Brontë's lonely spinsterhood. However, Zagarell's comments on such narratives certainly inform my thinking on Alcott's alternative communities.

11. Nina Auerbach implies that in *Jo's Boys*, Alcott creates a pseudo-Shaker community: "She seems quite deliberately to shape her father's Utopian vision to . . . the rival paradise that destroyed his own" (71). However appealing the more equitable division of labor that marked the Shakers might have been to Alcott, it seems unlikely, given her attachment to family, that their nonconjugal living arrangements would have appealed to her. Even Louisa's mother, the "beast of burden" at Fruitlands, wrote in her journal about her visit to the Shakers:

> Visited the Shakers. I gain but little from their domestic or internal arrangements. There is servitude somewhere, I have no doubt. There is a fat sleek comfortable look about the men, and among the women there is a still awkward reserve that belongs to neither sublime resignation nor divine hope. (2 July 1843; qtd. in Shepard 153)

Further, it would be a stretch to say that the Shaker community was responsible for the demise of Fruitlands. It had enough problems for it to collapse without any outside assistance.

12. Alcott's rendering of Steele as broken financially, mentally, and spiritually at the end of "A Nurse's Story" is a "blasting" to rival *Jane Eyre*'s Rochester. Alcott's heroine nurses, but does not marry, the broken man, however.

13. The question of Jo's marriage leaves few readers of the March trilogy neutral. Professor Bhaer has been repeatedly denigrated as a match for Jo, mostly on grounds of his passionlessness, by critics who either seem not to be able to forgive Jo for not marrying

Laurie or who can't forgive her for marrying *anyone* (see Showalter, *Sister's Choice* 61–62). Strickland, for example, calls him "an unfortunate male creation" (104). Some critics have more recently been kinder to him (see Elbert 210), including Showalter herself, whose position in *Sister's Choice* is more moderate than her own earlier assessment (e.g., in the Introduction to *Alternative Alcott*). I agree with Showalter that "As a couple, Jo and Bhaer have both values and feelings in common; they share an interest in educational reform, in new ideas, and in practical philanthropy. Most important, he understands her need to work" (*Sister's Choice* 62). Critics may not like Jo's choice, but I think there is little doubt that Alcott did: theirs is the kind of ideal marriage about which she writes constantly, and managed to create for a character very much like herself.

Incidentally, the newest (1994) film of *Little Women* provides Jo with an unquestionably virile (though beardless) Friedrich in the person of Gabriel Byrne.

Chapter 5. The Professional Life

1. Nursing, for example, though historically a suspect occupation for women in England (see Brontë's characterization of Grace Poole, for example), became much more respected after the efforts of Florence Nightingale and her nurses in the Crimean War. Journalism and feminism merged with the founding of the *English Women's Journal* in 1858; in 1859, the *Journal* began to share offices with the newly founded Society for Promoting the Employment of Women, which sought to establish schools in which women could be trained for "trades and occupations which are at present exclusively occupied by men" (Crow 159)—work such as clerks and cashiers, among other occupations.

2. Louisa Alcott, who died unmarried, even adopted her nephew, John Pratt, in order that he and his descendents might keep the rights to publications in the family and so continue to help support her family after her death.

3. According to Mary Poovey, the first Governesses' Benevolent Institution dissolved due to lack of funds after only nine years (1829–38) of trying to help former governesses who were infirm, elderly, or otherwise unemployed. When it reorganized in 1843, it also became increasingly class-specific, restricting its assistance to women who were truly from the upper classes and going so far as to establish separate residences and charities for lower-class women (129; 232n; also see Peterson 21).

4. This is not to suggest that Alcott—or American culture—was oblivious to issues of class. Christie, for instance, reminds the reader at several points that her father was a gentleman, though poor; Mrs. Wilkins, who takes her in at the lowest point of her despair, quickly notices her "unfitness for her present place" (209), Mrs. Wilkins's own working-class family. The narrator of *Work* comments at one point: "People wonder when such as [Christie] say they can find little to do; but to those . . . who tell them [poor gentlewomen] to go into factories, or scrub in kitchens, for there is work enough for all, the most convincing answer would be, 'Try it'" (W 149).

   Strickland (153–56) discusses how Alcott drew distinctions between what he calls "the 'worthy' and the 'unworthy' poor" (153) in both her work and her life. Ruth MacDonald notes the "class-conscious snobbery" (62) Alcott sometimes exhibits in the pairings-off in the children's novels, especially with Archie and Phebe of *Rose in Bloom* and Dan and Bess in *Jo's Boys*. Keyser, however, suggests that, at least in the case of Dan and Bess, Alcott's hesitation has less to do with class considerations and more to do with "how hard it is for even the most enlightened woman to relinquish the notion of separate spheres" (178) regarding marriage and career—that is, that she fears that Dan's sensuality would destroy Bess's passion for her artistic career. I think Keyser goes too far in suggesting that Mrs. Jo attempts to turn some of Dan's eroticism toward herself to mitigate the "onerous obligation" of her "passionless union with Professor Bhaer" (178). As I stated previously, I agree with Showalter's more positive assessment of Jo's marriage (*Sister's Choice* 57–62); nevertheless, I believe that Keyser is both insightful and accurate in detecting Alcott's internal conflicts regarding marriage and career, a theme she explored repeatedly in her fiction.

5. As Alcott was to turn her adoration of the great Charlotte Cushman into the magnanimous Miss Cameron of *Jo's Boys* (see below), Vashti—and Lucy's reaction to her—are almost certainly based upon Brontë's attendance at a London performance by the French actress Rachel Félix, "the greatest actress of her time" (Stokes 771). Brontë wrote of the experience:

   > I went to hear and see Rachel; a wonderful sight—terrible as if the earth had cracked deep at your feet, and revealed a glimpse of hell. I shall never forget it. She made me shudder to the marrow of my bones; in her some fiend has certainly taken up an incarnate home. She is not a woman, she is a snake; she is the ———. (June 2, 1851; qtd. in Gaskell 332)

As in "Behind a Mask," discussed below, Alcott uses the name Vashti as synonymous with "actress" on the first page of *Hospital Sketches,* a work otherwise not particularly indebted to Brontë. As heroine Tribulation Periwinkle is looking for "something to do," her "sister Vashti" suggests, "Turn actress, and immortalize your name" (3).

6. It should be noted that Alcott had at least one compellingly positive literary model for the uses of theatricality: Goethe. Goethe's Wilhelm Meister (whose tale Alcott said made Goethe her "chief idol" [*Journals* 60; comment added in 1885] ever after) spends nearly the entire first book of his apprenticeship tale relating the story of how he became enamored of theater at an early age, an interest that included writing and acting in Christmas theatricals in his home. Wilhelm spends nearly two-thirds of the novel in the company of a troupe of actors. Further, Goethe himself oversaw the court theater at Weimar for nearly forty years.

7. Keyser's analysis of Alcott's use of theatricality as a motif throughout her career is an impressive aspect of *Whispers in the Dark.* Of the works discussed here, Keyser includes examples of acting in *Work, Moods,* "Behind a Mask," and *Jo's Boys.*

8. This image from *Jane Eyre* and its implications interest Alcott greatly. In another story, "The Skeleton in the Closet," the heroine wears a bracelet "of steel, delicately wrought, clasped by a golden lock, the tiny key of which hung by a golden chain" (245). The key, as it turns out, unlocks the door to a part of her home where she helps and tends her mad husband. When the husband dies, the hero proposes:

> "Dearest Mathilde, you are a captive still, not to duty, but to love, whose thralldom shall be to you as light as the fetter I now bind you with." And as I spoke I clasped a slender chain of gold upon the fair arm where for nine bitter years lay the weight of that steel bracelet. (269)

Despite the love expressed, this ending is disturbing, for the narrator's voice and his final act suggest his control over Mathilde. Usually in Alcott's work, when power remains wholly in male hands, the relationship cannot be equal—and an unequal marriage, to use Jane Eyre's words, is merely a new servitude.

WORKS CITED

Alberghene, Janice M. and Beverly Lyon Clark, eds. Little Women *and the Feminist Imagination*. New York: Garland, 1999.

Albrecht, R. C. *Theodore Parker*. New York: Twayne, 1971.

Alcott, Abigail May. Diary, May 1869. Fragments of an Autobiography, Alcott collection, Houghton Library, Harvard University.

Alcott, Louisa May. *Alternative Alcott*. Ed. Elaine Showalter. New Brunswick: Rutgers University Press, 1988.

———. "Behind a Mask." 1866. *Alternative Alcott (AA)*. Introduction by Elaine Showalter. New Brunswick and London: Rutgers UP, 1988. 95–184.

———. *Behind a Mask: The Unknown Thrillers of Louisa May Alcott*. Ed. Madeleine Stern. New York: Avenel, 1975.

———. *Diana and Persis*. Ed. Sarah Elbert. New York: Arno, 1978.

———. "A Double Tragedy. An Actor's Story." 1865. *A Double Life*. Ed. Madeleine B. Stern, Joel Myerson, and Daniel Shealy. Boston: Little, Brown, 1988. 127–50.

———. "Fair Rosamond." Unpublished manuscript. Alcott Papers, Houghton Library, Harvard University.

———. *Flower Fables*. Boston: George W. Briggs & Co., 1855.

———. *Hospital Sketches*. 1863. *Alternative Alcott (AA)*. Introduction by Elaine Showalter. New Brunswick and London: Rutgers UP, 1988. 1–73.

———. *The Inheritance*. Ed. Joel Myerson and Daniel Shealy. New York: Dutton, 1997.

———. *Jack and Jill (JJ)*. 1880. London: Sampson, Low, Marston & Company, n.d.

———. *Jo's Boys (JB)*. 1886. London: Sampson Low, Marston, Searle & Rivington, Ltd., 1890.

———. *The Journals of Louisa May Alcott (Journals)*. Ed. Joel Myerson, Daniel Shealy, and Madeleine B. Stern. Boston: Little, Brown, 1989.

———. *Little Women (LW)*. 1868. Introduction by Elaine Showalter. New York: Viking Penguin, 1989.

———. *A Long Fatal Love Chase*. Ed. Kent Bicknell. New York: Random House, 1995.

———. *Louisa May Alcott Unmasked*. Ed. Madeleine Stern. Boston: Northeastern UP, 1995.

———. *A Modern Mephistopheles and Taming a Tartar (AMM)*. 1877 and 1867. Introduction by Madeleine B. Stern. New York: Praeger, 1987.

———. *Moods (M)*. 1864. Ed. Sarah Elbert, with an Introduction. New Brunswick and London: Rutgers UP, 1991.

———. "A Nurse's Story." 1865–66. *Freaks of Genius: Unknown Thrillers of Louisa May Alcott*. Ed. Daniel Shealy, Madeleine B. Stern, and Joel Myerson. Westport, CT: Greenwood, 1991. 29–114.

———. "Psyche's Art." 1868. *Alternative Alcott (AA)*. Ed. Elaine Showalter. New Brunswick: Rutgers UP, 1988. 207–26.

———. *Rose in Bloom*. 1876. Boston: Little, Brown, 1904.

———. *The Selected Letters of Louisa May Alcott (Letters)*. Ed. Joel Myerson, Daniel Shealy, and Madeleine B. Stern. Boston: Little, Brown, 1987.

———. "The Skeleton in the Closet." 1867. *Plots and Counterplots*. Ed. Madeleine B. Stern. New York: William Morrow, 1976. 239–60.

———. "V. V.: or, Plots and Counterplots." 1865. *Plots and Counterplots*. Ed. Madeleine B. Stern. New York: William Morrow, 1976. 41–130.

———. *Work (W)*. 1873. Introduction by Sarah Elbert. New York: Schocken Books, 1977.

Allott, Miriam, ed. *The Brontës: The Critical Heritage*. London: Routledge & Kegan Paul, 1974.

Auerbach, Nina. *Communities of Women: An Idea in Fiction*. Cambridge: Harvard UP, 1978.

Auster, Albert. *Actresses and Suffragists*. New York: Praeger, 1984.

Barish, Jonas A. *The Antitheatrical Prejudice*. Berkeley and Los Angeles: U of California P, 1981.

Barker, Juliet. *The Brontës*. New York: St. Martin's, 1994.

Baym, Nina. *Novels, Readers, and Reviewers: Responses to Fiction in Antebellum America*. Ithaca: Cornell UP, 1984.

———. *Woman's Fiction: A Guide to Novels by and about Women in America, 1820–1870*. Ithaca: Cornell UP, 1978.

Bedell, Madelon. *The Alcotts: Biography of a Family*. New York: Clarkson N. Potter, 1980.

————. Introduction. Louisa May Alcott, *Little Women*. New York: Random House, 1983.

Beer, Thomas. *The Mauve Decade*. New York: Knopf, 1926.

Black, Eugene C., ed. *Victorian Culture and Society*. New York: Walker and Company, 1974.

Bloom, Harold. *The Anxiety of Influence: A Theory of Poetry*. Oxford: Oxford UP, 1973.

Bodenheimer, Rosemarie. "Jane Eyre in Search of Her Story." *The Brontës*. Ed. Harold Bloom. New York: Chelsea House, 1987. 155–68.

Brodhead, Richard H. *Cultures of Letters: Scenes of Reading and Writing in Nineteenth-Century America*. Chicago: U of Chicago P, 1993.

Brontë, Charlotte. *Jane Eyre (JE)*. 1847. Oxford: Oxford UP, 1975.

————. *The Professor and Emma, a Fragment (P)*. 1857. London: J. M. Dent & Sons, 1985.

————. *Shirley (S)*. 1849. Oxford: Oxford UP, 1979.

————. *Villette (V)*. 1853. Hammondsworth, England: Penguin Books, 1979.

Brownson, Orestes. *The Works of Orestes A. Brownson, Collected and Arranged by Henry F. Brownson*. Detroit: T. Nourse, 1882–88.

Burlingame, Edward R. Rev. of *A Modern Mephistopheles*. *North American Review* 125 (Sept. 1877): 316–18.

Butcher, Patricia Smith. *Education for Equality*. Westport, CT: Greenwood, 1989.

Carey, Alice. "Louisa, We Hardly Knew Ye." *Boston Magazine* 86.12 (Dec. 1994): 58–61, 92–96.

Carpenter, Lynette. "'Did They Never See Anyone Angry Before?' The Sexual Politics of Self-Control in Alcott's 'A Whisper in the Dark.'" *Legacy: A Journal of Nineteenth-Century Women Writers* 3.2 (Fall 1986): 31–41.

Carrigan, Celine. "Versions of the Governess: Narrative Patterns in Ellen Weeton, Elizabeth Gaskell, and Charlotte Brontë." Diss. U of Notre Dame, 1988.

"Charlotte Brontë and the Brontë Novels." *North American Review* 177 (Oct. 1857): 295–329.

Cheney, Ednah Dow. *Louisa May Alcott: Her Life, Letters, and Journals*. 1889. Boston: Roberts Brothers, 1895.

Chesterton, G. K. "Louisa Alcott." *A Handful of Authors: Essays on Books and Writers*. Ed. Dorothy Collins. New York: Sheed & Ward, 1953. 163–67. Rpt. from the *Nation*, 1907.

Cobbe, Frances. "Female Charity—Lay and Monastic." *Fraser's Magazine* (Feb. 1862): 774–88.

Collins, Robert E. *Theodore Parker: American Transcendentalist*. Metuchen, NJ: Scarecrow, 1973.

Commager, Henry Steele. *Theodore Parker.* 1947. Gloucester, MA: Peter Smith, 1978.

"Contemporary Literature." *The Ladies' Repository* 28 (Dec. 1868): 472.

Cott, Nancy F. *The Bonds of Womanhood.* New Haven: Yale UP, 1977.

Craik, Dinah Mulock. *About Money and Other Things.* London: Macmillan & Co., 1886.

Crisler, Jesse. "Alcott's Reading in *Little Women:* Shaping the Autobiographical Self." *Resources for American Literary Study* 20.1 (1994): 27–36.

Crow, Duncan. *The Victorian Woman.* New York: Stein and Day, 1972.

Dalzeil, Margaret. *Popular Fiction 100 Years Ago: An Unexplored Tract of Literary History.* London: Cohen & West, 1957.

Douglas, Ann. *The Feminization of American Culture.* New York: Knopf, 1977.

Du Plessis, Rachel Blau. *Writing Beyond the Ending: Narrative Strategies of Twentieth-Century Women Writers.* Bloomington: Indiana UP, 1985.

"Editor's Table." *Godey's Lady's Book* Apr. 1855: 367–70.

Elbert, Sarah. *A Hunger for Home: Louisa May Alcott's Place in American Culture.* New Brunswick and London: Rutgers UP, 1987.

———. Introduction. *Moods.* New York: Schocken Books, 1977.

Emerson, Ralph Waldo. *Emerson Essays.* Introduction by Sherman Paul. New York: Dutton, 1976.

———. *The Letters of Ralph Waldo Emerson.* Ed. Ralph L. Rusk. New York: Columbia UP, 1939.

Estes, Angela, and Kathleen Margaret Lant. "Dismembering the Text: The Horror of Louisa May Alcott's *Little Women.*" *Children's Literature* 17 (1989): 98–123.

———. "The Feminist Redeemer: Alcott's Creation of the Female Christ in *Work.*" *Christianity and Literature* 40.3 (Spring 1991): 223–53.

Farr, Judith. "Charlotte Brontë, Emily Brontë, and the 'Undying Life' Within." *Victorians Institute Journal* 17 (1989): 87–104.

Foucault, Michel. *Discipline and Punish.* Trans. Alan Sheridan. New York: Vintage Books, 1979.

Francis, Richard. "Circumstances and Salvation: The Ideology of the Fruitlands Utopia." *American Quarterly* 25.2 (May 1973): 202–34.

Fraser, Rebecca. *The Brontës.* New York: Crown, 1988.

Gardner, Vivien. Introduction. *The New Woman and Her Sisters.* Ed. Vivien Gardner and Susan Rutherford. Ann Arbor: U of Michigan P, 1992. 1–14.

Gaskell, Elizabeth. *The Life of Charlotte Brontë.* 1857. Edinburgh: John Grant, 1924.

Gérin, Winifred. *Charlotte Brontë: The Evolution of Genius.* Oxford: Oxford UP, 1967.

Gilbert, Sandra M., and Susan Gubar. *The Madwoman in the Attic.* New Haven: Yale UP, 1979.

Gordon, Lyndall. *Charlotte Brontë: A Passionate Life.* New York: Norton, 1994.

Harper's Weekly 9 (21 Jan. 1865): 35. (Review of *Moods.*)

Harrington, Henry F. "Female Education." *Ladies' Companion* 9 (1838): 293.

Harris, Susan. "'But is it any *good?*': Evaluating Nineteenth-Century Women's Fiction." *American Literature* 63.1 (Mar. 1991): 43–61.

Heeney, Brian. *The Woman's Movement in the Church of England, 1850–1930..* Oxford: Oxford UP, 1988.

Helmstadter, Richard J., and Paul T. Phillips. *Religion in Victorian Society.* Lanham, Md.: UP of America, 1985.

Homans, Margaret. *Bearing the Word.* Chicago: U of Chicago P, 1986.

Hornblow, Arthur. *A History of the Theater in America.* 2 vols. 1919. New York: Benjamin Blom, 1965. Vol. 2.

Howe, Daniel Walker. "American Victorianism As a Culture." *American Quarterly* 27 (1975): 507–32.

Hudson, Aïda. "The Religious Temper of Charlotte Brontë's Novels." Diss. U of Toronto, 1980.

Hughes, Winifred. *The Maniac in the Cellar.* Princeton: Princeton UP, 1980.

"The Intellect of Women." *Saturday Review* 8 (Oct. 1859): 417–18.

Ireland, Annie. Introduction. *Selections from the Letters of Geraldine Endsor Jewsbury to Jane Welch Carlyle.* London: Longmans, Green & Company, 1892.

James, Henry. Rev. of *Moods. North American Review* 101 (July 1865): 276–81.

Johnson, Claudia. "A New Nation's Drama." *Columbia Literary History of the United States.* Ed. Emory Elliott, et al. New York: Columbia UP, 1988.

———. *American Actress.* Chicago: Nelson-Hall, 1984.

———. "That Guilty Third Tier: Prostitution in Nineteenth Century American Theaters." *American Quarterly* 26 (Dec. 1975): 575–85.

Keyser, Elizabeth Lennox. *Whispers in the Dark: The Fiction of Louisa May Alcott.* Knoxville: U of Tennessee P, 1993.

Kot, Paula. "Leading Women 'Out of the Bondage of Dead Superstitions': Alcott's Revision of the Christian Woman's Quest for Salvation." Unpublished essay, 1990.

Lane, Charles and A. Bronson Alcott. "The Consociate Family Life." In C. E. Sears, *Bronson Alcott's Fruitlands.* Boston: Houghton Mifflin, 1915. 40–52.

Langland, Elizabeth. "Female Stories of Experience: Alcott's *Little Women* in Light of *Work.*" *The Voyage In: Fictions of Female Development.* Ed. Elizabeth Abel, Marianne Hirsch, and Elizabeth Langland. Hanover: UP of New England, 1983. 112–27.

Latourette, Kenneth Scott. *Christianity in a Revolutionary Age. Volume II: The Nineteenth Century in Europe.* New York: Harper & Brothers, 1959.

Linton, Eliza Lynn. *The Girl of the Period and Other Social Essays.* 2 vols. London: Richard Bentley, 1883.

Logan, Mrs. John A. (Mary S.), ed. *The Part Taken by Women in American History.* Wilmington, Del.: The Perry-Nalle Publishing Co., 1912.

Lorimer, James. "Review." *North British Review* 11 (Aug. 1849): 455–93. Rpt. in Allott, 113–16.

MacDonald, Ruth. *Louisa May Alcott.* Boston: G. K. Hall, 1983.

Mahoney, Rosemary. "Sisterhood is Powerful." *Elle* (Dec. 1994): 144–50.

Mandelker, Ira L. *Religion, Society, and Utopia in Nineteenth-Century America.* Amherst: U of Massachusetts P, 1984.

Martin, Robert Bernard. *Charlotte Brontë's Novels: The Accents of Persuasion.* New York: Norton, 1966.

Martineau, Harriet. "Female Industry." *Edinburgh Review* 109 (Apr. 1859): 294–95.

Meltzer, Milton, and Patricia G. Holland, eds. *Lydia Maria Child: Selected Letters, 1817–1880.* Amherst: U. of Massachusetts P, 1982.

Miller, Nancy. "Changing the Subject: Authorship, Writing, and the Reader." *Feminist Studies, Critical Studies.* Ed. Teresa de Lauretis. Bloomington: Indiana UP, 1986. 102–20.

Moers, Ellen. *Literary Women.* Garden City, New York: Doubleday, 1976.

Moulton, Louise Chandler. "Louisa May Alcott." *Our Famous Women.* Harriet Beecher Stowe et al. Hartford: A. D. Worthington and Co., 1883; 29–52.

Nestor, Pauline. *Female Friendships and Communities.* Oxford: Clarendon P, 1985.

Newfield, Christopher J. "Loving Bondage: Emerson's Ideal Relationships." *ATQ* 5.3 (Sept. 1991): 183–93.

Nightingale, Florence. *Cassandra.* 1852. The Feminist P, 1979.

Niles, Thomas. Letter to Louisa May Alcott, 26 Oct. 1868, Alcott Papers, Houghton Library, Harvard University.

"Novels of the Season." *North American Review* 67.141 (Oct. 1848): 354–61.

Nye, Russell. *Society and Culture in America, 1830–1860.* New York: Harper and Row, 1974.

Palmer, Albert M. "American Theatres." *One Hundred Years of American Commerce.* Ed. Chauncey Depew. New York: Haynes Publishing Co., 1895.

Parker, Theodore. *Sins and Safeguards of Society.* Ed. Samuel B. Stewart. Boston: American Unitarian Association, n.d.

Paz, D. G. *Popular Anti-Catholicism in Mid-Victorian England.* Stanford: Stanford UP, 1992.

Peters, Margot. *Unquiet Soul: A Biography of Charlotte Brontë.* Garden City, NY: Doubleday, 1975.

Peterson, Jeanne. "The Victorian Governess: Status Incongruence." *Victorian Studies* 14 (1970): 7–23.

Phillips, Anne K. "The Prophets and the Martyrs: Pilgrims and Missionaries in *Little Women* and *Jack and Jill*." In Little Women *and the Feminist Imagina-*

tion. Ed. Janice M. Alberghene and Beverly Lyon Clark. New York: Garland, 1999. 213–36.

Pickett, LaSalle Corbett. *Across My Path: Memories of People I Have Known.* New York: Brentano's, 1916.

Porterfield, Amanda. *Feminine Spirituality in America from Sarah Edwards to Martha Graham.* Philadelphia: Temple UP, 1980.

Poovey, Mary. "The Anathematized Race: The Governess and *Jane Eyre.*" *Uneven Developments: The Ideological Work of Gender in Mid-Victorian England.* Chicago: U of Chicago P, 1988. 230–54.

Pratt, Annis. *Archetypal Patterns in Women's Fiction.* Bloomington: Indiana UP, 1981.

Reader 5 (15 Apr. 1865): 422–23. (Review of *Moods.*)

"Review." *Critic* 4 (July 1846): 6–8. Rpt. in Allott, 59–61. (Review of *Poems.*)

Reynolds, David S. *Beneath the American Renaissance.* New York: Knopf, 1988.

Rigby, Elizabeth. Review of *Jane Eyre: An Autobiography. Quarterly Review* 84 (Dec. 1848): 173–76.

Rohrer, Trish Deitch. "Sister Act." *US* 203 (Dec. 1994): 39–43.

Rostenberg, Leona. "Some Anonymous and Pseudonymous Thrillers of Louisa May Alcott." *Bibliographical Society of America Papers* 37 (2nd Quarter, 1943): 131–40.

Russ, Lavinia. "Not to Be Read on Sunday." *Horn Book* 44 (Oct. 1968): 521–26.

Russell, Lord John. Letter to the Anglican Bishop of Durham, 4 Nov. 1850. *Religion in Victorian Society: A Sourcebook of Documents.* Ed. Richard J. Helmstadter and Paul T. Phillips. Lanham, Md.: UP of America, 1985. 309–11.

Sanborn, Frank B. "Women of Concord." *The Critic* 48 (Apr. 1906): 338–50.

Saxton, Martha. *Louisa May.* New York: Houghton Mifflin, 1977.

Sears, Clara Endicott. *Bronson Alcott's Fruitlands.* Boston: Houghton Mifflin, 1915.

Shepard, Odell. *Pedlar's Progress, The Life of Bronson Alcott.* Boston: Little, Brown, 1937.

Showalter, Elaine. "Dinah Mulock Craik and the Tactics of Sentiment: A Case Study of Victorian Female Authorship." *Feminist Studies* 2 (1975): 5–23.

———. Introduction. *Alternative Alcott.* New Brunswick, NJ: Rutgers UP, 1988.

———. Introduction. *Little Women.* By Louisa May Alcott. New York: Viking Penguin, 1989.

———. *Sister's Choice.* Oxford: Clarendon P, 1991.

Smith, Anne. Introduction. *The Professor and Emma.* By Charlotte Brontë. London: J. M. Dent & Sons, 1985.

Smith, Daniel Scott. "Family Limitation, Sexual Control, and Domestic Feminism in Victorian America." Mary S. Hartman and Lois Banner, eds.

Clio's Consciousness Raised: New Perspectives on the History of Women. New York: Harper and Row, 1974. 119–36.

Smith-Rosenberg, Carroll. Disorderly Conduct: Visions of Gender in Victorian America. Oxford: Oxford UP, 1975.

Stern, Madeleine. Introduction. Freaks of Genius. Ed. Daniel Shealy. Westport, CT: Greenwood, 1991.

———. "Louisa Alcott, Trouper." New England Quarterly 26.2 (June 1943): 175–97.

———. "Louisa Alcott's Self-Criticism." Studies in the American Renaissance. Charlottesville: UP of Virginia, 1985: 333–82.

———. Louisa May Alcott. New York: Random House, 1996.

Stock, Phyllis. Better Than Rubies: A History of Women's Education. New York: G. P. Putnam's Sons, 1978.

Stokes, John. "Rachel's 'Terrible Beauty': An Actress Among the Novelists." ELH 51.4 (Winter 1984): 771–95.

Strickland, Charles. Victorian Domesticity. University: U of Alabama P, 1985.

Tanner, Tony. Introduction. Villette. By Charlotte Brontë. Hammondsworth, England: Penguin Books, 1979.

Thoreau, Henry David. Great Short Works of Henry David Thoreau. Ed. Wendell Glick. New York: Harper-Collins, 1982.

Tompkins, J. M. S. "Caroline Helstone's Eyes." Brontë Society Transactions 14 (1968): 18–28.

Tompkins, Jane. Sensational Designs: The Cultural Work of American Fiction, 1790–1860. Oxford: Oxford UP, 1985.

Turner, Lorenzo Dow. "Louisa May Alcott's 'M. L.'" Journal of Negro History 14 (Oct. 1929): 495–522.

United States Department of Commerce. Bureau of the Census. Historical Statistics of the United States: Colonial Times to 1970. White Plains, NY: Kraus International Publications, 1989.

Urbanski, Marie Oleson. "Thoreau in the Writings of Louisa May Alcott." Critical Essays on Louisa May Alcott. Ed. Madeleine Stern. Boston: G. K. Hall, 1984. 269–74.

Walsh, Walter. The Secret History of the Oxford Movement. 5th ed. London: Swan Sonnenschein & Co., 1899.

Walton, Jenny. "The Filming of 'Little Women'." Victoria Magazine (Dec. 1994): 115–17.

Weiner, Lynn Y. From Working Girl to Working Mother. Chapel Hill: U of North Carolina P, 1985.

Weisbuch, Robert. Atlantic Double-Cross: American Literature and British Influence in the Age of Emerson. Chicago: U of Chicago P, 1986.

Welter, Barbara. Dimity Convictions: The American Woman in the Nineteenth Century. Athens: Ohio UP, 1976.

Wendell, Barrett. *A Literary History of America.* New York: Charles Scribner's Sons, 1900.

Wise, T. J., and J. A. Symington. *The Brontës: Their Lives, Friendships, and Correspondences in Four Volumes.* Oxford: Oxford UP, 1932.

Zagarell, Sandra. "Narrative of Community: The Identification of a Genre." *Signs: Journal of Women in Culture and Society* 13.3 (Spring 1988): 498–527.

INDEX

Brontë, Charlotte, writing: works: *Emma*, 163; *Jane Eyre*, xv, xxi, xxii, 8, 15, 26, 31–49 passim, 53–57, 61, 62, 74, 76, 98–99, 103–4, 110, 115–17, 126, 130–31, 137, 146–47, 151, 153, 170, 174n, 176–77n, 180n, 188n; —, critical reception, 25–26, 28; —, *see also* Jane Eyre, Eliza Reed, St. John Rivers, Bertha Mason Rochester, Edward Rochester, Celine Varens; *Poems*, 14; *The Professor*, xxi, 7, 14, 73, 110, 117, 137, 141; —, *see also* William Crimsworth, Frances Henri, Mdlle Reuter; *Shirley*, xxi, 35, 99–102, 110, 111, 116–18, 130, 137, 139, 141–42, 160, 175n, 178n, 183n; —, *see also* Caroline Helstone, Shirley Keeldar; *Villette*, xxi, xxii, 26, 37, 39, 67–69 passim, 75, 76, 83–85, 102, 110, 125, 137–42 passim, 153–54, 176n, 180n, 181n; —, *see also* Madame Beck, Dr. John Graham Bretton, M. Paul Emanuel, Genevra Fanshawe, Paulina Home, Lucy Snowe, Vashti
Brontë, Emily, 7, 140
Brontë, Patrick, 4–5, 7–9 passim, 53, 82, 95, 173n
Byronic hero, 46, 49, 60, 176n

Cheney, Ednah Dow, xvii, xviii, xxi, 3, 70
Chesterton, G. K., xvii
Child, Lydia Maria, 25–26, 180n
Cobbe, Frances, 113, 117
Consociate Family, 132–33
Craik, Dinah Mulock, 112, 115, 120

du Plessis, Rachel Blau, 120–21

Elbert, Sarah, xix, xx, xxii, 33, 34, 121, 174n, 178n, 180n
Eliot, George, 75, 126
Emerson, Ralph Waldo, 6, 7, 88, 92, 105–6, 121, 137, 167, 174n, 178n; "Experience," 33, 49–50; "Friendship," 123; "Love," 123, 134; "Self-Reliance," 126, 171

Fields, James T., 12
Fruitlands, 6, 38, 129, 131–33, 137, 185n
Fuller, Margaret, 36, 132, 176n

Gaskell, Elizabeth, xxi, 3, 15, 25, 27, 53, 113, 173n, 185n
Godey's Lady's Book, 16
Goethe, Johann Wolfgang von, xxi, 75, 168, 174n, 188n; *Faust*, 58

Hawthorne, Nathaniel, 16, 87, 167, 168, 176n; *The Scarlet Letter*, 98

James, Henry, 18; reviews Alcott's work, xvi, xxii, 16–17, 33

Keyser, Elizabeth, xx, xxii, 54, 94, 157, 168, 176–78n, 187n, 188n

Lane, Charles, 132–33
Leslie, Frank, 18, 51–52, 61
Linton, Eliza Lynn, 112–13, 115

Nestor, Pauline, 119, 183n
Nightingale, Florence, 144–45
Niles, Thomas, 88–89, 180n
Nineteenth-century culture, 148; attitudes toward women, 57, 108, 129, 144, 183n; literacy, 124; missionary movements, 94–95; religion, 80, 97–98, 102; work ethic, 38

Louisa May Alcott and Charlotte Brontë was designed and typeset on a Macintosh computer system using PageMaker software. The text is set in Diotima and the chapter openings are set in Isadora. This book was designed by Angela Stanton-Anderson, typeset by Kimberly Scarbrough, and manufactured by Thomson-Shore, Inc. The recycled paper used in this book is designed for an effective life of at least three hundred years.